Salute thyself: see what thy soul doth wear.
Dare to look in thy chest; for 'tis thine own:
And tumble up and down what thou find'st there.
GEORGE HERBERT

It's a fool looks for logic in the chambers of the human heart.
FROM *O BROTHER, WHERE ART THOU?*

LOUISA YOUNG first came to prominence as author of *A Great Task of Happiness* (1995), her life of the sculptor Kathleen Scott. She followed that with her Egyptian trilogy of novels: *Baby Love*, *Desiring Cairo* and *Tree of Pearls*. She writes regularly for various newspapers, and lives in London with her daughter.

THE BOOK OF
THE HEART

Louisa Young

DOUBLEDAY
New York   London   Toronto   Sydney   Auckland

PUBLISHED BY DOUBLEDAY

a division of Random House, Inc.
1745 Broadway, New York, New York 10019

DOUBLEDAY and the portrayal of an anchor with a dolphin are trademarks of
Doubleday, a division of Random House, Inc.

First published in hardcover in the United Kingdom by Flamingo, an imprint of
HarperCollins Publishers, September 2002.

Book design by Helene Berinsky

Library of Congress Cataloging-in-Publication Data
Young, Louisa.
The book of the heart / by Louisa Young.
p.   cm.
Includes bibliographical references and index.
1. Heart—Popular works.   2. Heart—Folklore.   3. Heart—Mythology.
4. Heart—Religious aspects.   I. Title.
QP111.4.Y68 2003
398'.353—dc21   2002024496

ISBN 0-385-50173-0

PRINTED IN THE UNITED STATES OF AMERICA

February 2003

First Edition in the United States

1   3   5   7   9   10   8   6   4   2

To my father's heart,
and my mother's.
And in memory of Don Swift.

The heart of him that hath understanding seeketh knowledge.

CONTENTS

LIST OF ILLUSTRATIONS

ACKNOWLEDGMENTS

The human heart is an organ, a metaphor, a seed bed, a treasure chest, a pin cushion, a charm, a fountain, a house, a pump, a pine cone, a wheel, an electromagnetic entity, raw material, a rose, a pomegranate, a gift, a picnic spot, a significant ingredient in pâté. It flies, it sinks, it grows, it faints, it bleeds, it flutters, it burns, it rejoices, it breaks, it fibrillates, it stops, it fails. It is attacked, transplanted, sacrificed, given away, swept, polished, eaten, stolen. I have hardly begun to track what the heart is and does and has done to it, but I have wandered into many complex fields in its pursuit—fields in none of which I am expert. I am, specifically, not a cardiologist, an Egyptologist, a surgeon, a philosopher, an art historian, a Buddhist, a yogi, an expert on country and western, an anthropologist, a theologian, a literary critic, an undertaker; I don't read Dutch. Without these and many more limitations I would still be wandering and this book would still be an idea. I have had a mass of help and guidance; my mistakes are my own. My thanks are due to:

Professor Norman Stone, for pointing out twenty years ago that I would never make a serious historian (because I was a girl, he said—his reason was wrong but his prediction was right);

Dr. Richard Parkinson for ancient Egyptian pronunciation and definition;

Tim Reid for Grimm's Law;

Alex Morrison for paintings and voodoo;

Amira Ghazalla for Arabic and a garland;

Burt Caesar for poetry;

Charlotte Horton for pomegranates, legends, stringency and hospitality;

Wayland and Elizabeth Kennet for firsthand experiences, and my life;

Nick Crane for Mercator, Fine and the Family of Love;

Dr. Rodney Foale for cardiology and Sufi poetry;

Louis Adomakoh for cuttings, peace and quiet;

Jerome Burne for unlikely medical knowledge;

Jane Farrimond for Patanjali;

Sara Rossi for homeopathy;

John Walsh for George Herbert and Pádraic Pearse;

Stephen Clarke for French stamps;

Geoffrey Matthews for Latin and Greek;

Natasha for Cabbala and D. H. Lawrence;

David Flusfeder and David Cawthorne for songs;

Duncan Sprott for Louis XVI;

Alexander Fyjis Walker for Dr. Boyadjian;

Tom Whyte;

Clare Brennan for dispatches from Rwanda and Edinburgh and the Catholic faith;

Anna Stevenson for gory description;

Graham and Sally Greene for hospitality beyond the call;

The staff of the London Library, the Wellcome Institute Library and above all Humanities Two at the British Library;

Derek Johns, Anjali Pratap and the staff of A. P. Watt; Philip Gwyn Jones, Georgina Laycock, Karen Duffy, Terence Caven, Caroline Hotblack, Suzanne Collins, Nicole Abel, Laetitia Rutherford, Katja Alanen and the staff at Flamingo for doing their jobs so well;

Isabel Adomakoh Young, for intelligent comment, patience, interesting news and loving support.

INTRODUCTION

I met Magdi Yacoub once. He has performed more heart transplants than any other surgeon. We were introduced: he held out his hand to shake. I looked at his hand. I couldn't touch it. That hand had touched my father's heart. Mended it, to be sure, and saved his life—but touched it. I rationalized that I didn't want my rough hand to threaten that delicate and clever one—what if I broke it? I just didn't want to touch what had touched my father's heart. It didn't seem right. It seemed disrespectful—a little heretical.

We are not meant to touch hearts. Hearts are away, hidden, at the center where they can't be got at. Protected. Vital. The seat of the soul. If a heart is touched, it can only be a miracle. When Christ's heart appears to a medieval saint; when the heart of a miser is touched with mercy; when a surgeon opens a rib cage and mends a heart, it is a miracle. Otherwise do not touch.

We all have one; most of us will never see one. We all know what it is, very few of us can explain exactly how it works. There is a universal human fascination with the heart which no other organ has inspired—not the brain, which is more interesting as an organ, not the eyes, which are so beautiful and visible. The heart is simply a lump of muscle, a pump, and yet it is the home of love, and courage, and religion, and soul, and almost any other human feeling you care to think of. Everybody knows this; sometimes they wonder why, though more often, as R. A. Erickson put it, "the heart is so taken for granted that it is the quintessentially marginal organ . . . so central to our physiological and symbolic functioning that for the most part we hardly pay attention to it." I think about the human heart a lot: its efficiency, its strangeness, its physical strengths and weaknesses. The blood it is filled with, and the symbolism, and the duties it has to perform. Two, basically: to keep you alive, and to let you love someone, as a six-year-old once said. And from that so much flows.

This is why I have written this book of the heart. Because it *is* the heart—the heart of things, the heart of the matter. And because, as the heart, not the surface, it remains mysterious. Every culture and every age has had ideas and beliefs about the heart which overlap, support and undermine each other. Every age and every culture has known its vital importance, and each has assigned similar reasons for it. Every art form has used it; every religion uses it. It is ever present in poetry and lyrics, libretti, literature, advertising, kitsch, everyday language and imagery. We love the heart, because it is the organ of love. Here is its story. It is not a story with a beginning or an end. Nor does it—quite—go round in circles. It is more like soup. If you find one bit not to your taste, move on, feel free—all the flavors connect up.

Louisa Young
London, 2001

PROLOGUE

Why did you pick up this book? Because you are a romantic? Or because you have a historical curiosity? Is it love you want to know about, or knowledge? The history of the heart weaves these two together over thousands of years: in disentangling the web for you I spend a lot of time with both, and in the overlapping areas. But I'll start with love. Here is a poem:

My heart flutters hastily,
When I think of my love of you;
It lets me not act sensibly,
It leaps from its place.
It lets me not put on a dress,
Nor wrap my scarf around me;
I put no paint upon my eyes, I'm not even anointed.
"Don't wait, go there," it says to me,
As often as I think of him.
My heart, don't act so stupidly,
Why do you play the fool?
Sit still, the brother comes to you,
And many eyes as well!
Let not the people say of me:
"A woman fallen through love!"
Be steady when you think of him.
My heart, do not flutter!

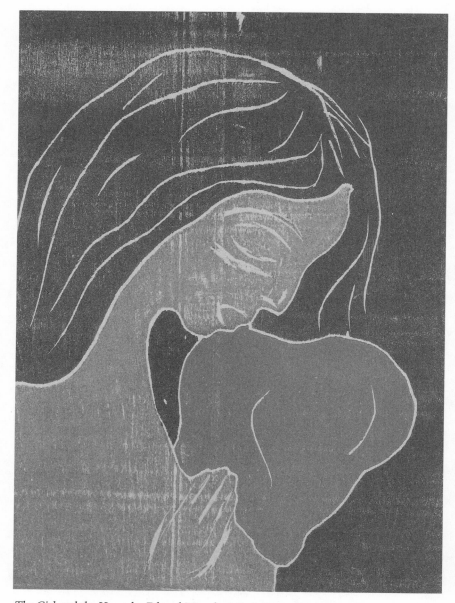

The Girl and the Heart, by Edvard Munch. © *Scala/Museo Munch/DACS 2002*

It is ancient Egyptian (from the Chester Beatty Papyrus I), several thousand years old, but its double message is immortal. A hundred years ago they'd say: "Be still, my beating heart!" Thirty years ago: "Heartbeat, why do you miss when my baby kisses me?" The message is the same: the heart is extraordinarily independent for a bodily organ, and the heart is the home of humanity's great mystery, great energy, great blessing: love.

And were love and the heart always associated? I always assumed that somewhere in the dim untraceable past, earlier than writing, love and the heart had become irretrievably associated in the human mind—but that is because I have been brought up rational, and encouraged to think that everything happens in the mind. Now, having read what the greatest (and lowest) minds have had to say over millennia on the subject of the heart and love, even my rational mind is inclined to think that love does genuinely belong in the heart—we didn't put it there; we found it there.

Here is another poem, from the twentieth century this time, by Lilian Moore:

Sometimes
when I skip or hop
or when I'm
jumping
Suddenly
I like to stop
and listen to me
thumping.

As soon as mankind knew anything about itself, it knew that it had a heart. For two million years we were hunters and gatherers. When we chased an animal, we felt our hearts beat faster. When we caught the animal, we felt its heart beat frantically in fear. When we killed the animal—through the heart was quickest—we felt the heartbeat cease and the breath stop. When we brought it back to the family, we may have fancied that our own hearts swelled with pride. When we cleaned it, we saw the trickly intestines, the gleaming liver, the curious frilly lungs and—this: this little, hard, shiny thing, with pipes going in and out of it. Fifty thousand years ago a Cro-Magnon somebody painted a mammoth on the wall of what is now known as the cavern of Pindal, in Spain, and there on the left-hand side of its thorax is a red ochre splodge which may or may not have been its heart. Some say this is the first representation of a heart (others that it is just an ear, or a splodge).

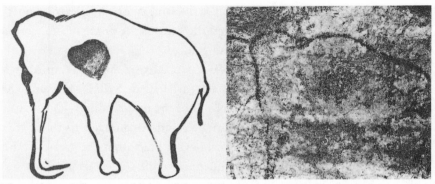

The prehistoric "mammoth's heart" found in 1911 in a cave at Pindal, Spain, by Abbé Henri Breuil: here is his drawing and his photograph. *From H. Alcalde del Rio, Henri Breuil, Lorenzo Sierra, Les cavernes de la région Cantabrique (Espagne), Monaco 1911*

Sometimes the hunter would have seen the contractions of a dying heart—hearts hate to stop, even after throats have been cut or necks wrung. How could he not relate this animal thing, warm and mobile and beating, to the beating he felt inside his own chest? He could see for himself that he had pipes going up and down his own neck. Perhaps they joined up inside him to the kind of pipes he could see coming out of the heart. He knew perfectly well, from fighting and hunting and being wounded, that these pipes had blood inside them. He knew that blood came from the heart. Or went to the heart. And he knew that breath had something to do with it, because the heartbeat and the breath increased and decreased together, like well-matched dancers.

He could clearly feel his heart beating harder and faster whenever anything big or exciting happened: fear, sex, childbirth, anger, surprise, violence, physical exertion. He could feel its pulses around his own body and his companions', and their absence in death, as cold immobility crept in, and breath disappeared. And did he feel a kind of pang there when this happened to someone he loved . . . did he love?

The earliest mentions of the heart in poetry are emotional. The Babylonian/Sumerian goddess Ishtar went down to the Underworld to rescue her husband Tammuz from the dead: her heart nearly broke with grief, and only joyful melodies could calm it. Gilgamesh, hero of the oldest known work of literature, felt his heart beating with pride. He too was trying to bring a beloved—his friend—back from death.

The emotional content of the heart is older than writing, and so too is the spiritual. How natural and obvious to prehistoric man that this beating thing, so responsive to action and feeling, right there at the front of the middle of his chest, should be seen, as soon as he came to think about that kind of question, as the seat of life, and, before you know it, the residence of the soul. As soon as he noticed his own individuality and intelligence, the idea of the soul emerged to name and define it. That the soul should be immortal was the whole point of having one (or two for the ancient Egyptians; four in other parts of Africa). As soon as the soul emerged, it needed somewhere particular to live. The immortal soul lives in the body during mortal life—but where in the body? For most cultures, for millennia, there was no question: in the heart (though for some Australian tribes in the fat of the kidneys). For thousands of years before mankind had a clear idea of what the heart really does, and why, people across the world had a spiritual and magical role for it.

Our modern view of the heart comes directly from ancient Egypt, and so before heading off into what the heart means now, and how it came to do so, we have to understand something of what it meant on the banks of the Nile 5,000 years ago. Here is a story—one of the oldest in existence, written down 3,000 years ago. It introduces ideas about the heart which echo down the centuries.

THE TALE OF THE TWO BROTHERS

Anubis and Bata were brothers. Anubis was the elder; Bata worked for him and was like a son to him. All was well until one day Anubis's wife looked at Bata and "her heart recognized him, as you recognize a young man." She invited him to lie with her, whereupon he became "like a cheetah of the south in his hot rage" and rejected her. Angered by this, and afraid that he would speak of her proposition, the woman rubbed herself with grease and ash so she looked bruised, and told her husband that Bata had attacked her. Anubis sharpened his knife and hid behind the door of the stable to kill his brother when he returned with the cattle. The cows saw Anubis there and as Bata approached, they warned him. Terrified, Bata fled, calling on Pre-Harakhti to protect him. The god laid down a body of crocodile-infested water between Bata and Anubis, and from the far side Bata cried out to his brother that he was going to the faraway Vale of the Pine.

The following morning Bata told Anubis his side of the story, and then

"He took a billhook for cutting reeds, he severed his phallus, he cast it into the water, where the electric catfish devoured it." At this the elder brother cursed his heart, and Bata said: "I shall take out my heart by magic and place it on the top of the flower of the pine; and when the pine is cut down and my heart falls to the ground you will come to seek for it." Bata told Anubis to put the heart in fresh water when he found it, and he, Bata, would return to life. In the meantime, so long as the heart was safe atop the flower, Bata was safe too.

Meanwhile the gods gave Bata a wife, a woman so beautiful that even the sea desired her. When she washed in the waves, the sea took a lock of her hair and carried it to Egypt where it got into the Pharaoh's laundry. He searched her out and took her as his principal favorite. She told him about the pine and the heart, and made him have the tree cut down to destroy Bata.

When this happened Anubis's beer frothed and his wine became clouded; thus he knew it was time to search for his brother's heart. After many years "he found a fruit, and lo! It was the heart of his younger brother." He brought a cup of fresh water and placed the heart in it. By nightfall the heart had absorbed the water, and Bata, lying dead on his bed, trembled in all his members, and gazed fixedly at his elder brother, whilst his heart was in the cup. "Anubis seized the cup of fresh water in which was the heart of his younger brother, who drank and his heart was in its place and he became as he was before."

Bata became a bull and went to court to frighten his wife; when she saw him she had his throat cut. Where drops of blood fell to the ground, two great and beautiful persea trees sprang up. When she sat beneath one, Bata murmured to her, so she had the trees cut down and made into coffers. As the carpenters cut the wood, a splinter leapt into her mouth, and "she perceived that she had conceived." She bore a son, to whom, when he came of age and inherited the crowns of Egypt, Bata told the whole story. The wicked wife was punished, Bata lived happily ever after.

This story seems so strange to modern eyes, but it brings up many, many aspects of the heart which recur through history. It speaks of eating the heart and washing it in water in order to win life after death, prefiguring the Christian sacraments of baptism and holy communion. The correlation between the heart and the phallus—the love/sex connection—is clear. There are connections with the Osiris legend, where Osiris was killed by his brother and dismembered before being brought back to life by his sister/wife Isis; and with Dionysus, who was dismembered by Titans, and rescued by his father Zeus who snatched his heart and brought him back to life by feeding the heart in a glass of water to the nymph Semele, or in another version by bearing the child himself, in his thigh. The trees sprouting from fallen drops of blood, the soul separating from the body, either to spy or to be kept safe, and the heart as a fruit appear in all folklores. The story foreshadows the virgin's conception, the treacherous kiss, the sacrificial death of a son and his resurrection. Already, 3,000 and more years ago, the heart embodies identity, life, fertility, loyalty and love.

The emotional territory of the ancient Egyptian heart was as wide as, or even wider than, our own: "Man's heart is his life-prosperity-health!" It could be happy or frivolous, it could match your tongue, it could be "big," meaning proud, or "great," meaning high-minded and magnanimous, or "wide," meaning patient. You could be master or mistress of it (it was good for a wife to be mistress of her heart); it could be inflamed (making you what we think of as a "hothead"—a "hot-heart" is a person out of control); or it could be content: advising that when drinking with a drunkard you should not take a drink yourself till his heart was content.

The heart could ponder the truth, or even rest on Maat, the feather of truth. It could make its owner not hear words of wisdom. When you studied, you put what you had learned in your heart (you learned it "by heart"). Queen Hatshepsut built "two obelisks of electrum whose summits would reach the heavens" in honor of her father, Thutmose I, and her heavenly father Amun. She entered, with a loving heart, into the plans of Amun's heart, and then when the obelisks were completed her heart turned "to and fro, in thinking what will the people say": her heart encompassed love, belonging, consideration and pride. The love was to do with duty and devotion as much as romance: 4,000 years ago Weni of Abydos recorded in his tomb that King Pepi I's heart "was filled with me beyond any other servant of his . . . I was worthy in His Majesty's heart . . . I was excellent in His Majesty's heart, I was rooted in his heart." Special advisers and courtiers were given gold and silver hearts engraved with the name of their ruler, which they wore around their necks: they were then the "conscience" of the Pharaoh, being trusted by him.

The heart could desire, fear, rejoice, bathe, fill, empty, retreat, worry and be sad. It could be appeased by kind words, it could incline to accept them, it could be brave and bronze, it could be broken and weak, it could be lifted up and reaffirmed, it could be disobedient and stubborn, it could jump and be like a bird in its flightiness, it could be greedy, troubled, angry; it could lean or turn toward somebody in sympathy, but it was dangerous for it to move further than that. You could put it on someone, or toward them, in love and desire. You could put it behind them, which meant you worried about them. To wash the heart meant to relieve your feelings (which is part of the process of being reborn). Intelligence, understanding and knowledge lived there. It was where memories were kept (or lost). There seems to be no end to its duties: it was even used in the humble signing-off of a letter to a superior: *réjouir le coeur*. These expressions recur throughout Egyptian writings, stories, inscriptions and poetry.

Above all a heart could be delighted: Harkhuf, a sixth-dynasty official buried at Aswan, recorded in his tomb at length how the heart of Pepi II was gladdened by the prospect of seeing the dancing pygmy Harkhuf had brought from the land of the horizon dwellers. His heart was so delighted that he mentioned the pygmy four times.

The vital importance of the heart comes up over and over in the sayings of Ptolemaic instructors. Reading them now some seem almost truisms, like something from Shakespeare or the Bible:

The impious man who is proud of himself is harmed by his own heart.
The life that controls excess is a life according to a wise man's heart. A small good news makes the heart live.
He who knows how to hold his heart has the equivalent of every teaching.
Do not let your tongue differ from your heart in counsel when you are asked.
The heart cannot rise up when there is affliction in it.

Others have an altogether wilder and more ancient air:

Wine, women and food give gladness to the heart—he who uses them without loud shouting is not reproached in the street.
Do not scorn the voice of your heart; he who does makes a stench in the street.
Do not speak to God when there is anger in his heart.
Do not be close to one in whose heart there is hatred.
The evil man whose heart loves evil will find it.

Do not open your heart to your wife or your servant; open it to your mother, she is a woman of discretion.

For the heart then, as now, contained our secrets and mysteries:

One does not discover the heart of a man if one has not sent him on a mission.

One does not discover the heart of a friend if one has not consulted him in anxiety.

One does not discover the heart of a brother if one has not begged from him in want.

One does not discover the heart of a son until the day when one seeks goods from him.

One does not discover the heart of a servant as long as his master is not attacked.

One does not ever discover the heart of a woman any more than one knows the sky.

FROM THE INSINGER PAPYRUS

Then, as now, romantic love was in the heart. And then, as now, love was foolish:

My heart thought of my love of you
When half my hair was braided;
I came at a run to find you,
And neglected my hairdo.
Now if you let me braid my hair,
I shall be ready in a moment.

FROM PAPYRUS HARRIS 500

One Egyptian concept we have entirely lost: the heart of man is the nose of god. I have tried to work out what this could possibly mean, and failed. The subject is never-ending. So let's begin.

CHAMBER ONE

THE
ANATOMIST'S
HEART

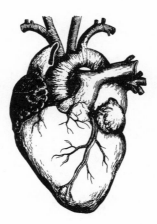

1

THE HISTORY OF THE
ANATOMICAL KNOWLEDGE
OF THE HEART

Before embarking on the uplands of the heart's emotional and spiritual manifestations, let's look at what it undeniably is. It is a pump made of muscle, and it moves blood around the body. It took us a very long time to discover this, and the story of this discovery is both strange and beautiful.

The spiritual significance of the heart, in Egypt and elsewhere, contributed directly to anatomical ignorance of it: religious and magical beliefs precluded finding out more. The hope of, desire for and belief in some form of life after death was universal among human cultures. Who could swear it would not involve the resurrection of the body? Cutting up the body to see how it worked was, for generation on generation and across the world, taboo. Anatomical knowledge therefore depended on what butchers saw inside the animals they slaughtered, and what priests saw in the animals they sacrificed and in whose innards they fossicked for knowledge of the future. None of these was necessarily interested in anatomy; none that we know of kept a record or tried to educate others beyond passing on professional skills. The medicine men of primitive societies did sometimes open a body, but only to look for signs of magic: anatomical knowledge was not a useful thing to them.

THE ANCIENT EGYPTIANS

The Egyptians specialized in cutting the human body: their religious rites specifically required them to open the thoraxes of corpses in the course of mummification, and to remove certain organs. So why didn't they garner anatomical knowledge along the way? Those doing this cutting were embalmers, unconnected with medicine. Their job was to preserve the body for eternity, not to uncover its secrets. The disemboweling rites, out of respect for the body, involved only tiny cuts. Ancient Egypt had sophisticated medical and surgical practices, but they were based on limited and prescribed ancient knowledge; when the Egyptians started writing things down, contemporary anatomical investigation was not something they considered. The heart—which anyway was not removed during embalming—was above all for them a spiritual entity.

The twenty-meter-long Ebers Papyrus (1550 B.C.) contains a book which opens thus:

> The Beginning of the Secret of Medicine. Knowledge of the pulse of the heart. Knowledge of the heart . . . There are vessels for every part. In each place where each healer, each priest of Sekhmet, each magician puts his fingers—on the nape, on the hands, on the place of the heart, on the two arms, on the two feet—everywhere he encounters the heart, by its channels to all the parts.

They had identified the heart, the vessels and the pulse. They were not the first: the forty clay tablets of the *Mesopotamian Treatise of Medical Diagnosis and Prognosis*, which is dated circa 650 B.C. but records far older Sumerian and Assyrian healing traditions, also recognized that the pulses were informative in diagnosis. (This knowledge was *completely* bound up in magic: a tablet from 2000 B.C. reads, "When a woman gives birth to an infant that has the heart open and has no skin, the country will suffer calamities." The Mesopotamians believed the liver to be the seat of life, and used it in divination, before it lost its status forever under Christianity: it was associated with pagan divination and low, base urges—concupiscence and lust and greed.)

Another Egyptian text, *Der Grosse Medizinische Papyrus der Berliner Museum*, speaks of "The system of circulation of man in which is found all his maladies . . . [the vessels] bring air to his heart and it is they that give air to every part of his body." Now, the circulation of the blood per se was not discovered and proven until William Harvey demonstrated it in 1618, but it seems the ancient Egyptians may have had an idea of it (the Atharvaveda—see page 9—mentions circulation in the vessels 2,500 years before Harvey). The Egyptians knew that air came in through the nose to the heart and lungs, and was circulated to all the limbs—which if you read oxygen for air is true, though they hadn't clarified the complexities.

The Egyptians believed that the body was fashioned by Khnum, the potter god, who "knotted the flow of the blood to the bones" and formed "the spine to give support, the testicles to move, the arm to act with vigour . . . The heart to lead, the loins to support the phallus in the act of begetting . . ." and so on, all "by the will of his heart." The heart, they thought, slowly grew larger and heavier until the age of fifty, and then began to shrink again, just as slowly. It spoke in pulses to the organs and body parts through the *metu*, which included blood vessels, tendons and long thin muscles, respiratory vessels and possibly the digestive system too, as they all joined together at the anus, and this speech could be interpreted by taking the pulse. (*Debdeb*, the ancient word for the noises made by the heart, is charmingly similar to the *lubdub* used by modern Western doctors.) The vessels carried secretions, humors, blood, sperm, feces, air, the breath of life and the breath of death.

These fluids moving through the vessels were considered similar to the Nile and its canals: Herodotus observed that "every month for three successive days [the Egyptians] purge themselves, for their health's sake, with emetics and clysters"—the equivalent of clearing an irrigation ditch. If the feces backed up toward the heart, you could become very sick. The heart governed the flow, and had a life, moods and requirements of its own. If it wandered—and it might—it was important to persuade it back into position: a heart in its place denoted good health. Even now, our heart can be in our mouth, or in our boots, neither of which gives us the same comfort and security as knowing that our heart is in the right place. (In the sixteenth century the equivalent was: "Your hert is in your hose, all in despaire.")

For doctors, dealing with diseases rather than wounds (doctors and surgeons traditionally carried out different functions and were often a little adversarial), the heart was paramount. Many terms for sicknesses of the heart survive in hieroglyphs. Paragraph 855 of the Ebers Papyrus is a series of explanations of terms used to describe heart sicknesses. The heart can suffer from *wiauyt,* old age; *wegeg,* weakness; *fet,* turning aside; *maset or mas,* kneeling; *ad,* decay. It can be weary as though from traveling far, constricted, small: all these descriptions have been associated with what we now term heart failure. Congestive heart failure might be indicated by *igep, bah* and *meh,* meaning "flooded" and "drowned." "The heart is covered up," or "a liquid of the mouth" suggests pulmonary edema and left ventricular failure, which can in extreme cases lead to frothing at the mouth. A heart that is *deher, rut* or *nepa* (bitter, dancing or fluttering) is considered by modern medical diagnosis to be enlarged or displaced, though poets and people in love might recognize the symptoms as something else. Other descriptions, eloquent if unplaceable, include *sesh*, the heart that spread itself out, with its *metu* holding feces; *wesher*, where it dries up; *aq*, where it perishes; *meht*, where it is forgetful (these two are caused by the breath of the lector priest); *djednu*, hot; *depet*, powerless, dark because of anger; *neba*, unclear, something entering from the outside; and *wekh*, shrouded in darkness.

The Ebers Papyrus includes what is possibly a description of angina: "He suffers in his arm, his breast and the side of his stomach. One says concerning him: It is the *wadj* disease. Something has entered his mouth. Death is approaching." The prognosis and symptoms are correct; *wadj* can mean green, arguably the skin color of someone suffering an attack of angina. What "enters" is usually a disease-causing demon. Fascinating work has been done in this area, but in many ways we remain *wekh*, partly because though there were separate words for the heart/soul—*ib*—and the organ—*haty*—there was a great deal of shared territory between the physical and the spiritual: the body had not yet been artificially separated from the soul. A description of what sounds like a physical heart condition might equally be an emotional or spiritual condition, or a combination of the two.

The Egyptians were themselves fairly *wekh* when it came to treatment: remedies to cool the heart were among the most common; amulets were popular, in the shape of an admired animal or body part—hearts appeared frequently. The amulets would be made of red stone—jasper, carnelian or red glass—or porcelain, or wax, and inscribed with a human head or with verses

from the Book of the Dead to give the wearer power in the afterlife. Another "timely remedy" was "to prevent illness by having the greatness of god in your heart."

A heart scarab with a human face from Late Middle Kingdom Egypt. © *Werner Forman Archive*

ANCIENT CHINA

The earliest Chinese medical texts, 3,000 years old, speak, like those of the ancient Egyptians, of the significance of the pulse. *The Inner Classic of the Yellow Emperor* explains how the flow of *qi*, vital energy which could be compared with the Greek *pneuma* (see page 11), round the body is vital to good health, and is measured by the pulse. When the Yellow Emperor declared that he "should like to be informed about Nature to the utmost degree and to include information about man, his physical form, his blood, his breath of life, his circulation and his dissolution; and I should like to know what causes his death and his life and what we can do about all this," his adviser Ch'i Po started to explain: "According to the final calculations Nature begins as one and ends as nine . . ." and proceeded to divide man into three, and each part into three (the heart, for example, is attended to by the element of man in the middle regions). The liver controls the soul; the heart controls the *shên*, the spirit or "divinely inspired part"; the spleen controls ideas and thoughts; the lungs control the inferior or animal spirits; and the kidneys control the will and resolution, aspects commonly associated with the heart in the West. The *shên*

> cannot be heard with the ear. The eye must be brilliant of perception and the heart must be open and attentive, and then the spirit is suddenly revealed through one's own consciousness. It cannot be expressed through the mouth; only the heart can express all that can be looked upon. If one pays close attention one may suddenly know it but one can just as suddenly lose this knowledge. But shên, the spirit, becomes clear to man as though the wind has blown away the cloud.

This system is wonderfully complicated, exact and poetic, based on the system of yin and yang (the two principles of nature, female and male respectively), the four seasons and the five elements. The heart also plays the role of the king or master—*xin zhu*—in charge of the blood. *Xin zhu*, however, is an activity, not a thing. It is yang, rather than yin, and concords as follows:

> Red is the colour of the south, it pervades the heart and lays open the ears and retains the essential substances within the heart. Its sickness is located within the five viscera; its taste is bitter, its element is fire, its animal are sheep, its

7

grain is glutinous panicled millet, it conforms to the four seasons and corresponds to the planet Mars. And thus it becomes known that its diseases are located in the pulse, its sound is *chih* [a note in the pentatonic scale], its number 7 and its smell is scorched . . . The bitter flavour strengthens the heart . . . Extravagant joy is injurious to the heart, but fear counteracts happiness.

Again the spiritual and the physical are closely bound. Ailments were attributed to disharmony and lack of balance, caused by the wind and the weather, "noxious emanations" in heaven or wrong living.

The heavenly climate circulates within the lungs; the climate of the earth circulates within the throat, the wind circulates within the liver, thunder penetrates the heart, the air of a ravine penetrates the stomach, the rain penetrates the kidneys . . . violent behaviour and scorching air resemble thunder.

For example, "the south wind arises in the summer; its sickness is located in the heart and there are disturbances in the chest and ribs." Those who disobey the rules of summer (which include getting up early, not being weary during the daytime, not allowing yourself to get angry, enabling "the breath to communicate with the outside world" and acting "as though they loved everything outside") "will be punished with an injury of the heart," intermittent fevers during the autumn and grave disease at the winter solstice. "Those who do not conform with the atmosphere of summer will not develop their greater *yang*." The atmosphere of their heart will become empty.

Evil influences can follow into this emptiness. The ancient Chinese *Art of the Heart* shows how to keep it

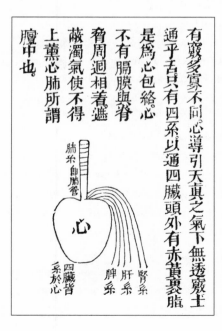

A Chinese diagram of the heart from the *Inner Classic of the Yellow Emperor*. The vessels pointing down connect to the kidneys, liver and spleen (r. to l.). The vessel above connects to the lungs and trachea. *From Ling Shu Su Wen Chieh Yao*

open to the good spirits which give essences and powers to the blood. The emptiness was not purely physical: the ideogram for heart, *xin*, shows the form of the heart and the beginning of the aorta, but unlike ideograms for other organs, it includes no radical indicating flesh.

The Yellow Emperor and his advisers were clearly wise; when he asked why people don't live to the age of one hundred any more, Ch'i Po answered:

> Nowadays people . . . use wine as a beverage and they adopt recklessness as usual behaviour. They enter the chamber of love in an intoxicated condition, their passions exhaust their vital forces, their cravings dissipate their true [essence], they do not know how to find contentment within themselves . . . they devote all their attention to the amusement of their minds . . .

Plus ça change . . . Ch'i Po harked back to a time when "hearts were at peace" and men were "pure at heart."

MEANWHILE IN INDIA

In India early knowledge was mostly magical, poetical and optimistic. According to the Upanishad of the Embryo:

> The establishment of the seven *dhatu* [blood, flesh, fat, tendons, bones, marrow, sperm] occurs in the heart. In the heart there is an inner fire, and where there is fire, there is bile, and where there is bile, there is wind, and where there is wind there goes the heart. The inner fire gathers in the form of bile, and is fanned by the wind (which blows through the respiratory and digestive systems). The heart is the seat of breath, and of blood vessels.

Around 1200 B.C. the magico-religious Atharvaveda was written. This is a collection of 731 hymns in twenty books, incorporating herbal drug remedies, goblins, evil spirits, sorcery, archaic medical history, popular practices of the time and a suggestion of circulation in the vessels, 2,500 years before William Harvey identified it. Veda means knowledge, sacred lore, revealed by Brahma to sages. Most of the Vedas were ancient even before they were written down; many are still active today.

Here's a chant to get rid of jaundice and *hrddyota*, a "heart affliction" which may or may not have been angina pectoris. The patient is to drink water mixed with hair from a red bull and to wear a piece of the bull's skin, soaked in cow's milk and anointed with ghee, as an amulet round his neck.

> Up to the sun shall go thy heart-ache and thy jaundice; in the colour of the red bull do we envelop thee! We envelop thee in red tints, unto long life. May this person go unscathed, and be free of yellow colour! The cows whose divinity is *rohini*; they who, moreover, are red—in their every form and every strength we do envelop thee. Into the parrots, into the thrush do we put thy jaundice, and furthermore into the yellow wagtail do we put thy jaundice!

Flowing blood was stopped with this charm: "The maidens that go yonder, the veins, clothed in red garment, like sisters without a brother, bereft of strength, they shall stand still!"

Heart disease is mentioned: *balasa,* which has a connection to emotional states, and *hrddyota,* but it is not possible to tell exactly what is what. Here is a charm for general well-being, including getting rid of *balasa*:

> We charm away the *balasa* out of your heart and limbs . . . let the *balasa* become ash; let the pain-causing one become urine . . . Let those who surge on the heart and who extend along the vertebrae stream forth, harmless and without causing pain, out of the anal orifice . . . let the pangs who surge across your chest stream forth, harmless and without causing pain, out of the anal orifice . . .

This charm was presumably accompanied by a purgative.

After Atharvaveda came Ayurveda, a more medicinal and less magical system (*ayur*: the science of longevity). It worked on the balance of three *dosa*s, rather like humors, connected with the wind, the sun and the moon. From the thirteenth century, when Indian medics began to study Islamic/Galenist medicine (see page 24) and to incorporate it under the name Yunani (Ionian), reading the pulse began to play an important role. Ayurvedic teachings recognized 600 types of pulse, and associated a slow pulse with, among other things, depression. If the dosa Vayu is disturbed, this could result in palpitations, slowed heart rate, fainting fits and murmuring noises in the heart, all of which are familiar symptoms; other sicknesses showed a confusion with the stomach (burping and a bitter taste in the mouth), and another was thought to be caused by parasites in rotten food which invaded the heart and destroyed it. Throughout this period the god Brahman lived in the heart and, as in Europe, the literality of this image of God caused beautiful poetic confusions in anatomical beliefs.

THE ANCIENT GREEKS

It was the ancient Greeks who divided the body and the soul and started the process of sorting out the relationship between them. For millennia, only the heart remained both body and soul: a vestigial remnant of a simpler undivided humanity. In many ways, to many people, it still is, despite the brain's creeping takeover of the soul, rationalizing and restructuring it, usurping some roles and trying to abolish the rest.

The Greeks were not immune to the primeval reasons for valuing the heart: its warmth, centrality in the body, mobility and system of connections. To those reasons they added their own, based, for the first time, on physical observation and natural philosophy. Once this admirable Hellenic clarity was in place, the history of the knowledge of the physical heart might have developed into a simple narrative of ever-increasing knowledge and understanding, as scholars and physicians learned from each other, but this was not to be: the heart itself may seem relatively simple, but it is the center of a complex system and coming to understand that system is taking thousands of years.

For a start, the physical heart was no more separate from the spiritual for the Greeks than it was for anyone else at that time. Its prime duty was to be the home of the soul. One very important observation, made very early, was that you could be unconscious without being dead and that this was particularly likely to come about if you were hit on the head. The Greek system dealt with this by dividing the soul into two: the *psyche*, which was your individuality and personal immortality, and lived in the head, and the *thymos*, which was your heat, motion and physical life, your "breath soul," and lived in the heart. At death, your *thymos* would return to the *pneuma*—the life spirit of the world, mankind and the universe—and your *psyche* would live on. (The *psyche*, incidentally, was also known as the *nous*, though they mean very different things in modern English.) This system accepted that even if your *psyche* was damaged, your *thymos* could continue to keep your body alive: "the lights are on but nobody's home." It was largely because of the question of unconsciousness that the brain first became a contender for seat of the soul. This division of soul duties between the head and the heart, and the question of

A WORD ON MICROCOSM AND MACROCOSM

Man is heaven and earth, and lower spheres, and the four elements, and whatever is within them, wherefore he is properly called by the name of microcosmos, for he is the whole world . . . know then that there is also within man a starry firmament with a mighty course of planets and stars that have exaltations, conjunctions and oppositions. The heart is the sun; and as the sun acts upon the earth and upon itself, so also acts the heart upon the body and upon itself.

PARACELSUS

The body has long been used to make sense of what is around it. Patterns of reality, based on the nature of the body, have been created since antiquity. The simple one is that man is a little universe, the universe is a big man. The heart is the sun, the sun is the heart. Between the two, created on the same model, lay the state: here the king is the heart (or the head), and the nation is the body or the universe. Scholars and political theorists defined and redefined this basic model for centuries: arguments about which was better and stronger, the heart or the head, the king or the pope, and which was which, resound down the ages. Blood can be justice, nerves the ecclesiastical hierarchy. But the heart was almost always the center of the body politic, as it was of the body physical. As the surgeon Henri de Mondeville wrote in the first years of the fourteenth century: "It is located in the very middle of the chest, as befits its role as the king in the midst of his kingdom." Sometimes the heart is the world itself (see "A Word on Maps," page 230). It's there again in John Donne's *An Anatomy of the World*: "The First Anniversary":

> And learnst thus much by our Anatomie,
> That this worlds generall sicknesse doth not lie
> In any humour, or one certaine part;
> But as thou sawest it rotten at the heart.

The body politic has repeatedly been explained through the body itself, and vice versa. This is not a purely European idea: in China "The heart is like the minister of the monarch who excels through insight and under-standing"—for once not the monarch itself, the Ayurvedic dosas—and in Ayurveda the three dosas connect with the sun, the moon and the wind—are a version. In Islam Adam, the first man, received his name from *adim*, the upper layer of earth from which he was made; his heart was made from the earth of the Kaaba, the central shrine of Islam in Mecca. The twelfth-century Sufi Al-Ghazzali wrote: "The body may be figured as a kingdom, the soul as its king."

which organ is the seat of life, continued to exercise philosophers for millennia, and indeed still arises each time a brain-dead person is put on—or taken off—a life-support machine.

Tell me, where is fancy bred
Or in the heart or in the head?

In *Timaeus* Plato recorded many pre-Socratic beliefs about the human body. He was most interested in the heart as one of the seats of the soul and as the center of his philosophical microcosm, but he also reported a selection of traditionally held beliefs about the body: that blood was made in the liver, and that the soul—*pneuma*—was breathed in from the air and carried in the vessels. He also introduced the idea—which lasted in Europe until the end of the sixteenth century—that the body existed primarily as a vessel for the soul, and could not be considered separately from it. This was not a specially peaceful arrangement, particularly when it was adopted by Christianity: the body tormented and imprisoned the soul with its base desires and carnal re-quirements; the soul was a bad guest in the body with its parasitism, moral bossiness and yearning for release from the evils of the world and the flesh. Before rational science began to question the arrangement, the body stood be-tween the soul and God. Al-Ghazzali agreed: "The body, so to speak, is simply the riding animal of the soul, and perishes when the soul endures. The soul should take care of the body, just as a pilgrim on his way to Mecca should take care of his camel; but if the pilgrim spends his whole time in feeding and adorning his camel, the caravan will leave him behind and he will perish in the desert."

The early Greeks assumed that the *pneuma* was drawn into the brain via the nose and sent around the body in the vessels, possibly mixed with blood. Having seen the main vessels—what we now call the vena cava and the aorta—in animals, they assumed that a simplistic and symmetrical two-vessel system arose in the brain and went down the body like a tree (this was one beginning of a long-lasting image—see page 246), stopping off at the heart, the liver and the spleen. Some felt that the heart must be more important than this: they looked for some direct anatomical route for the soul-bearing breath to reach the heart. Before there was any genuine anatomical knowledge, it was easy to imagine whatever you needed to prove your theory: Empedocles, in the sixth century B.C., believed that the vessels themselves, when they reached the skin, could breathe air in and out as the blood rose and sank; others believed that the network of vessels carried air, blood and fire.

Around 430–330 B.C. a collection of medical works, known as the Hippocratic Corpus, came together. Until the mid-nineteenth century (when Rudolf Virchow developed the theory of cellular pathology, the basis of modern medicine), the Hippocratic system of humors pertained. Like Eastern medicines, it held that health was balance and illness was imbalance; health was stability, illness was an upset. What had to be in balance were the humors or *chymoi*, the four fluids in the body: blood (sanguineous), phlegm (phlegmatic), yellow bile (bilious) and black bile (melancholic). If too much of the blood (a plethora) flowing out (in a defluxion) from the heart gathers at the extremities, bearing too much of one humor or the other, the subject will be made ill. Vomiting, diarrhea, catarrh, pus and nosebleeds were seen as the humors trying to level themselves out, which suggested the remedy of bloodletting: tying a ligature around a limb, allowing the vessel to swell up and then lancing it to relieve the pressure, the excess humor and therefore the sickness. Bloodletting was invented by the Hippocratics, perfected by Galen, and still highly popular 200 years ago.

The Hippocratics declared quite clearly that the heart was a muscle with two ventricles and two auricles wrapped in the pericardium. The right ventricle fed blood to the lungs and received air in exchange. The left ventricle, containing only air, was the seat of the innate heat which generated the humors from food, kept them in balance and moved them around the body. The vessels "are the springs of man's existence, from them spread throughout his body those rivers with which his mortal habitation is irrigated, those rivers which bring life to man as well, for if ever they dry up, then man dies." Inside the heart are

> the hidden membranes . . . a piece of craftsmanship deserving description above all others. There are membranes in the cavities, and fibres as well, spread out like cobwebs through the chambers of the heart and surrounding the orifices on all sides and emplanting filaments into the solid wall of the heart . . . these serve as the guy-ropes and stays of the heart and its vessels, and as foundation to the arteries. Now there is a pair of these arteries, and on the entrance of each three membranes have been contrived, with their edges rounded to the approximate extent of a semi-circle. When they come together it is wonderful to see how precisely they close off the entrance to the arteries . . .

Clearly, someone had seen inside some kind of heart and seen the valves. They had noticed that veins and arteries are different: arteries (from *aer tereo*—carriers of air, as they were believed to be) are much tougher. Aristotle, who was the first consciously and decisively to base systematic anatomical theories on dissection (albeit animal, not human), distinguished between their structures but not their functions, and for him both—and indeed everything else—originated in the heart. The Hippocratic view was that the heart was the seat of man's intelligence, "the principle which rules over the rest of the soul," but they were quite firm

> that the source of our pleasure, merriment, laughter and amusement, as of our grief, pain, anxiety and tears, is none other than the brain. It is specially the organ which enables us to think, see and hear, and to distinguish the ugly and the beautiful, the bad and the good, pleasant and unpleasant.

Aristotle did not agree. The heart was the prime mover of life, he said, and "the motions of pain and pleasure, and generally of all sensations, have plainly their source in the heart, and find in it their ultimate termination." All the blood vessels originated there, blood was made there. As the heart was the first organ to form in the embryo, it was the parent of all other organs. Observing embryos in eggs, he saw the first heartbeat as the first sign of life, and the last as death. For him even sight went to the heart. He believed also that *pneuma* was innate and that breathing in air was simply a way of cooling the natural animal heat of the heart, on which life depended.

Unfortunately, he also held that large warm-blooded animals had three chambers to their hearts, small animals only one, and middle-sized ones, two. "One would a little wonder," wrote the seventeenth-century anatomist Nehemiah Grew, with the benefit of hindsight, "how so observing a man should discover so many mistakes in so few words."

Dissection was of great help to the advance of anatomical knowledge, but it was not without flaws. The dead, immobile heart looks nothing like the flexing living organ. Also, the method of killing an animal affects the nature and amount of blood in its heart and vessels. Strangling (which Aristotle favored) stops blood in its tracks; throat-cutting drains at least some off. This is why arteries seemed to contain not blood but air. No one could know that this was not the case when the creature was alive—it seemed more likely to the cerebrocentrists that the tough, seemingly empty vessels contained invisible *pneuma*, or vital spirits. Moreover the fetal heart—which is probably the only kind of human heart Aristotle ever saw—is different from the adult heart: it has the foramen ovale, a small hole in the septum between the atria, and the ductus arteriosus, a passage connecting the pulmonary artery and the aorta, both of which disappear in the adult heart (the hole closes up, the duct becomes a ligament). Animal hearts can also be very different from human hearts. In fetal hearts and apes' hearts the right atrium looks like a mere swelling in the tube of the vena cava. The issue of the number of chambers perplexed scholars down the ages. Even when you know how many there are it can be hard to make them out: cutting through different planes can produce very different-looking cross sections. As Julian Barnes put it in *A History of the World in Ten and a Half Chapters*, "The heart, I'm afraid, looks a fucking mess."

Aristotle had faith in the ancient knowledge, but he identified for the first time that the blood vessels were a connected system going from the heart throughout the body and that there were different kinds of blood in the different chambers of the heart—what we now know to be the bright red oxygenated arterial blood and the heavy blue deoxygenated venous blood.

THE ALEXANDRIANS

The first known and recorded human dissections took place in Alexandria in the third century B.C. Herophilus (c. 300 B.C.), who compared pulses to musical rhythms and invented a water clock to time them, is said to have dissected human bodies in public, and Cornelius Celsus (fl. A.D. 60) reported that Alexandrians experimented on living people too.

Why, despite the taboos, did human dissection become possible? Because Alexandria was a cosmopolitan city, where Egyptian traditions of mummification and Greek philosophical theories (which held that only the soul, not the body, could expect immortality) combined with the presence of a medical school in a society where slaves and condemned criminals were not considered entirely human—except in body. As a result of the opportunity this threw up, the Alexandrians learned to distinguish between blood vessels and nerves; and they recognized the systole—contraction—to be the active phase of the heart's action, by which blood is expressed from the heart. They also discovered the central nervous system and recognized through experiment that it was the organizational center of the body—so much for Aristotle's central and sensory heart. Using Aristotle's ideas of working rationally and through observation, the Alexandrians displaced his theories. But old ideas die hard: Praxagoras tried to reconcile Aristotle's ideas with the Alexandrian discoveries by saying that blood vessels became nerves when they grew too thin for blood to pass through.

The Alexandrians also examined the cardiac valves. That is not to say that they understood how they worked. Still, the traditional view—that the heart and the lungs were symmetrical, with blood and air being exchanged on both sides—was superseded when it became apparent to some that blood entered the right side through the vena cava and exited the left through the aorta. One of the pair of fundamental vessels was an artery, one was a vein. Confusion over this led to terms such as "venous artery" and "arterial vein" for vessels which looked like the one but were held to behave like the other.

This constantly shifting balance between what was observed and what was assumed to be the case greatly increased the length of the voyage to understanding. Thus Erasistratus, one of the great Alexandrians, could believe that the arteries contained only vital spirit, which had been concocted out of *pneuma* in the left ventricle, and which in the arteries of the brain became psychic spirit. The heart he held to be two-chambered, the atria (or auricles) being just extensions of the vessels, with one side respiratory and one sanguineous. But in that case, why do arteries bleed when you cut them, rather than ooze spirit? The finest veins, he surmised, too fine to hold blood, intercommunicated with the finest arteries, which when damaged lost their *pneuma*, and drew blood from the veins into the resulting vacuum. This is

Hippocrates and Galen; a medieval fresco from the cathedral at Anagni. © *Scala*

only one splendid example of cutting your anatomy to fit your theory. And yet—the finest arteries do link up with the finest veins, via the capillaries, and how this works was not solved until after Harvey discovered circulation 2,000 years later, and then only with the aid of a microscope.

Erasistratus conducted another interesting experiment: when Prince Antiochus of Syria was melancholy and his pulse slow, the doctor had the ladies of the court parade past his couch. When the prince's stepmother Stratonice appeared, his pulse picked up, and when dispensation was given for them to marry, sphygmic stability was achieved. A similar observation is used in an early twenty-first-century car advertisement. A young man's ECG reading goes wild because, we are led to assume, of the beauty of the young cardiologist's bottom; in fact—depressingly—he's looking out the window at a car.

The Roman Claudius Galen used merely to recite the names of likely sweethearts while holding the wrist of patients he suspected of being lovelorn (the name Pylades produced a "turbulent pulse" in one heartsick wench). Galen, known as the Prince of Physicians, was born about A.D. 129 in Pergamon, the son of an architect and a woman who, he said, used to bite her serving maids. He studied in Alexandria, but was too late to benefit directly from human dissection:

the physicians had been expelled by the Ptolemy of around 200 B.C., and for medical students it was back to animals (apes, pigs, goats and an elephant), skeletons and fortuitous circumstance. He was also for a while physician to the gladiators, which gave him plenty of opportunity to look inside the body through wounds. Galen revised the old image of the tree by upending it: he rooted it in the liver and had it grow upward toward heaven. He also held, with the Alexandrians, that the brain, not the heart, was the source of the nerves, and of their powers.

In his book *On the Causes of Pulsation* he described the body as he saw it. Incoming food, he said, was made into chyle in the stomach and intestines, which was then turned into blood by the liver. Blood was the food of the body, sent out in one direction in the veins and assimilated by the parts of the body that needed it. Assimilation means, literally, making similar, so the parts would take from the blood that which was similar to them. The lung, as he called it, was, however, too light and delicate to accept anything from heavy venous (deoxygenated, as we now know it to be) blood, so the blood had to be "concocted" in the heart to make it "subtle." "Heavy" blood from the liver entered the heart through the vena cava (A in the diagram below), sucked in by the heart's natural expansive movement (as he thought the diastole, the resting stage, to be), as a bellows draws in air, from the liver. It passed through the right auricle (B) and the valve into the right ventricle (C), where by a special "faculty" (Galen called anything he hadn't fully worked out a faculty) it was concocted, and then sent to the lung through the pulmonary artery (D), which he called an arterial vein, because he needed it to be a vein to carry this rarefied venous blood. He explained that the blood was so special the vein needed to be as strong as an artery to make sure it didn't escape. The arteries, which he held to originate in the heart, also contained blood, which mixed with air (*pneuma*) in the left ventricle (E) and then proceeded to the body via the aorta (F), ebbing and flowing through the vessels.

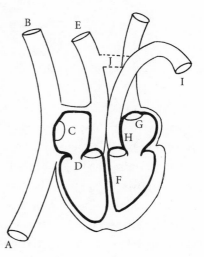

How the heart worked, according to Galen.

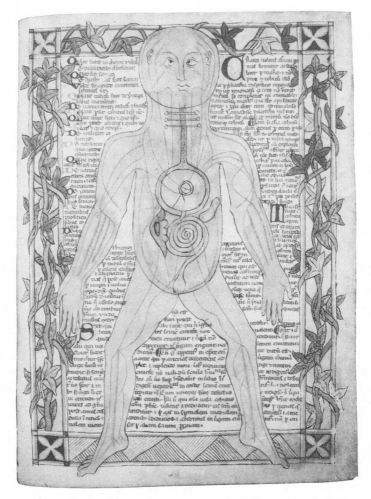

Veinman, from a thirteenth-century set of English anatomical diagrams. *MS. Ashmole 399, fol. 18r, Bodleian Library, University of Oxford*

Galen thus held that there were in effect two separate blood systems: nutritive (venous), based on the liver, and respiratory (arterial), based on the air-breathing heart, which goes back to the traditional view of the two main vessels running the length of the body. The heart was to him a single organ divided in two to deal with the two systems. He proved by experiment that arteries contained blood, not just pure spirit. But now he had a problem. If the thick venous blood was nutritive and the thin arterial blood was spiritual, and the two systems were entirely separate, and if Erasistratus was wrong about

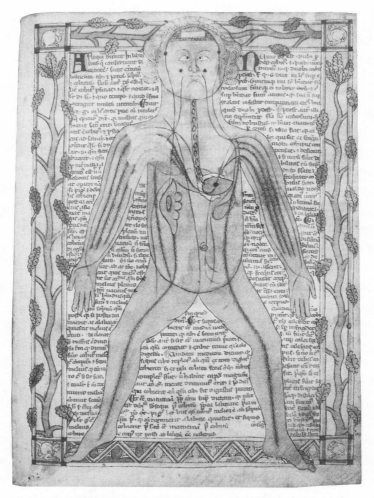

Arteryman: Veinman's brother. Note the black grain in his heart.
MS. Ashmole 399, fol. 19r, Bodleian Library, University of Oxford

the transference of blood at the fine ends of veins and arteries, as Galen also insisted, then how did blood get from its sole place of production, the liver, into the arterial system? It couldn't come back from anywhere because blood was assimilated by the body; it couldn't transfer from vein to artery because he'd just denied that possibility . . . so he postulated tiny holes in the septum between the ventricles (G), through which a little venous blood could seep, in order to undergo the vital process of mixing with *pneuma* to make vital spirits, which would carry vital heat through the arteries to the body.

He saw these pores, he said, with "the Eye of Reason." The little pits he saw on the septum had to go all the way through because otherwise they were without purpose, and nature does nothing without purpose. (He was right in that—but he had no way of knowing what nature was dealing with when it formed the human heart. Nobody designing a heart from scratch would come up with the complex system that nature evolved as creatures crept up out of the sea and learned to breathe air.) The mixing of blood and *pneuma,* he said, would produce sooty wastes, which would be expelled—whoops! Another problem. The waste could only escape by going back up through the mitral valve (F)—which worked in the opposite direction. Moreover—how could the lung get the arterial blood it needed without that blood having to go back through the valve too? Galen had landed himself with spirit, blood and sooty wastes moving in two different directions through valves whose direction favored only the least substantial of them. This is what provoked Harvey, 1,500 years later, to cry out: "Good God! How do the mitral valves hinder the return of air, and not of blood!"

Galen's ideas dominated knowledge of the heart for so long because his ideas were satisfying, because nothing new was discovered and because much of what had been discovered was forgotten after the fall of the Roman Empire. Dissection was no longer, Greek texts were neglected. Cicero knew nothing later than Aristotle. Aretaeus of Cappadocia described the different kinds of blood, but knew no Galen. The Dark Ages descended on Europe.

Drops of light shine through: in the fourth century Vindicianus described the heart as muscular, shaped like a pine cone, inclined to the left and having four veins, two sanguineous and two spiritual, and two "ears," in which live the mind and soul of man. If he meant the auricles, the "little ears," this is the first time the soul was placed there rather than in the ventricles—indeed when last heard of the right auricle was a mere expanded bit of blood vessel. But Vindicianus tells us that everything worthy of our attention comes through these ears. Lactantius, an early Christian writer who sought to reconcile the Greeks with the Bible, stated that the heart was the seat of wisdom and though the soul was located in the brain, it traveled to the chest in times of abstraction and concentration, which is why we don't notice things when we're deep in thought. Isidore of Seville, in about 600, offers some anatomical information in his encyclopaedia Libri Differentiarium: veins and arteries are not distinguished and the chambers of the heart are called arteria. From the heart "two arteries emanate, the one on the left having more blood, and the one on the right having more spirit. This is why we take the pulse on the right arm." In the dark he'd got it the wrong way round.

Such knowledge as was passed on became corrupted through copying and, in particular, through the multiple translations involved in its sojourn in the East. Greek medicine was taught at Alexandria up until the eighth century, and (much copied) diagrams from the twelfth to the fifteenth centuries open: "Here begins the description of dissection, just as in Galen, that most skilful physician . . ." Many are hugely corrupted: the Veinman has no heart at all; the Arteryman's heart contains something called a "black grain," which is meant to be the source of arteries: "where the spirit lives and from where arises a great vein that goes in two parts, left and right." Galen did use the analogy of a seed in the heart being the origin of the arterial tree (of ancient image); this may be where the black grain came from (see page 247 for more on this).

THE ARABS

What we think of as Greek culture in fact developed in what is now known as the Middle East as well, and was inherited there by the Arabs and the Muslim world. Knowledge that in the West remained lost for generations was preserved and naturalized in its Arab branch by Arab scholars. A Christian priest, Sergios, who translated Galen's anatomical works into Syriac, started a process of translating, condensing, misunderstanding and retranslating that became at times almost ridiculous. Take the principle of reduplication: an anatomical structure for which there was no word in the language often had a name invented for it by the translator, and so on throughout however many languages it was translated into. When it was translated into a language which *did* have a word, there would be two words and only one structure. The next translator would try to find structures to be called by the name that had been invented. In this way the thoracic body-wall membranes, for example, multiplied when Greek, Latin and Arabic versions were finally assimilated.

The Arab term for artery was "pulsatile vein." Galen's "arterial vein" and "venous artery" came out as "the pulsatile vein that looks like a non-pulsatile vein," and vice versa, ultimately leaving the Arab reader having to deal with the idea that the pulmonary artery was "a pulsating non-pulsatile vein that re-

A nineteenth-century Spanish portrait of Ibn Sina (Avicenna). © *Museo Real Academia de Midicina/Bridgeman Art Library*

sembled a pulsating vein and which Galen said did not pulsate," as R. K. French puts it in his admirable *History of the Heart.*

The Arab scholars—al-Razi (Rhazes in Latin), Ali ibn al-Abbas al-Majusi (Haly Abbas) and Abu Ali al-Husain ibn Abdullah ibn Sina, known in Europe as Avicenna—were of necessity inter-preters, compilers and reconsiderers of the theories of Hippocratic, Galenic, humoral medicine. "The veto of the religious law and the sentiments of charity innate in ourselves alike prevent us from practising dissection," as Ibn al-Nafis put it. "This is why we are willing to be limited to basing our knowledge of the internal organs on the sayings of those who have gone before us."

Despite this limitation, Ibn al-Nafis was the first to make the clear allegation that Galen was wrong about his septal pores, "for the substance of the heart is solid, and there exists neither a visible passage, as some would suppose, nor an invisible passage which will permit the flow of blood, as Galen believed." He agreed with the rest of Galen's physiology, and came up with a solution: blood crossed the lungs "so that it can spread out in their substance and mix with the air" and thence to "the venous artery, and from there to the left ventricle." This came to be called the pulmonary transit; it is what happens and Ibn al-Nafis was the first to identify it. Al-Majusi, on the other hand, held that only one big pore existed (presumably the others were lost in the translation), which was wider on the right side of the heart and became narrower toward the left, so as to prevent any but the finest parts of the blood from entering the left ventricle—a fine example of the sort of magnificent bollocks produced by the combination of intelligence and partial information. (Another splendid one comes from Johannes Mesue, who said that the three "pouches" of the heart were stacked vertically.)

Ibn Sina (978–1036), meanwhile, suggested that the all-important heart might act through other organs—the brain for psychic functions and the liver for nutrition. This was the first glimmer of a way of reconciling Aristotle's and Galen's views of the heart. In a micro/macrocosmic way, it also makes room for the idea that God, rather than being omnipotent, acts through humans; for individual responsibility over fatalism.

Despite the prohibition on dissection and on reproducing living things in art (which was seen as putting oneself in competition with God, maker of all things), there are some very beautiful Arab anatomical illustrations: embellishing scientific texts was exempt. In 1396 Mansur ibn Muhummad ibn Ahmad published *Tashrih-i badan-i Insan* (*The Anatomy of the Human Body*), the illustrations from which were still being transcribed in the nineteenth century, and were based on the same five-figure series from which we have already seen the Veinman and the Arteryman, with its squatting figure and great round head: skeletal, muscular, nervous, digestive, cardiovascular.

The heart holds a very important role in Islam, uniting *jism*, the body, and *rooh*, the vital force or spirit. Classical Greek medical knowledge has been absorbed into forms that were acceptable to Islam—"religiously correct medical lore." In Islamic medicine *rooh* issues from the left ventricle. It is made up of *latif*, subtle particles of the *akhlaat*—the four humors, also known as the daughters of the elements; the heart is particularly associated not with blood (*dum*), as you might expect, but with yellow bile (*safra*). Consequently *rooh* can be adjusted by changing the diet, by medicines and by attention to behavior and the emotions. "The vital force diffuses itself into the remotest parts of the organism," wrote Muhammad Salim Khan in 1986, "and resembles the sun in luminosity. An imbalance or disharmony within

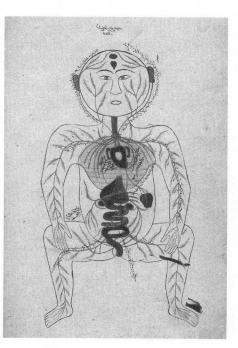

Late fourteenth-century anatomical drawing showing the heart and arteries, by Mansur. © *The Art Archive / British Library*

the vital force is the very beginning of disease." The pulse is the movement and contraction of the heart, and can be read for temperature, strength, duration, fullness, constancy, size, quality of impact, speed of cycle and elasticity. This informs the *hakim* (healer) of the balance or otherwise of the humors so he can make his diagnosis.

Part of the vital force, *rooh Haiwana*, comes from the left side of the heart. It is the vital faculty, and maintains life. *Rooh Nafsania*, the part of the vital force concerned with cognition, movement and sensation, is based in the brain. Cognition is divided into *zahir*, the external or conscious, and *ghaib*, the internal or subconscious: they are then subdivided into thinking, imagination, memory, intuition and reasoning, all of which, originating from internal or external sources, according to Khan, "are referred to the heart, which . . . deals with them according to the condition of the self. Thus we can begin to see that the idea of unity permeates throughout Islamic pathology with the heart as its pivotal point." If the vital force makes a sudden violent internal movement, coma or even death can be the result, and "any prolonged movement towards negative aspects can predispose an individual towards mental-emotional and physical illness."

Sharia forbids the use of magic, but geomancy and astrology used to be significant. *The Arabian Nights* tells how "When your father said to me, 'Draw my blood,' I fetched the astrolabe and found that the constellation of the hour was unfavourable." And bleeding of the neck is unfavorable, according to a twelfth-century Fatimid doctor in Cairo, when the moon is in the sign of Taurus; that of the back when the moon is in the sign of Leo; "and generally when the moon is in the sign of that limb which is to be cupped." Astrology was significant in European medicine too.

MEDIEVAL KNOWLEDGE

In the second half of the eleventh century Constantine the African was translating back from the Arabic, and a medical school at Salerno was instructing how to dissect a pig, because, they said, "although some animals such as monkeys are found to resemble ourselves in external form, there are none so like us internally as the pig." In these instructions the vena cava is said to enter the "lower auricle" from below; apart from that there is no mention of the heart at all. Other surviving knowledge from Salerno harks back to Plato's upside-down tree idea—as if Galen had never turned it back on its roots. Scholars tended to be divided into philosophers, following Aristotle, and physicians, following Galen. Peter of Abano, writing in 1303, tried to reconcile the two, and like Ibn Sina decided that the heart was the center of the body and seat of the soul because it was the source of the other parts.

> For the heart is like the sea [Peter wrote], agitated by winds, and from it flow three great rivers, one of which flows through the whole body carrying spirit and blood through the great river called aorta . . . Another river flowing thence rises to the brain so that the nerves may be generated from the brain, from a matter related to a matter of the heart and that of the brain . . . This river, held back in its progress by an upper obstacle, produces a lake, that is, the brain, from which, laterally, originate smaller rivers, of which the largest is the spinal medulla, and the seven smaller rivulets are the seven pairs of nerves . . . also from this sea arises, at the right auricle of the heart, another river . . . by which the matter of the heart is connected to the matter of the liver.

Medieval scholars tended to feel inferior to the great ancients: not only intellectually—which made them doubt their own understanding instead of questioning the Greeks' authority—but also physically. Perhaps, some thought, the human body had changed, for the worse, since the days of Aristotle, and this was why the ancient wisdom didn't add up.

Only when the idea emerged that scientific knowledge could be cumulative did scholars give precedence to the methods, rather than the findings, of Galen and Aristotle, and start again to use reason and observation, and to make progress. In other words, the Renaissance began.

In 1300 Pope Boniface VIII had issued a bull, *De Supulturis*, forbidding people from boiling up the bones of dead crusaders in order to transport them back to Europe for burial (see page 325). For a while this was taken as a ban on human dissection, which had just started to creep back into legitimacy: in 1302 there were postmortems held for legal and medical reasons in Bologna. By the early 1400s dissection was recognized by university statutes there and in Padua and Florence. (In 1540 Henry VIII allowed four hanged felons a year to the united Company of Barbours and Chirurgeons, for the purpose of anatomical study: a corpse given for dissection, like one drawn and quartered, would have no Christian funeral, which was seen as a most particular

A sixteenth-century French anatomy of man, showing the relation of the organs to the stars (note the heart and the sun) and recommending that "when the moon is in Taurus, Virgo and Capricorn it is good to bleed the melancholic." © *Musée Condé / Bridgeman Art Library*

punishment.) In 1525 a comprehensive new edition of Galen was published in Greek. Erasmus translated some of it into Latin—indeed 590 editions of works by Galen appeared in Europe during the sixteenth century. In Bologna Mondino produced his *Anatomia*, a guide to dissection for the education of surgeons, which incorporated Aristotle, Galen, the Arabs and the knowledge uncovered in Salerno. Though this cleared up much of the confusion, the original purpose of these dissections was still to prove and illustrate the accepted texts. This presented scholars with a new intellectual challenge: reconciling the ancient knowledge with the dissected body. Silvius declared that if the body contradicted Galen, the body was wrong. Even Mondino, for all his practical experience, still held the heart to be three-chambered, and furthermore believed the auricles to be reserve tanks in case too much blood or spirit entered the ventricles. The other great challenges were to "familiarise the heart with a certain necessary Inhumanity" required by surgery in the days before anaesthesia and antiseptics, as William Hunter put it in the late eighteenth century, and to get as much work done on a corpse as you could in the few days before it began to rot.

THE AGE OF ENLIGHTENMENT

As the sixteenth century dawned, perfect knowledge did not descend like sunbeams from behind a Tiepolo cloud, raining enlightenment on all and sundry. (As late as 1806 Nicholas Corvisart was still complaining that doctors "abstain carefully from finding in the dead body the mistakes which their ignorance of anatomy caused them to commit.") The pulse of a patient was still often measured against the unreliable clock of the physician's own pulse, which was assumed to be 60 beats per minute, based on Copernicus's law. Johannes Kepler took his astronomical readings by his pulse: "In the space of time in which the artery in a double pulse dilates once, and again contracts, the largest circles will be revolved 7,500,000 miles, and Saturn, in a 2000 times narrower orbit, passes generally through 4000 miles." One only hopes he was feeling calm and well all the time he was working. He did have a biblical precedent: "The heart proclaims the hour to the people." And there exists a theory that it was the combination of the movements of the stars and the beat of his own pulse that set the first mathematician thinking in the first place.

In the late fifteenth century Gabriele de Zerbis was referring to a sinew as real which was in fact nothing more than a translation error from Galen centuries before, and the existence of those invisible septal pores continued to be accepted, despite the fact that whatever the Eye of Reason beheld, the cold eye of reality had now looked on the human heart (albeit boiled, as was the custom, almost until it fell apart) and found no such thing. On the subject of the number of cavities, de Zerbis's contemporary Niccolò Massa decided that most hearts have two, but some have three, as the human body is very variable. He claims to have seen a third cavity in 1534, at the dissection of "the biggest heart I have ever seen." Later, Harvey was "frankly amazed" by the variety in the hearts he saw, but he found them nothing but conservative in the number of chambers they had. (Milton Helpern, chief medical examiner for New York City, agreed: "No two hearts are alike.")

IN THE course of the sixteenth century two matters most occupied anatomists. One was the purpose of valves in the veins, more and more of which were being discovered. It was widely and erroneously believed that the purpose of a valve was to prevent too-swift movement of blood *away* from the heart. The other great issue was the pulmonary transit, the passage of the blood from one side of the heart to the other by way of the lungs. Ibn-Nafis had suggested it centuries before; now the idea reemerged in curious forms.

The Spaniard Michael Servetus (1511–53) was most interested in the idea that the blood was the seat of the soul—the Holy Spirit as breathed into man by God. How, he wondered, could enough spirit get into the blood? The left ventricle, where traditionally *pneuma* or spirits from outside were mixed and concocted with the blood, seemed illogically small. Surely the lungs were more appropriate places for blood and spirit (or air) to meet, being larger, nearer to the outside air, and well served with blood vessels. Also, if the pulmonary artery's only job was to take blood to nourish the lungs, why was it so big? The coronary vein (artery, in fact), which took blood to the heart's own fabric, was much smaller. Everything for Servetus pointed to blood going to and somehow through the lungs, then back to the heart for distribution through the arteries. His Eye of Reason saw that there must be a way through the lungs. Servetus's religious beliefs, although they led him to this breakthrough, also denied him its fruits. In 1538 he had been condemned in Paris for lecturing on astrology; in 1553 he was denounced as a heretic by Calvin and burned at

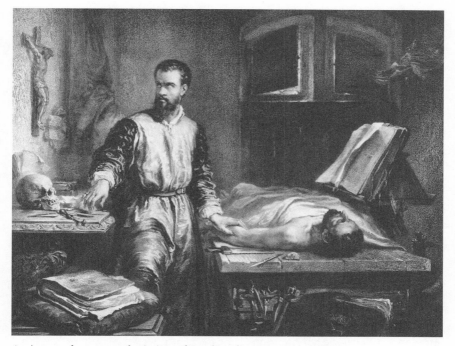

A nineteenth-century depiction of Vesalius dissecting a corpse. © *Corbis*

the stake. His work had little effect on the general increase of knowledge as it was burned too, either by him or with him.

Servetus didn't care if Galen's septal pores between the ventricles existed or not. Vesalius (1514–64) doubted them out loud. His *Tabulae Anatomicae Sex* were among the first anatomical drawings made specifically for medical students, and his *De Humana Corporis Fabrica* (1543), illustrated with large, beautiful, clear woodcuts from his own drawings by Jan Stephan van Calcar, was a systematic exercise in challenging Galen. His weapon? The human corpse. Here he is on acquiring one:

> While out walking, looking for bones in the place where on the country high-ways eventually, to the great convenience of students, all those who have been executed are customarily placed, I happened upon a dried cadaver . . . I climbed the stake and pulled off the femur from the hip bone. While tugging at the specimen, the scapulae together with the arms and hands also followed . . . After I had brought the legs and arms home in secret . . . I allowed myself to be

shut out of the city in the evening in order to obtain the thorax, which was firmly held by a chain. I was burning with so great a desire . . . that I was not afraid to snatch in the middle of the night what I so longed for . . . The next day I transported the bones piecemeal through another gate of the city.

Among other developments, in Book VI Vesalius was "driven to wonder at the handiwork of the Almighty by means of which the blood sweats from the right into the left ventricle through passages which escape the human vision." His contemporary Realdo Colombo at Padua declared that those who believe in septal pores "err by a long way," and followed on, through vivisection experiments, to prove the pulmonary transit. Blood was heavy and blue when it entered the lungs, bright scarlet when it left. He also showed that the systole (contraction) was stronger than diastole, and thus the forceful stage of the heart's movement.

Colombo's idea of pulmonary transit, published in 1559, was revolutionary to say the least, and led to a flurry of discussion, denial and hurriedly produced alternative possibilities (such as Varolius's idea that blood went both up and down in both the aorta and the vena cava) as it was gradually realized that Galen had been quite profoundly wrong in this. It was the first time that Galen had been discredited, and it shook the framework of Western medical knowledge. It did not, however, stop people from making desperate attempts to reconcile opposing views. Many, indeed, were still trying to accommodate Aristotle too. Consider Caesalpino, who evolved the theory that while we are awake and active, blood comes to our sensory organs through the arteries, bringing with it heat and spirit, and then while we sleep our veins take the cooled blood back to the heart. It is a kind of circulation, based on the Aristotelian theory that heat rises and coolness sinks back. But it was wrong.

All the information was there for William Harvey (1578–1657) to discover the circulation of the blood. The valves had not only been identified but considered at length by Harvey's teacher at Padua, Fabricius; the pulmonary transit and the nonexistence of the septal pores had been established; nebulous notions of circulation of some kind had been mooted, and knowledge was now shared, published and debated. Harvey's was the first generation of scientists to understand how valves actually work—no more nonsense about them letting things in or out when they felt like it. The Aristotelians—of which Harvey was one—disagreed with the Galenists, and the Galenists were

HARVEY

Harvey's imagery is far from revolutionary: the heart as a fountain and as a house are biblical; the heart as the sun is Platonic; the heart as a father figure goes back to Jeremiah. Harvey was a royalist in the Civil War, and he dedicated *De Motu Cordis* to Charles I with a quasi-flattering micro/macrocosmic comparison between heart and king. In Chapter 14 he writes: "It must therefore be concluded that the blood in the animal body moves around in a circle continuously, and that the action or function of the heart is to accomplish this by pumping. This is the only reason for the motion and beat of the heart." On one hand this might be a warning to poets; but in light of later developments it might also be read as a reminder of a king's responsibilities. Harvey lost many papers during the Civil War: "No grief was so crucifying to him," observed John Aubrey. He was not altogether delicate, however: "He was wont to say that man was but a great mischievous baboon," and had a reputation for being too swift with his dagger "upon every slight occasion."

William Harvey demonstrating to Charles I his theory of the circulation of the blood, by Robert Hannah, 1848 (note the dead deer on the table to the right). © *Royal College of Physicians / Bridgeman Art Library*

in disarray. *Autopsia*—seeing for oneself—had replaced the Eye of Reason, and dissections were held in public: at Bologna they were part of the annual carnival. It was time for a coup de grâce.

Harvey put it all together, took a great leap of imagination and reversed the direction of blood in the veins so that it flowed back to the heart. As he did so, everything else fell into place. With circulation, the problem of the venous artery and the arterial vein is resolved, as each is given back its proper job and title. The unsatisfactory notion that the heart does two jobs, serving two systems, when it is clearly one organ, was removed. So was the question of why, if half the heart were respiratory, it was not built like the trachea and the lungs rather than like its own other side.

The heart was a muscle, Harvey said; its contraction was its active phase; the notion of pulmonary transit was correct, and as for pores, "Damme, there are no pores and it is not possible to show such." Sooty wastes did not exist, air did not enter veins or arteries, animal vivisection showed that far too much blood passed through the heart for it all to be absorbed by the body—more passed through in an hour than could be contained by the whole animal. The amount of blood traveling fast in "flux and reflux, thither by the arteries, thither by the veins" made it "absolutely necessary to conclude that the blood . . . is impelled in a circle, and is in a state of ceaseless motion."

> It comes to pass in the body [he wrote in *De Motu Cordis* (*On the Movement of the Heart*)], that all the parts are nourished, cherished and quickened with blood, which is warm, perfect, vaporous, full of spirit, and, that I may so say, alimentative: in the parts the blood is refrigerated, coagulated, and made as it were barren, from whence it returns to the heart as to the fountain or dwelling house of the body, to recover its perfection, anFd there again by naturall heat, powerfull and vehement, it is melted, and is dispense'd again through the body from thence being fraught with spirits, as with balsam. And that all the things do depend upon the motional pulsation of the heart: so the heart is the beginning of life, the Sun of the Microcosm, as proportionately the Sun deserves to be called the heart of the world, by whose virtue, and pulsation, the blood is mov'd, perfected, made vegetable, and is defended from corruption, and mattering; and this familiar household god doth his duty to the whole body, by nourishing, cherishing and vegetating, being the foundation of life, and author of all.

In the face of Harvey's work, the old Galenist theory of two systems fell apart completely. He provided what had up till then been lacking: a cogent theory to replace what he was destroying.

ONLY IN one area was Harvey reduced to the Eye of Reason. Capillaries are invisible to the naked eye, and Harvey held that veins and arteries, however small, could not generally meet mouth to mouth because arteries are much smaller than veins. So how did the blood get from arteries to veins? Galen had spoken of "certain invisible and extremely narrow passages" through which blood and *pneuma* could be exchanged between arteries and veins; Harvey was not too proud to fall back, in this matter, on Galen's ancient knowledge and the Eye of Reason.

Harvey outlined his discovery in lectures in 1616 and published *De Motu Cordis* in 1628, but making a great leap did not stop speculation and discovery. Harvey described how blood circulated, but he did not describe why, which was something of an offense to his critics. "How" is all very well, but "Why" was considered a more noble question. Harvey sniffed at that: start with how, he said, and when you have the facts you can proceed to the causes. Aubrey reported: "I have heard him say that after his book of the Circulation of the Blood came out that he fell mightily in his practice, and it was believed by the vulgar that he was crackbrained, and all the physicians were against his opinion, and envied him, and many wrote against him." For his part, he liked to sit on the roof to think; he told Aubrey to read Aristotle, Cicero and Ibn Sina, and called the modern authors "shit breeches."

MECHANISM

In the meantime, in France, René Descartes (1596–1650) had begun to put forward his theories that the body was a machine; that the soul was an immortal and insubstantial source of consciousness, responsible for thought and decision; and that the two were completely separate. (This didn't answer the question of how the two related—according to Descartes, the pineal gland was the link.) The heart, whose beat was an involuntary (if regular) action, was an important part of the machine, the source of movement. God, he held, placed a dark fire in the heart which vaporized blood as it entered. This produced heat which opened the arterial valves, the vaporized blood went through the valves, round the arteries and veins, as Harvey had described, reliquefying in the process before returning to the heart. Meanwhile nervous spirits had separated off from the blood through their great speed, and the fastest traveled to the brain, where they entered the nerves and caused sense and movement. Effectively, he reclaimed some very ancient notions and gave them mechanistic methods and raisons d'être. The heart was the body's engine. Thomas Hobbes (1588–1679) took the materialist attitude even further, suggesting that only matter existed. "What is the heart but a spring?" he asked in *Leviathan*. In 1653 the poet Margaret Cavendish itemised the new knowledge:

> That all sound, sent, sight is created in the Braine . . . That the bloud goeth in circulation . . . That all passions are made in the head, not in the heart. That the soul is a kernal in the Braine. That all the old Philosophers were fooles, and knew little. That the moderne Philosophers have committed no errours.

There developed something of a division between French and English thought on these matters.

A curiosity of the time, demonstrated relatively easily, was how a viper's heart kept on beating after being removed from the viper. Everyone knew that the heart was fundamental to life, yet could not be controlled by the conscious brain; so if the soul resided in the brain and the heart could be separated from it and still beat, what did that mean? Surely that the heart was a purely mechanical thing? But in that case, why did it respond to emotion? And why was it so responsive also to the body—exertion and sickness affected it, and its changing pulses were believed to help the body to deal with, for example, fever.

In time it became more or less accepted that the body *was* a machine: the heart pumped blood, blood gave power to nervous spirits, which moved the muscles by contraction from within, and the whole thing was an exercise in perpetual motion based on the heart. Nobody had an answer for where the motion came from in the first place. Then Isaac Newton presented his theories of physics, which most scientists at the time did not understand, and the body machine became a more complicated postulation. If the body was simply a hydraulic machine, it needed an external driving force. So what was that force? Newton showed that motion is forever being lost to friction, collisions and so on, and held that it might be replenished by gravity, natural fermentations and reactions caused by ether; many people, not surprisingly, felt that a soul with physical power over the body was if nothing else an easier explanation.

Meanwhile at Montpellier in France, according to R. K. French, it was being taught that

> while the direct meeting of equal masses moving at equal velocities was assumed to result in total loss of motion, their indirect meeting was held to produce constant oscillation about a point. The heart was said to move in a libration of this type as a result of . . . blood entering, blood leaving, gravity, pressure from the body and so on. The result was said to be true perpetual motion, without any internal or external input.

Wild and beautiful interpretations of the heart's physical activity did not cease with advancing knowledge; they simply became more scientific and more complex.

Chemistry began to play a part, though oxygen was not identified until the middle of the nineteenth century: Thomas Willis at Oxford described how movement in the muscles occurred when nervous spirit originally from the blood but resident in the muscle was joined by nervous spirit sent down the nerves from the brain at the soul's command, and they effervesced together in the muscle. The Italian Borelli held that the soul understood that the heart was overheated by the blood within it, and from the embryonic stage sent messages to expel the hot, heavy blood and thus relieve the heart. As the blood filled the heart again, through the veins, so the soul would send messages to have it expelled. After a while this response became so familiar that the soul put it, as it were, on automatic, which is why it was no longer under our conscious control. The soul did this because its purpose was to do good, and removing discomfort in the heart was part of that duty. This assumed powers of the flesh—a kind of memory and wisdom—which was utterly unacceptable to those who believed the body was a machine.

Curiously, the animists and the mechanists ended up with very similar beliefs about the physical nature of the body. The animists believed it was a machine, powered by a soul; the mechanists believed it was a machine, powered in some still-incomprehensible way by its own natural forces. After a while, for all practical purposes, they simply merged into each other, so that now the most exact research scientist can be devoutly religious and know that God created every gene, every cell, every wiggle of DNA and how it all fits together.

R. K. French points out one extraordinary fact about this entire history. In all that time, and despite the ubiquity of bloodletting, so unquestioned was the belief that blood flowed *from* the heart only that nobody noticed that the *veins* swelled up on the outside of the ligature, furthest from the heart. The wrong side.

ONCE THE circulation had been correctly identified, a few details needed clearing up. Further discoveries were made: that blood is made in the bone marrow, not the liver; that the role previously played by *pneuma* is actually performed by oxygen; how exactly the blood is "perfected"; and how it distributes to the parts what they need. Antoni van Leeuwenhoek (1632–1723) invented the microscope, and the Bolognese anatomist Marcello Malpighi used it to spot capillaries. "Such is the wandering about of these vessels," he wrote in 1661, that "there appears a network . . . it was clear to the senses that the blood . . . was not poured into spaces, but was always contained within tubules, and that its dispersion is due to the multiple winding of the vessels." With this, the heart's role as a magnificent pump was pretty much finalized: except for the little detail of what made it go.

A new discipline, electrophysiology, came into being as scientists noticed what electricity could do to muscle. In 1770 the Italian Louis Galvani accidentally applied an electrical current to a frog that he was preparing to dissect, and its muscles began to leap and spasm: he found that thunderstorms made amputated frogs' legs twitch, and electricity became the life force du jour. (In 1760 Christopher Smart wrote: "The electrical fire is the spiritual substance which God sends from heaven to sustain the bodies both of man and beast.") In 1774 a small boy fell out of a window in London. He was given an electric shock which as it happened jolted his fibrillating heart back into the rhythm of life. Stannius (1803–83) systematically investigated the heart's electrical system and identified its intrinsic pacemaker. In 1856 von Kolliker and Muller put a bit of frog nerve and muscle on a beating heart and noted that it twitched with each contraction. By 1889 Willem Einthoven had come up with the electrocardiograph, through which the heart's actions lie ever open to knowledge and medicine.

2

THE ANATOMY
AND WORKINGS OF
THE PHYSICAL HEART

So, after all that, how does the heart work exactly?

The heart is a muscle, a single organ made up of two pumps, Siamese twins working side by side to move blood around the body. An adult human heart is the size of a clenched fist and weighs about 300 grams (9 oz). It lies under the sternum, between the lungs and a little to the left. It contains four chambers: one left and one right ventricle, and one left and one right atrium. The right side (which is on the left as you look at a diagram) is the pulmonary heart; it is slightly smaller as it sends blood only to the lungs. The left (on the right in diagrams), the systemic heart, is bigger because it needs to send blood (2,000 gallons a day) all around the body (through 60,000 miles of tubes per day). The atria are above the ventricles.

The heart's walls are made up of three layers: the actual heart, the striated muscular myocardium, the central layer which contracts, and the surrounding membrane, the double-layered pericardium, the inner layer of which fits snugly round the heart and then doubles back on itself at the base to form the outer layer. Between the two pericardial layers—in the pericardial cavity—there is a fluid which prevents friction during the heart's contractions, as the pericardial layers slide over each other.

During diastole—the relaxation of the heart—blood which has circulated the body and given up its oxygen enters the thin-walled right atrium through the superior and inferior vena cava, and deoxygenated blood from the heart's own muscular flesh enters through the coronary sinus. The left atrium, also thin walled, receives oxygenated blood from the lungs via the pulmonary veins. Blood from the atria moves down into the right and left ventricles simultaneously through the atrioventricular orifices. The right orifice is

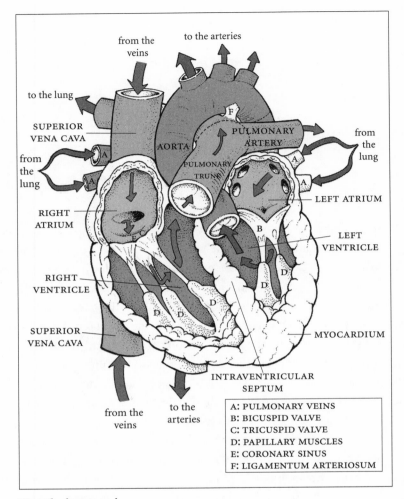

How the heart works.

guarded by the tricuspid (three-cusp) valve, the left by the bicuspid (two-cusp) valve. The cusps are like panels of a parachute, and are attached by tendinous cords to the papillary muscles in the ventricles.

Systole (the contraction of the ventricles) is prompted by the sinus node, a small group of cells, about 12 mm long, in the wall of the right atrium; this generates an electrical impulse which moves through the heart via highly conductive nerve fibers and stimulates the ventricles to contract (the node is in turn controlled by the nervous and hormonal systems). When it does so ventricular blood—deoxygenated on the right, oxygenated on the left—is pumped from the right ventricle along the pulmonary trunk to the lungs for reoxygenation and simultaneously from the left ventricle into the ascending aorta to circulate the body again via the arteries. When this is happening the papillary muscles contract, tensing the cords, which hold the valves closed, preventing the blood from reentering the atria. During diastole two pocketlike semilunar valves—the pulmonary and the aortic—close to prevent blood from falling back from the pulmonary trunk and the ascending aorta into the ventricles, which should now be filling up with the next batch of blood from the atria.

The arteries take the oxygenated blood round the body, dividing as they go into smaller and smaller vessels. The smallest arteries become capillaries, tiny vessels in which blood cells not only go single file but have to bend a little in order to fit through at all. The blood now travels at one thousandth of the speed at which it burst from the heart, which allows time for oxygen and nutrients to move through the capillary walls to the body's cells and for cell waste products such as carbon dioxide to enter the blood. The capillaries then gradually join up again to form veins, which take the deoxygenated blood back to the heart and thence, as we have seen, to the lungs for reoxygenation. (There is also a loop round to the liver and kidneys to offload the waste.)

Our bodies contain about 4.5 liters (8 pints) of blood. The heart beats about once every eight-tenths of a second—faster with exertion; a blood cell takes only a minute to go all around the body and back to the heart again. Blood enters the heart at a pressure of about 5 mm Hg; it leaves the right ventricle for the lungs at 25 mm Hg and the left ventricle for the body at about 120 mm Hg (enough pressure to shoot water about six feet in the air). For this reason the left ventricle has thicker muscular walls than the right; both ventricles have thicker walls than the atria. Blood pressure is the force generated by the heart to move the blood: 90/60 would mean a systolic pressure of 90 and a diastolic pressure of 60.

The heart has its independent synchronicity, but it also speeds up and slows down in response to signals from the body: either through the autonomic nervous system or directly through hormones adrenaline and noradrenaline (to speed it up and increase pressure) and acetylcholine (to slow it down).

Blood vessels are present in the ovum even before it becomes an embryo. The heart forms as a dilatation on the arteries which later produce the aorta, and is originally double: the two hearts soon fuse into one. An embryo's heart appears about six weeks after conception, and starts beating about three months in. What makes the cells start to beat together at the same time is not known. As fetuses before birth take no nourishment from the bowels and breathe no air, their circulation is different from that of an adult. Two large vessels pass out through the navel and convey blood to be fed and cleansed by contact with maternal blood, and another brings it back. There is a gap in the septum between the right and left atria (the foramen ovale) and a link— the ductus arteriosus—between the pulmonary artery and the aorta. At birth the ductus arteriosus becomes a ligament; the foramen ovale and the extra vessels swiftly close up and shrivel away as the child, like a prehistoric creature, moves on from a watery to an airy life.

The heart's electromagnetic field is 5,000 times stronger than that of the brain. Its normal electrical frequency is 250 cycles per second (most of the brain's electrical activity is between 0 and 30 cps), and its cells are the only ones in the body to pulsate.

Sometimes the heart is positioned to the right rather than the more usual left. This happens when the fertilized embryo which splits to produce identical twins creates a mirror-image pair rather than a "same-parity" pair. One of the pair will be a cardiodexter, and probably left-handed.

If the heart stops beating for more than a few seconds, we lose consciousness. If it stops for more than about six minutes, we die (usually—but see pages 62–63). A heart disconnected from its brain and body will continue to beat for several minutes.

3

❧

WHAT GOES WRONG
WITH THE HEART?

Three things: wounds, congenital defects and acquired disease.
The symptoms of heart disease have been observed since the beginning of observation. Was that horrible Babylonian tablet from 2000 B.C., referring to "an infant that has the heart open and has no skin," a reference to ectopia cordis? When the Egyptians detected every malady through the heart, were some of those maladies heart disease as we know it today? In 569 B.C. General Tzu-Chung was greatly distressed after a military failure and died of *hsin chi*, which has been identified as angina brought on by anxiety. Hippocrates observed that "sharp pains irradiating soon towards the clavicle and back [a fair description of angina] are fatal." Pliny recommended powdered rock crystal as a medicine for heart disease; Ibn-Sina described heart failure. In Yi-dynasty Korea (1433) nine different kinds of heart pain were listed. In 1632 Robert Burton's *Anatomy of Melancholy* referred to "Borage and hellebore . . . soveraigne plants to purge the veines of melancholy, and cheare the heart of those black fumes which made it smart."

Giovanni Battista Morgagni (d. 1771) described angina, heart block and other heart diseases; physician William Heberden wrote of angina in 1768 ("the patients . . . suddenly fall down and perish"); Jean-Nicholas Corvisart, Napoleon's physician, wrote in 1806 that "it is sometimes possible, I think, to prevent [heart] disease, but never to cure it." Toward the end of the nineteenth century Julius Cohnheim worked out that the failure of the blood supply to the heart damaged it; but the first description of a blocked artery in the heart was published only in 1910. Though symptoms of heart disease have been recorded for centuries, before it was understood how the heart worked, heart disease could not be recognized for what it was.

In 1892 Sir William Osler said that heart disease was relatively rare; four years later Sir Stephen Paget said that "surgery of the heart has probably reached the limits set by nature to all surgery; no new method, and no new discovery, can overcome the natural difficulties that attend a wound of the heart." Even looking at a living heart would destroy it. How could surgery possibly cure it? How wrong they have proved to be. On the one hand, despite the ancient references, noncongenital heart disease is almost entirely a phenomenon of the twentieth century (and, no doubt, of the twenty-first), an artificial phenomenon. During that century it proved to be almost epidemic. On the other hand, our knowledge of and treaments for heart disease have in that same century achieved gobsmacking levels of intricacy and depth. How did we go in a hundred years from hardly having it, and knowing nothing about it, to so many people having it, and such sophisticated responses to it? So sophisticated that, for example, a German doctor, Rudiger Dahlke, has recently written a long book correlating the microcosm of heart disease in the individual to the macrocosm of an overpopulated world, and companies are taking out patents on the genes of the human heart.

Osler also observed that rich people got heart disease, and held this to be because of their rich diets. Atherosclerosis, the hardening and narrowing of the arteries, was "the Nemesis through which nature exacts retributional justice for the transgression of her laws"; the typical patient was "a keen and ambitious man, the indicator of whose engine is always at 'full speed ahead.'" This sounds pretty much like the modern notion of stress and the type-A behavior recognized by doctors today as a factor in cardiac disease: over identification with personal accomplishment as a symbolic—yet unattainable—victory in the quest for self-worth. In 1886 it was reported that, a century before, a "hairy heart" was believed to occur "especially in bold and adventurous men." Today it is poor people in rich countries who get it, and get it in droves. More people die of cardiovascular disease (of the heart and circulation) in the U.S. than die of cancer, AIDS and all other diseases put together; this despite the fact that between 1982 and 1992 the death rate from cardiovascular disease went down by 24.5 percent. Cardiovascular disease is more common in older people; ironically as our life expectancy increases so do our chances of getting one or more of these conditions. At the same time, the modern industrialized society which has given us this increased life expectancy also provides the threats to the quality of our health while we are alive: lousy diet full of animal fats and processed food, propagated by aggressive, stress-inducing advertising and marketing;

pollutants which promote the formation of free radicals (these damage the heart cells as well as all the others); smoking; the evil twins of unemployment and overwork; pressure; cheap and easily available addictive pleasure-drugs and love substitutes such as heroin and alcohol; overdependency on the car for getting around and the decline in physical exertion as a normal part of everyday life. I am reminded of Tithonus, the Trojan prince who accepted eternal life as a gift from Zeus so that Aurora, who had fallen in love with him, could marry him: unfortunately they neglected to mention eternal youth, and he grew older and older, more and more wrinkled, bent and desiccated, and ended up a sort of grasshopper.

HEART DISEASE

Heart disease is a great tangled pile of interconnecting conditions and symptoms: many discoveries have been made about these during the past century, and yet we tend to be ignorant about them. For example, what does a hole in the heart mean to you? That the blood gets out into the body? Congestive heart failure—how can something with a name like that not be terminal? (It isn't.) Complete heart block is not a fatal blockage of blood in the heart, it is a blockage in the electrical communication between the atria and the ventricles—a symptom, not a killer.

Here are some of the conditions:

Atherosclerosis (from *atheros*, porridge, because the plaque looked like old dried-up gruel, and *sclerosis*, hardening—although it is the narrowing, not the hardening, that causes the problems): healthy arteries have smooth walls for blood to pound through, taking goodness and oxygen (and "L" energy—see page 103—if you're into that kind of thing) around the body. But if the lining is damaged, perhaps by nicotine or by free radicals (molecules produced by our bodies in response to outside irritants such as pollution, cigarette smoke, pesticides and food additives, which cause chemical chain reactions throughout the body, including in the arteries), it becomes sticky. Then proteins, cholesterol and fats start to stick to it; blood platelets and finally muscle cells from the artery wall get caught up too, making a gloopy, fatty obstacle (some doctors compare it to pizza, rather disgustingly) which after a while grows big enough to stop the blood in its tracks. An artery can be 90 percent blocked by this plaque before any symptom becomes apparent, and the first symptom may be failure of the part that was being fed by the artery that is now blocked: failure of the brain, say, which is a stroke, or of the heart itself. Heart attacks are usually caused by atherosclerosis of the coronary arteries.

Angina pectoris, heart attack, myocardial infarction, or heart death: angina pectoris (from the Latin *angere*, to choke, and *pectus*, chest) is a symptom, not a disease, a severe constricting pain in the chest which can extend to the left shoulder and down the arm, caused by *ischemia* (lack of blood) in the heart muscle due to coronary heart disease—atherosclerosis in the coronary (from *corona*, crown) arteries. The heart is an active muscle and as such needs blood, which it receives through the coronary vessels. If these are narrowed, the blood supply is diminished, the heart under stress cannot cope, and it "suffers painfully," as the heart transplant pioneer Christiaan Barnard put it. Angina attacks pass when the heart's demand for oxygen is diminished: with rest and calm. But too much stress on the heart for too long, or too frequently, or total occlusion of blood supply, results in a total ischemia: the lack of oxygen causes an electrical problem in the heart's conductive system, and the heart, instead of beating as it should, begins to fibrillate (ventricular fibrillation—atrial fibrillation is something else, see page 49). The muscle twitches and quivers rapidly and helplessly, still alive, but unable to do its job. (Vesalius recognized it in animals; he said the fibrillating heart was like a bag of worms. Christiaan Barnard used a similar phrase: "Each fibre went into its own rhythm, tiny spasms within spasms. What had been a rolling sea became a lake of worms.") This is a heart attack. Unless the heart can be set back on course and made to pump again, the patient dies. If on the other hand some blood continues to get through, only part of the heart dies, leaving the rest to carry on under greater stress. (My father went into ventricular fibrillation during an angiogram. "It's a long process and goes on and on, you're lying there sedated but conscious, and they're plunging nozzles in every coronary artery, so they were plunging away and I thought this is odd, the ceiling is going brown, I wonder if there is an electrical brownout . . . then I lost consciousness. And then I was aware of messages on the TV screen too fast to read, and Dr. Foale nonchalantly pumping my chest, and a smell of burning in the air"—from the electrical defibrillator.)

MOUTH-TO-MOUTH RESUSCITATION

Mouth-to-mouth resuscitation was traditionally used to start newborn babies who needed help breathing. It was known as the "biblical method": in II Kings 4:18–37, the Shunammite's boy dies and Elisha "put his mouth on his mouth, and his eyes upon his eyes, and his hands upon his hands . . . and the flesh of the child waxed warm . . . and the child sneezed seven times, and the child opened his eyes." It has been pointed out that with his hands upon the child's hands Elisha could not have been holding the child's nose; however, when resuscitating babies it is best to cover both nose and mouth with your mouth, and we don't know how old the Shunammite's boy was. The method was already being practiced in the eighteenth century: Napoleon's surgeon Baron Dominique Jean Larrey (see page 66) did it using bellows: "How is the surgeon transported," he wrote, "when he sees . . . that the heart palpitates, and respiration is restored. It is the rapture of a Pygmalion, when he see the marble becoming animated under his fingers!" It made a general comeback during the 1930s. Compression of the chest to restart the heart was first suggested in 1883, but received with derision. Not until 1960 was the technique accepted.

Angina is usually brought on by exertion, and also by emotional upset, anger, excitement, cold, hurrying, time pressure and exertion too soon after eating or getting up.

One and a half million U.S. citizens each year have heart attacks, of which half a million die. Heart attacks come by day or night; they can be painless or agonizing; there may be no previous symptoms or there may have been warning aplenty. A heart attack will kill you, or leave you shocked, pale, breathless, sweaty—and, ultimately, grateful, as you realize a) that you have survived and b) that, now you know, you can do something to prevent it happening again. Half of heart attack victims who die do so within a couple of hours. If someone is having a heart attack, call an ambulance. If they are unconscious and without pulse, give mouth-to-mouth resuscitation and heart massage (learn how at a first aid course). People die because ventricular fibrillation sets in, and like a computer or a curdling mayonnaise they need to be restarted. An electrical defibrillator is used for this. Ambulances carry them.

The cause of angina—the cutting off of the blood supply to the heart's own fabric, caused by a blockage in one or more of the coronary arteries—was first correctly identified by Adam Hammer of St. Louis in 1876. "I have never heard such a diagnosis in my life," said his colleague. "Nor I also," replied Hammer—giving between them a perfect example of how medicine progresses.

Other factors can contribute to the blockage: a blood clot or a coronary artery spasm.

High blood pressure (hypertension): a complicated chemical interaction among heart, blood vessels, kidneys, hormones and the nervous system determines the blood pressure, telling the heart how much blood to let through. The kidneys affect blood pressure by controlling fluid levels in the body: if the kidneys retain salt and water, they raise the fluid levels. The excess salt and water is stored in the body's cells, making them stiffer. This makes it harder for blood to get round the body (60,000 miles of blood vessels a day, remember), which means the heart must work harder. Thus it becomes bigger, thicker and more muscular. Then it needs more oxygen, which it can't necessarily get, and it runs less efficiently. Meanwhile blood pushing through arteries at high pressure can damage the linings, contributing to atherosclerosis or producing a blood clot which can cause a heart attack or stroke; or the constant pressure can weaken the artery wall, leading to an aneurysm, when a weak spot in the wall gives way and swells up in a kind of balloon, which can pop, and kill.

Heart failure: high blood pressure can lead to heart failure. If a heart doesn't get enough oxygen, it has a heart *attack*. Heart *failure* happens when there is too much demand on the heart: it weakens, and cannot keep the blood going round at the rate the body needs. With high blood pressure, as we have seen, the heart has to work harder. Sometimes it can't manage it. It grows bigger with the effort and weakens as it swells. Blood that is meant to return to the heart backs up in other parts, causing swelling and exhaustion and congestion—fluid—in the lungs. This happens, for example, when a heart attack—or series of heart attacks—has been survived: instead of working muscle, where the infarction occurred there is only scar tissue. Alcohol and cigarettes can weaken the muscle, and valve problems which reduce the effectiveness of the pumping can, in the end, cause the heart to give up.

Valve problems: the blood pulsing through the heart makes noises which can be heard from outside through a stethoscope. There is a sound, *lubdub,* which doctors look for: the sound of healthy valves snapping back into place, swinging shut behind each dollop of blood as the heart does its job. Sometimes they hear a murmuring rushing sound—a sign that all is not right with the valves. Some murmurs are innocent: half of all children have a murmur at some stage as their heart grows. Pregnant women, dealing with an extra load, can get a temporary murmur. But the murmur may be saying that a valve is damaged. Narrowing (stenosis) of the valves or a reluctance to open or close fully can cause backflow. This may be the result of a heart attack or an infection. Some valves are "relatively slackly and carelessly" made, as Harvey puts it. Some are congenitally prolapsed: they just don't close very well. The mitral valve (so-called because it is supposed to look like a bishop's miter), between the left atrium and the left ventricle, is prolapsed in about 6 percent of people, most of whom have no symptoms.

Arrhythmia: this is when the heart's natural beat, as instructed by the sinus node, goes awry. It can be caused by anxiety, by too much drink and cigarettes and staying up late, by too much caffeine from cola drinks and chocolate and coffee. It's just one of the damaging side effects of cocaine. Or it can be a symptom of heart disease. Tachycardia is when the ventricles beat too fast to fill up with blood: without treatment, it can lead to heart failure. Bradycardia is when the heart beats too slowly; not enough blood is pumped around the body. Fibrillation is when the heart's electrical systems become confused and the heart panics, and cannot beat at all. With atrial fibrillation, the atria can beat up to 500 times a minute, while the ventricles increase their rate to only about 150 per minute. The difference is that atrial fibrillation goes away, with time, treatment or conscious relaxation, whereas ventricular fibrillation, unless it is put right within four to six minutes, kills you. (There is a tale of a London cardiologist who went into atrial fibrillation regularly. "Feel my pulse," he'd say to students down at the pub. "Been fibrillating since Wednesday." "It is a terrifying and appalling feeling," says my father, "until you remember that you've had it five times before and it hasn't killed you . . . and before you remember that sometimes it goes ventricular. But relax and it goes away. It's difficult when it happens in your sleep.")

Rheumatic heart disease: this is a result of untreated rheumatic fever, an inflammatory condition in connective tissues in, among other places, the heart, which is itself a result of streptococcal infection. An untreated streptococcal sore throat—more common in third-world countries—can be the cause. Early diagnosis and antibiotics can easily prevent it happening—if they are available, that is.

Bacterial endocarditis: this can develop when bacteria enter the bloodstream via tooth decay, and cause infection in the valves and the heart lining. Symptoms include night sweats, weight loss, aches and pains. Sometimes an abscess can form in the heart, or a rotten part of an infected valve may be carried away and cause a blockage in the circulation, which can result in a heart attack or a stroke. Antibiotics are necessary, and sometimes a replacement valve.

Pericarditis: this is inflammation and infection of the pericardium, the double-layered sac in which the heart lies. The pericardium cannot move properly; in extreme cases it becomes hard and tight, constricting the heart's movement; its watery filling can become too effuse, which also puts physical pressure on the heart. Sometimes it needs to be removed (see also pages 130–31, "circumcision of the heart").

Atrial myxoma: because the heart is a muscle it doesn't generally get cancer, but it can get tumors, the most common of which is atrial myxoma, on the septum at the site of the foramen ovale. It is a gleaming, multicolored, gelatinous lump, not malignant, but recurrent if not fully removed. It looks—revolting. Other tumors—rhabdomyosarcoma and hemangiosarcoma—are extremely rare. Secondary cardiac tumors are more common; multiple small nodules, resulting from breast cancer, malignant melanoma or bronchial tumors. Inside the ventricles looks very like inside a pumpkin, the tendinous cords of the valves strung like fibers, or cobwebs; the secondary deposits look like the mold inside an aging jack-o'-lantern two weeks after Halloween.

Soldier's heart: during the First World War a condition was identified called "soldier's heart," involving breathlessness, fatigue, a feeling of impending doom and a heart murmur. At the start of the war it was assumed that these were symptoms of heart disease, and bed rest was prescribed. By the end, when there were fewer soldiers left to go off and fight, it had been reclassified as "effort syndrome," and the soldiers were prescribed exercise and returned to service. Sometimes diagnosis is led by social requirements.

CONGENITAL HEART DISEASE

Congenital conditions you are born with; of course, given the differences between a fetus's and a child's heart, some of them are more common in premature babies. Holes in the heart, for example: in his 1513 series of anatomical drawings Leonardo da Vinci drew a defect of the septum between the atria and noted: "I have found from a) left auricle to b) right auricle, a perforating channel from a to b which I note here to see whether this occurs in other auricles of other hearts." Sometimes this gap between the atria in the fetus, the foramen ovale, does not completely close when the child is born. Blood leaks from atrium to atrium, shunted from side to side as each becomes overloaded, and the lungs flood. Depending on the size of the hole, it can be serious and require surgery. My little cousin Phoebe was born with this, but by the time she went for surgery, when she was eight, her heart had to all intents and purposes mended itself: instead of one 12 mm hole she had two 1 mm holes, which had practically no effect on her at all. Her sister Zoe says she's a changed character now. Sometimes the ductus arteriosus does not close up completely. (One tenth of heart surgery is performed on children: repairing congenital defects, sewing up holes and replacing faulty valves.)

Valve problems: Faulty valves are the most frequent congenital defects: too many cusps (flaps) on your valve, or too few; cusps too small or too big, or unequal. It may not matter, but if faults allow leakage or stenosis they need surgery to correct them. Ebstein's anomaly, for example, is a congenital misplacement of the tricuspid valve. The valve is partially inside the ventricle; the ventricle is thus out of proportion with the rest of the heart, and too small to pump properly, so pressure builds up and its walls grow thin. A condition like this would probably need a replacement valve: a transplant or an artificial valve.

Problems with the aorta: Sometimes the aorta and the pulmonary artery are transposed, and enter the heart in each other's places. The blood returning from its voyage round the body does not go through the pulmonary artery to the lungs as it should, but straight out through the aorta and back round the body again, without having been reoxygenated. In effect there are two separate systems instead of one linked system: venous blood goes round and round, oxygenated blood goes round and round, and the two never transfer. This lack of oxygen is what makes a "blue baby" or "blue child": "cyanotic" is the technical term. In a curious echo of Galen and the invisible pores which made his two-system circulation viable, if there is also a rupture of the septum, blood passes from side to side of the heart and the child can survive for a few years. If there isn't, the child is probably born dead or miscarried.

Coarction of the aorta is a pinching which compromises the blood flow. Hypoplastic heart is when the heart is not completely formed. This is rare, and used to be fatal, but surgery now offers a 44 percent chance of survival even for the most serious type, hypoplastic left-heart syndrome. Marfan's syndrome, an inherited disorder, involves a range of abnormalities, including a prolapsed mitral valve, mitral regurgitation, an atrial septal defect, and aneurysms. Even if these problems are corrected surgically, patients continue to decline: 90 percent of Marfan's sufferers die of cardiovascular disease.

The Tetralogy of Fallot is a complex rearrangement of the heart whereby there is a hole in the septum and the aorta is positioned over the hole (thus taking up unoxygenated blood for circulation) plus the pulmonary valve is narrowed and to make up for it the right ventricle becomes enlarged. It was identified by Arthur Fallot in 1888, who accurately described what he would expect to find inside his patient at autopsy. The condition had been recorded much earlier, by the Dane Niels Stensen (1638–86), who noticed an aorta forming "a double orifice in the middle septum of the heart," and by Sandifort, in 1777, who described "a Blue Boy, a clever boy," with a "very rare disease of the heart." He had had "blue fingers" and "sinking spells" from the age of one: at autopsy the aorta was

springing from both ventricles, and had to receive all the blood from both . . .
How great was the surprise of the onlookers, how great equally was my own
surprise, when we saw the point of the finger to stretch into the aorta, which is
not at all accustomed to maintain communications with the right ventricle, in
conformity with the otherwise constant laws of nature!

In 1784 William Hunter described a sufferer who survived to the age of
thirteen with "a peculiarity of constitution about the heart . . . which we could
not suppose that any medicine would reach." He asked that people refrain
from "bleeding, blistering, vomiting, purging, cutting tissues, applying caus-
tics, in a word torturing a miserable and incurable human creature," and
noted that he had been "reared with the utmost attention, and his affection-
ate parents hardly ever durst entertain hopes of his arriving at the age of manhood." This did not stop him "hinting to the father . . . if he should be carried
off in one of these fits, that it would be unpardonable to neglect the opportunity of discovering the cause of his ill-health."

Nearly 200 years later the heart surgeon Christiaan Barnard treated the
same condition by inserting a tube from the pulmonary return directly into
the right ventricle and removing the atrial wall, creating a single atrial chamber; blood is forced from it down the only remaining opening into the left
ventricle. Look at the diagram on page 40. It works. It is simply plumbing of
a high order.

DIAGNOSIS

The heart is not secret as it was. It is now possible to look at it without killing
it. If we can persuade our doctors to let us look, and if we know how to recognize what we see, we can spy on our own workings.

Since the early nineteenth century doctors have been able to estimate the
size of the heart by percussion, tapping the chest. Old methods still hold good:
stethoscope, taking pulses, health history and family health history, looking at
gestures, walk, eyes, color. It has been said that a particular crease on the ear-
lobe is informative. The eyes reflect the health of the circulation and thus the
heart: a doctor may see fatty deposits or bleeding in the retina. Measuring the
blood pressure is routine: cut off blood supply to arm with inflatable cuff. Ap-

THE STETHOSCOPE

In 1817 the stethoscope was invented by René Theophile Hyacinthe Laennec (1781–1826):

> In 1816, I was consulted by a young woman presenting general symptoms of heart disease. Owing to her stoutness little information could be gathered by application of the hand and percussion. The patient's age and sex did not permit me to resort to direct application of the ear to the chest. I recalled a well-known acoustic phenomenon: namely, if you place your ear against one end of a wooden beam the scratch of a pin at the other extremity is distinctly audible. It occurred to me that this physical property might serve a useful purpose in the case with which I was then dealing. Taking a sheet of paper I rolled it into a very tight roll, one end of which I placed on the pericardial region, whilst I put my ear to the other. I was both surprised and gratified at being able to hear the beating of the heart with much greater clearness and distinctness than I had ever before by the direct application of my ear.

ply stethoscope to inner elbow to hear the sound of the blood. Loosen cuff: as blood starts to come through measure blood pressure at systole (contraction) using a sphygmomanometer, with its mercury-filled gauge measured off in millimeters; as the sound stops, measure pressure at diastole. More than 140 systolic over 90 diastolic (140/90 mm Hg) is considered high.

Electrocardiograms: these measure the electrical activity in the heart and can show abnormalities from coronary artery blockage, muscle damage or heart enlargement. Ten electrical leads are attached to the patient's chest and arms; each lead picks up a pattern of impulses produced by a different angle on the heart and displays it on a graph. A healthy heart produces a recognizable printout. Analyzing it, the cardiologist looks at five waves—P, Q, R, S and T—representing the heart's electrical impulses at various stages of its cycle. Particular disorders produce particular recognizable patterns. Measuring is best done during exercise, because much that wouldn't show up at rest appears when the heart is stretched. Portable monitors—the Holter monitor—can be worn for up to 48 hours to get a full picture. In 1876 Augustus Waller in London invented an ECG machine for measuring electricity in the heart; in 1902, William Einthoven of Leyden connected the electrodes to a string galvanometer and gave the waves their initials—the patient had to sit with his feet in a tub of salt water for it to work. Einthoven won a Nobel prize in 1924.

Cardiac catheters: the cardiac catheter, a tube inserted via a vein up into the heart, is used to make an angiogram: an opaque dye, which will show up on x-ray, is injected into the heart or coronary arteries to show up movement, areas of blockage or defects, the site and severity of stenosis, the function of the valves. It can be filmed for reference. A blood pressure monitor can be attached to the end of the catheter, to measure the blood flow between the cavities.

The cardiac catheter was invented by a twenty-five-year-old German called Werner Forssman in 1929. Having been inspired by previous work on horses, and having practiced on corpses, he was discouraged—nay, forbidden—by his professors ("Remember your mother!" said his superior, when he suggested doing it to himself). So he persuaded a nurse, Gerda Ditzen, to help him, by "prowling round her like a sweet-toothed cat round the cream jug," and lending her anatomy books. Indeed he persuaded her so well that in the end *she* suggested they do the experiment themselves, and volunteered to be the subject. After she had prepared everything, he persuaded her to lie down (because of the anesthetic, he said), then tied her to the operating table and cut into his own elbow, injected the catheter into his vein and sent it up his arm and down into his heart. Then he untied her and they went down several floors to the x-ray room so that he could photograph it, having kicked the shins of a colleague who tried to pull the catheter out. The process wasn't introduced for human patients until the 1970s, and is now widely used.

X-rays: invented in 1895, these can give information about the size and shape of the heart and show up some congenital defects and also congestion of the lungs (with fluid), which may be a consequence of heart disease.

Ultrasound can also be used to measure heart size, the function of the heart valves and chambers, and to gauge how well the heart is performing. High-frequency sound waves are bounced against the heart, and the echoes are converted into a clear and detailed image of the shape of the heart. Doppler ultrasound measures the flow of the blood within the heart, which is useful for assessing leakage, narrowing of the valves (aortic stenosis, mitral stenosis, aortic regurgitation, mitral regurgitation). Transesophageal ultrasound looks at the heart from behind: the patient swallows an ultrasound probe. Ultrasound can be used on fetuses to see if they have a congenital defect.

Magnetic resonance imaging—putting the heart into a magnetic field and exposing it to various levels of radio frequency—gives a three-dimensional image on a screen, and a radioisotope can be injected into the blood and then photographed as it travels around the system, showing up blood flow and pumping action. This is a nuclear scan.

TREATMENTS

John Fothergill (1712–80) recommended "a plan of restricted food, and to restrain excesses of passion and anxiety" on the appearance of chest pain. Avoidance, they all say now, is the way forward. Avoid particular kinds of fat, avoid stress. Prehistorically we needed stress reactions: the quickening breath, increasing heartbeat and blood pressure, and the tensing muscles as blood rushes to them. This is the "fight-or-flight" response needed when hunting mammoths, which was identified by Walter B. Cannon in 1914. At the same time, cholesterol levels go up, blood platelet activity increases and arteries get tighter: this makes blood clot more easily—our bodies are preparing to be wounded. Today it's all too much—we don't need this, it makes us ill. Avoid laziness—exercise keeps the heart strong. Avoid obesity and at the same time avoid great weight change. Avoid smoking, which kills more people through heart disease than it does through lung cancer. Nicotine damages artery linings, setting off the pizza-gunk blockages of atherosclerosis; it contributes to blood clots; and carbon monoxide occupies the place in blood which should be full of lovely oxygen. Other chemicals in tobacco increase the heart rate. Within two or three years of stopping smoking, the risk of heart attack drops to the same level as that of nonsmokers. Avoid these and you can probably avoid acquired heart disease.

But 50 percent of people having their first heart attack have none of the common risk factors of high blood pressure, obesity, smoking and high cholesterol levels; and eight out of ten people with three of these factors never have a heart attack. A predisposition to heart disease is hereditary.

For those who have it, there are drugs, and there is surgery. New proce-dures, interventions and drugs are discovered all the time. They don't cure you, but they give you a second chance to get your habits in order. A new science—cardiac psychology—has built up around the need to treat the whole person—including our appetites, our weaknesses, our addictions—in order to support a mended or replaced heart. Gene science will turn everything on its head.

DRUGS

Digitalis—foxglove—has been prescribed since the seventeenth century, per-haps longer, as a diuretic and to slow the pulse rate, and is still the drug of choice for atrial fibrillation. In the 1770s William Withering got hold of an old family recipe, a herbal infusion used for treating swollen legs, from a Shrop-shire woman, and detected digitalis as the active one of the twenty ingredients. There are many more antiarrhythmic drugs now.

Warfarin, a blood-thinner, was originally discovered in North Dakota when moldy hay provoked internal bleeding in cattle that ate it. It's used as rat poison for the same reason, and is prescribed with caution. Aspirin is a more digestible blood-thinner: it makes platelets less sticky. Clot-dissolving drugs are more powerful, and can help when you're actually having a heart attack. Cholesterol-dissolving drugs can be used if diet and exercise fail to improve cholesterol levels—but one of the side effects is high blood pressure. Also there is still a lot of debate about how guilty cholesterol actually is (and even if it is guilty as hell it is still a substance essential to the human body, used in nerve function and hormone production, present in cell walls, and, funnily enough, it protects us from free radicals. Then there are nitrates (to relax mus-cle in the veins and arteries, effectively dilating them), beta-blockers (to dilate blood vessels and slow down the heart rate), alpha-blockers, calcium-channel blockers (to prevent calcium, which is responsible for muscle contractions, from being absorbed into blood vessels), angio-converting enzyme inhibitors, and rt-PA. I could go on. I won't. The aim of whatever cocktail the sufferer is given is to help and support the sick heart, to make it easier for it to do its job. Every day my father, who has had twenty years of angina and seven bypasses in the course of two operations twelve years apart, plus angiograms and an-gioplasties till the cows come home, takes Adizem, against clotting, and Im-dur, a form of glyceril trinitrate (which has been prescribed for 100 years for the purpose), to dilate the arteries, and a tiny thing called Ikorel which his doctor called "our last big gun" but Dad can't remember what it's for. He also has an emergency supply of another form of glyceril trinitrate, in case of angina, and a bronchiole dilator to increase his oxygen pickup, because his heart has been weakened.

ALTERNATIVE THERAPIES

Alternative therapies include antioxidants against free radicals: vitamin E, vitamin C, beta carotene, selenium, zinc, manganese and copper. Some believe in co-enzyme Q10, present in normal cell chemistry and deficient in many heart disease patients. Garlic and onion lower blood pressure, hawthorn berry (available as tea) is a source of compounds that lower blood pressure and cholesterol and decrease arterial plaque buildup. Mistletoe is said to decrease blood pressure. The right kind of fat—fatty acids from oily fish in particular—is good, as are walnuts. Chelation therapy—in which heavy metals present in the blood are rounded up and cleared out—has its fans.

MINOR INVASIVE TREATMENTS

Pacemakers are little electronic gadgets, operated by lithium battery, which every five seconds give the heart the electric jolt normally given by the sinus node, in cases where arrhythmia cannot be helped by drugs. A long insulated wire with an uninsulated tip leads from the gadget into the muscle of the right ventricle, which accepts the electrical stimulation. Batteries need changing every ten years or so. Temporary ones are external: you are plugged in via a wire which goes in through a vein in the arm or neck; permanent ones go under the skin below the collarbone. Some pacemakers recognize when the heart is producing its own electrical impulses correctly and will only intervene when the heart is slow. However, these pacemakers can't always tell a heart from a metal detector, and mistake the metal detector's emissions for the heart's electrical signal.

Some arrhythmias—those associated with abnormal electrical conduction between the atrium and the ventricle—can be treated by ablation: the unnecessary pathways are precisely located, wires introduced, and pathways destroyed by heat using a radio frequency ablation catheter.

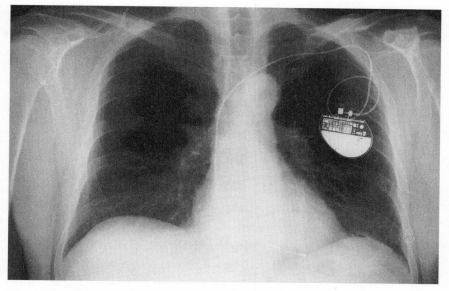

X-ray of a pacemaker in position. © *Corbis*

Cardioversion is a procedure whereby an electric shock is administered to shock the heart back into its correct rhythm (this was first performed on a human—a fourteen-year-old girl—in 1947 by Dr. Claude Beck. The defibrillating device had only ever been used on animals and was only in the operating theater by chance). People at risk of recurring life-threatening fibrillation can (very rarely) be fitted with an implanted cardioverter defibrillator, which recognizes the dangerous disturbances in rhythm and, if necessary, will deliver the electric shock.

Balloon angioplasty involves a tiny balloon being fed up a catheter to the blocked bit of an artery and blown up in situ. The atherosclerotic blockage—the pizza of cholesterol, fats, cells and platelets—is squashed against the artery wall, so the blood can flow through freely. Sometimes the artery is exhausted and like a precarious mineshaft needs support from within; then doctors put in a stent—a little tubular support, erected remotely like a ship in a bottle—so that the artery doesn't just collapse back on itself. It can be done under a local anesthetic, with heparin, aspirin or warfarin and glyceril trinitrate to relax the coronary arteries. A quarter of all angioplasties need to be done again later, and a stent provided.

And mechanical help can be given. Intra-aortic balloon counterpulsation is used to boost a weak heartbeat after a heart attack or during heart failure: a balloon is inserted into the aorta by catheter, connected to an air pump, and rhythmic inflation pushes the blood through the aorta. The patient can stay on it for two weeks. Left-ventricular assist devices provide temporary pumping support after an operation: blood flows through a tube from the left ventricle into an external artificial left ventricle and is pumped back through a second tube into the aorta by a power supply.

THE RELAXATION RESPONSE

Cannon's fight-or-flight response, also known as ergotrophic reactions—the heightened arousal of the sympathetic branch of the autonomic nervous system—has its opposite. The trophotropic or relaxation response decreases the arousal of the sympathetic nervous system: it lowers blood pressure and decreases muscle tension and respiration. You can provoke the latter response in order to counteract the long-term effects of the former. To avoid road rage, practice yoga; for every perceived slight, meditate or pray; for every moment you are kept waiting on the telephone by a machine, repeat your pelvic floor exercises. The physiological response to these deep, peaceful, rhythmic mental and physical activities helps to counteract the effects of the fight-or-flight response, in an age when most individuals neither fight nor flee.

The basis is mental focusing and a passive attitude toward distracting thoughts. Sit still, be comfortable, close your eyes, breathe through your nose. Count. Let your thoughts move on past you. Be gentle. Do it for about twenty minutes. Don't use an alarm—look up to check the clock. It can't possibly hurt, and there's a great deal of evidence to suggest that it helps.

Dean Martin knew all about it years ago when he sang that excellent ode to antistress, "Relax-Ay-Voo." So did Galen: the importance of the influence of "passions or perturbations of the soul" on general health was known to all his pupils. According to Moses Maimonides, the Spanish Jew of Cairo (1135–1204): "It is known that passions of the psyche produce changes in the body that are great, evident and manifest to all." The wise and anonymous author of the Ptolemaic Papyrus Insinger put it succinctly: "If the heart worries about its owner it creates illness for him. When worry has arisen the heart seeks death itself." Ankhsheshonq, a Ptolemaic priest of Ra at Heliopolis, had good advice too: "Do not fret so long as you own something. Do not fret at all." And: "A crocodile does not die of worry, it dies of hunger." Psalm 4 suggests that you "commune with your own heart upon your bed, and be still."

As we shall see, almost every religion offers ways of calming the heart, and the soul, through rhythmic repetition, self-knowledge and calm union between the self and its maker. Meditation, contemplation, deep prayer, yoga, pranayama, Buddhist chanting, rosaries, repetitions of the names of God, prostrations—all these practices connect the physical and the spiritual. Their physical effects have been measured: accomplished yogis can reduce their consumption of oxygen and elimination of carbon dioxide, and Zen monks slow down their cortical alpha wave (brain wave) activity. The most advanced yogis are said to be able to stop their hearts at will and start them again. Certainly they can breathe so lightly and slow their heart rates to a point where they appear dead to the casual observer. Sri Krishna Macharya lowered his heart rate to such a degree that he utterly confused the machine measuring it. It broke.

LOVE

High-cholesterol-consuming rabbits which are stroked and loved have healthier hearts than low-cholesterol-consuming rabbits which are lonely and unloved. There are hormones and chemicals associated with love, comfort and happiness: serotonin and endorphins. These are good for your heart and your circulation. People who feel lonely and isolated are more likely to suffer from heart disease—to such a degree that cardiac psychologists now consider social isolation to be one of the psychosocial risk factors for coronary heart disease, alongside smoking, a sedentary lifestyle, type-A behavior (aggression and susceptibility to time pressure), stress, bad diet and obesity. A loving spouse and good friends can make all the difference. A type-A person chasing desperately after self-esteem and a sense of personal security is more likely to achieve them through love, family and friendship than through workaholism and constant "new challenges" which become unimportant once they have been achieved. Love and the heart are not unconnected.

FROM DR. GEORGE CHEYNE'S
THE ENGLISH MALADY, 1733

Colonel Townshend, a gentleman of excellent natural parts, but nearing his death from a kidney condition, told Dr. Cheyne of an odd sensation: that

> he could die or expire whenever he pleased, and yet by an effort, or somehow, he could come to life again, which it seems he had some-times tried before he had sent for us. We heard this with surprise . . . We all three felt his pulse first: it was distinct, tho' small and threedy: and his heart had its usual beating. He compos'd himself on his back, and lay in a still posture some time: while I held his right hand, Dr. Baynard laid his hand on his heart, and Mr. Skrine held a clean look-ing glass to his mouth. I found his pulse sink gradually, till at last I could not feel any, by the most exact and nice touch. Dr. Baynard could not feel the least motion in his heart, nor Mr. Skrine the least soil of Breath on the bright Mirror he held to his mouth; then each of us by turns examined his arm, heart and breath, but could not by the nicest scrutiny discover the least symptom of life in him. We reasoned a long time about his odd Appearance . . . judging it inexplicable and unac-countable, and finding that he still continued in that condition, we be-gan to conclude that he had indeed carried the Experiment too far, and at last were satisfied that he was actually dead, and were just ready to leave him. This continued about half an hour . . . As we were going away, we observ'd some motion about the Body, and upon Examina-tion, found his pulse and the motion of his heart gradually returning: he began to breathe gently and speak softly: we were all astonish'd to the last Degree at this unexpected change . . .

The colonel then called for his attorney, added a codicil to his will, and died later that day. His heart after death was "big and strong." Cheyne, "con-founded and puzled," and "not able to form any rational scheme that might account for it," leaves it to the Philosphyck Reader to make what Inferences he thinks fit.

FROM THE *GUARDIAN*, JANUARY 2000

A young doctor who was clinically dead for three hours was brought back to life after she became trapped under ice and her body temperature dropped to a record low of 13.7 centigrade—23 degrees below normal. No-one is known to have lived after becoming so cold before. Anna Bagenhom, 29, a trainee surgeon, was skiing offpiste near Narvik, in northern Norway, when she fell through a frozen river and became trapped under the ice for 40 minutes . . . On arrival at hospital she was not breathing, her blood circulation had stopped and her pupils did not respond to light. Doctors rewarmed her while her circulation was maintained on a heart-lung machine until her heart started to beat again. She spent 60 days in intensive care . . . Mads Gilbert, of the Tromso University Hospital, said the key to surviving . . . included "a spirit not to give up."

BY THE WAY

You can die of fear. Of course, if you have atherosclerosis, the artery-tightening in the fight-or-flight response is a particular risk to you, but completely healthy people can die of fear too. The response prompts nerve cells to release catecholamines (adrenaline and noradrenaline) into the bloodstream to help clotting in the case of wounding, to dilate pupils so you can see what's going on and to divert oxygen-bearing blood from the digestion to the muscles. Catecholamines can also be released directly into the heart, which opens the channels that admit calcium. If a massive amount of catecholamine is released the heart cells flood with calcium, to the point where the muscle fibers contract dramatically and seize up. At autopsy, the heart fibers are torn and turned, in effect, to stone. The heart is calciated—petrified.

Very rarely, autopsies of suicides have shown their hearts to be studded with hundreds of tiny hemorrhages: through the same process, fear of the death they were about to inflict upon themselves had made their hearts bleed. Neurologist Martin A. Samuels, of Harvard Medical School, is quoted in *New Scientist* 6.3.99 as saying that cocaine can also stimulate the brain to produce this response. Because cocaine imitates fright, cocaine-induced deaths are "almost certainly due to this." It could also explain why people can die of a curse—if they believe in it.

And the future? Laser angioplasty, gene therapies, customized enzymes, embryonic stem cell technology, nanotechnology, genetic engineering, cloning organs, a computerized virtual heart for experimenting on, artificial hearts, heart-breeding, organs for sale, organ futures . . . The future is another book. I'll leave you with just one thought: scientists are investigating the venom of the Chile Rose tarantula, which may be able to stop ventricular fibrillation.

4

HEART SURGERY BEFORE
TRANSPLANTS

So much for the drugs and the minor invasive treatments. Sometimes hearts need serious surgery: mechanical healing.

Hippocrates and Galen believed that any wound to the heart would be fatal. And so they were, not least because of that belief. In Islam, the thorax could not be opened; and if it were opened by a wound, the *hakim* could do nothing to help. Occasionally, voices in the wilderness suggested that if a wound did not actually penetrate the ventricles, a patient might survive. As postmortem examinations became possible, scarred hearts turned up in people who had died of other causes: Zacchias, physician to Pope Innocent X in the seventeenth century, wrote of a mad priest who castrated himself and then speared himself over and over in the heart with a stout needle. He lived for six days, and the postmortem revealed that his needle had punctured his heart with every blow. But not until 1824 was fluid drained from a stabbed heart and the victim saved. The surgeon responsible was Larrey.

Then in 1872, during a fight in a pub, a young Englishman lost a needle that he usually kept on his lapel; it was removed from his heart muscle via an incision between the ribs. In 1894 an Italian, Simplicio del Vecchio (it means Simplicity of the Old), made wounds in dogs' hearts and stitched them up again; in 1896 the German Ludwig Rehn successfully stitched together a heart wound—stitching the heart and the pericardium had been done before, but, as they say, though the operations were successful the patients died. The next year Herbert Milton in Cairo described splitting the sternum to get access to the chest, and declared that "it requires not a great stretch of fancy to imagine the possibility of plastic operations in some, at all events, of [the heart's] valvular lesions." In 1902 Sir Thomas Lauder Brunton suggested going into the ventricle with an instrument and separating the fused cusps of the mitral

BARON DOMINIQUE-JEAN LARREY

As well as Napoleon's surgeon Larrey was surgeon-in-chief to the Grande Armée: at the Battle of Borodino he performed 200 amputations in twenty-four hours, and at Waterloo he was left for dead. Later, mistaken for

Napoleon by the Prussians, he was sentenced to be shot, until recognized by a former pupil and sent to Field Marshal Blücher, whose son's life he had once saved. He was given safe conduct and survived to write his most interesting memoirs. Napoleon left him 100,000 francs in his will and called him "the most virtuous man I have ever known."

Baron Dominique-Jean Larrey, by P. J. B. Guérin. © *Château de Versailles / Bridgeman Art Library*

valve by touch: the idea was greeted with horror, particularly because he was a physician and not a surgeon.

Harvey's great detractor Jean Riolan had suggested in 1653 that when "copious humour collects and the heart is embarrassed [i.e., a buildup of serum, blood or pus in the pericardium prevents the heart from functioning properly] is it not lawful to open the sternum with a trephine?" It's not known whether he ever tried to answer his question. In the 1820s a Spaniard, Francisco Romero, made a practical attempt: he went in between the fifth and sixth ribs, snipped the pericardium with scissors, drained it, drew off with gauze for three days and then let the wound heal naturally. He was particularly careful to let no air enter the wound, and two of his first three patients survived. A Swede, Skielderup, tried Riolan's method of drilling through the breastbone, but without anesthesia it didn't catch on. Incising the pericardium, however, did.

Going inside the chest at all was a huge leap forward. The heart has never been just any old bit of muscle: it was, as the other sections of this book explain, the seat of love, the divine part of man, the connection with God, the home of the soul. In the nineteenth century the most scientifically minded doctor was still likely to be a religious person, and alongside the technical problems of access to the heart there were, across the world, pervasive religions and cultures which held the heart in immense respect. But once surgical treatment of thoracic conditions, and of wounds to the heart, had been conceived, surgical treatment of a diseased or malformed heart itself was the next step. There were other cultural obstacles too: heart disease was seen as a medical problem, inappropriate for surgery, so the traditional doctor/surgeon divide would have to be breached. The progress of heart surgery was not a steady one.

In 1907 Alexis Carrell was grafting and patching veins in dogs and transplanting kidneys in cats; in 1910 he was experimenting with grafts to bypass the aortic arch. In order to avoid creating bulky clot-attracting internal seams when sewing blood vessels together, he learned delicate stitching techniques from a lacemaker. (In 2000 two of the first batch of cloned piglets grown for organ transplant purposes were named after him—Alexis and Carrel; another was called Christa, for Christiaan Barnard.)

In 1908 Friedrich Trendelenburg removed a pulmonary embolism: he went through the ribs, cut off the blood supply with a rubber tube round the aorta and pulmonary artery, and then, in forty-five seconds, cut open the pulmonary artery, pulled out the clot and closed up the incision with forceps. Again, the operation was a success, but the patient died (an artery was injured in the process, and he hemorrhaged). In 1912 Tuffier dealt with a stenotic aortic valve by opening the rib cage and approaching the valve via the aorta but from outside, clothing his finger, as it were, with the wall of the aorta, and poking it down through the obstructed valve. It helped the patient—but it is another example of the lengths to which surgeons would go to avoid facing up to the big question: having to go inside.

Going inside the heart is something else. The history of learning how to do it during the late nineteenth century is not a pretty one, as dogs were paralyzed with curare, their arteries tied up, their valves artificially lacerated and lesioned, their ribs opened, their lungs inflated with bellows, and valve stenosis and incompetence induced. All this was by design; with human beings, it was very hard to be sure, before someone died, what it was that they were suffering from.

The First World War demystified the human body. In a situation where thousands were dying in appalling circumstances, and survivors were terribly damaged, doctors had opportunities for do-or-die (and probably die anyway) experimentation. Effective anesthesia, bacteriology and x-rays allowed surgery in all fields to advance swiftly, and after the war thoracic surgery reemerged in the U.S., armed with a lot more knowledge. (Blood transfusion and antibiotics weren't effective till the 1940s.)

The first successful operation to repair a valve took place in 1923, on an eleven-year-old girl, using a kind of knife passed in from the outside and operated remotely. As was so often the case, further attempts failed. Then in 1925 Henry Souttar, a general surgeon at the London Hospital, sectioned off a young woman's left atrium with clamps and sutures, and put his finger inside her heart, through her mitral valve, to ease her stenosis and loosen some adhesions. As he removed his finger, a suture tore and a "voluminous gush of blood" came out; he clamped it, and all was well. Did she live? For a while, but she remained altogether unwell, and though the operation was successful—as well as historical—Souttar's colleagues were fearful, and he had no more patients. Meanwhile in Edinburgh William Wilson had worked out a way of giving dogs mitral stenosis (fixing strips of rolled-up pericardium against the orifice) which could then be operated on.

Early surgical treatments for coronary heart disease included Claude Beck's operation, in 1935, in which both the heart and the pericardial sac in which it lives were scratched—in the hope that they would grow together and that the heart would thus receive some of the sac's blood supply. Beck wanted to induce a sterile inflammation of the pericardium, as a form of adhesive pericarditis which would produce lots of new extra blood vessels from the pericardium to the heart. To this end he introduced carborundum, sand, powdered beef bone, kaolin, asbestos, iron filings, alcohol, formaldehyde, human skin, ether and cotton to the sac in which the heart sits. Talc was the most effective. Apparently, this sometimes worked, though it's not known how. "The operation has never achieved a widespread acceptance," wrote Robert Richardson in 1969, almost as if surprised.

Arthur Vineberg implanted a portion of the internal mammary artery directly into the heart muscle, to bleed freely into the myocardium. This produced high hopes at the time, as the artery seemed to take root in the heart. It was effective up to a point for coronary artery disease, but it didn't help once the heart muscle was dead. Swooshing it with blood won't bring it back.

In 1938 Robert Gross, at the Harvard Medical School, successfully closed up an open ductus arteriosus—where blood leaks through from aorta to pulmonary artery, via what in fetuses is the ductus arteriosus but should have become a ligament. The patient—a seven-year-old girl—lived; the operation worked, everybody understood it. That same year, the right contrast medium to make the heart show up on x-ray was identified, and the chambers of the heart and the blood vessels became visible from without. Everything was coming together.

In 1944 Helen Taussig, a pediatric cardiologist who had been refused entry to Harvard because she was a woman, noticed that blue babies who had a persistent ductus were healthier than those who hadn't, and deduced that an artificial ductus, or shunt, which would let blood bypass the narrowed pulmonary valve which was causing the blueness in the first place might be the answer. Surgeon Alfred Blalock tried the operation in that same year; by 1950 1,000 had been done and mortality for this kind of blue child was down to 5 percent.

In 1953 the first artificial valve surgery was performed, by Dr. Charles Hufnagel. Now faulty valves are replaced every day—the replacement valves are artificial, or from pigs, or human donors, or made from calf's pericardium. Artificial ones last longest, but need anticoagulant drugs because blood clots on to alien artificial objects. With animal or human valves, as with any transplant, the patient needs to take antirejection drugs.

One big problem delayed these extraordinary advances: time. The brain can survive without oxygen for about four minutes. Surgeons can achieve a lot in four minutes, but not as much as they could if time were no object. Moreover, a pumping heart is a moving target. It's like trying to service a car with the engine going. What was needed was free access to the immobile heart, to get inside: the heart's full cooperation, if you like. But how could that be had when the heart was perpetually beating? This was the double bind which had Paget thinking that heart surgery could go no further.

Selective use of hypothermia slows down all the functions, and was used to give more time in surgery, but it was not enough. Lillehei invented a cross-circulation technique, which worked by linking the patient's heart and lung functions to those of another living person by means of a system of catheters.

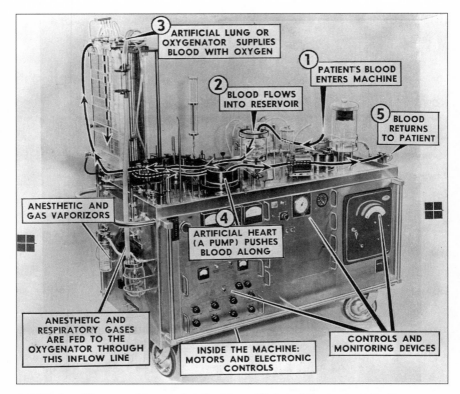

A 1950s heart/lung machine used at the Mayo Clinic in Minnesota. © *Corbis*

This was daring, revolutionary and, as G. J. Haupt put it, "the only known procedure associated with a possible mortality rate of 200 percent."

But meanwhile John Gibbon was working on his heart/lung machine, which took twenty years to perfect. Using this, he performed the first successful open heart surgery in 1953. (General Motors was also building a heart/lung machine at the time, for F. W. Dodrill, in Detroit. It looked like a car.) For twenty-seven minutes Cecelia Bavolek was breathed for and pumped by the machine, while Gibbon mended a hole in her heart. Blood from the right atrium—deoxygenated blood coming into the vena cava, on its way to the lungs—is instead pumped through a series of membranes which oxygenate it just as the lung would, then return it direct to the aorta for sending round the body again. The heart is bypassed altogether. (This is one use of the term "heart-bypass" operation, though not the usual one, which refers to the extra vessels sewn in to bypass blocked vessels. Denton Cooley, president and surgeon-in-chief of the Texas Heart Institute and a cardiology legend, offers a third: the disease is "temporarily bypassed," to give the patient a chance to stop smoking, lose weight and straighten up.) Somewhere in the common mind is the idea that the heart and lungs are connected to the machine, which is not the case: their services are performed by the machine, and they do nothing. The heart stops for the duration.

THE HEART stops. This, to many of us, whether the brain is alive or not, simply means that we are dead—albeit temporarily. And later, we are brought back to life. Literally, it is life after death, which is the great miracle, or the great fantasy, on which all religions and mythologies, and most art and literature, are based. It is the purpose of sacrifice and the role of God. Patients going in for open heart surgery know that they are going to be dead for a while. It is a *hell* of a thing.

The technical ability to stop and start a heart raises the question: What is death? "No-one knows," wrote R. G. Richardson, "and it is not really satisfactory to define it as the end of life, for what is life? . . . all we can do is recognise death when it comes, and that is not always easy." A surgeon who was about to have cardiac surgery once said, "I know they keep your vital functions going when they use that pump—I have used it myself—but with your heart stopped, you are *really* dead." Many heart surgery candidates fear that they might go to heaven during the operation, even see their parents, and be torn when they have to return to their living families. This is particularly likely with people whose parents died when they were young, or died of heart disease.

SURGEONS CLAMP the aorta shut close to the heart and inject/perfuse the heart with a solution that stops it beating and preserves its cells for up to six hours, during which time it can be cut and stitched, replumbed and mended. Once the effectiveness of the heart/lung machine was proven, heart surgery was free to advance as swiftly as the ideas came to the surgeons. Blocked arteries were replaced; valves from corpses inserted; and in 1967 coronary arteries themselves were approached for the first time.

René Favaloro grafted a vein from the patient's leg round a blocked artery—the first coronary bypass. The procedure was perfected for coronary bypass in the 1960s by Dr. Michael DeBakey and Dr. Edward Garrett. In a CABG—coronary artery bypass graft, known as "cabbage," of course—operation, the blockages in the coronary arteries are bypassed, as a town is, or a traffic jam. Usefully, and for unknown reasons, the blockage tends to happen not along the length of an artery, but in one or a few specific places, leaving the rest of the artery clear and healthy. A vein taken from the leg (where there are plenty to spare) or an artery diverted from the breast (in men and postmenopausal women, the usual subjects, these arteries are no longer needed) is brought in and one end is attached to the aorta and the other downstream of the blockage. Double bypass means that two blockages have been bypassed, quadruple means four, and so on. Today, it's one of the most frequent surgical procedures. It is a piece of plumbing: it restores the flow and reduces angina, but it cannot reverse the effects or development of atherosclerosis; habits do that.

Many people suppose that the "open" of open heart surgery refers to the chest, or the rib cage. This is a strange enough image at the best of times: the sternum sawn through and the ribs clamped open, like a cathedral with its roof off, open to the winds, flying buttresses flying. But it refers also to the heart itself. The insides of our physical hearts remain a mystery to most. How many of us, on first asking ourselves, assume that the valves are in the vessels, not inside the heart?

ARTIFICIAL HEARTS

The first permanent artificial heart was tried out in 1982. Barney Clark, aged sixty-one, was suffering from heart failure. He was too old for a transplant, and the drugs were not working. In an eight-hour operation he was given a Jarvik-7 artificial heart, which pumped his blood with a flexible diaphragm operated by lines of compressed air—the heart is implantable, but you have to remain attached to machines. (One was used temporarily in 1969, on a patient awaiting a transplant donor.) Mr. Clark lived for 112 days, suffering seizures, kidney failure, lung problems and other disorders. Three more were tried, but they were not successful, and in 1990 the approval of the U.S. Food and Drug Administration was withdrawn, though the heart is still being used elsewhere in the world.

In 1999 Professor Sir Magdi Yacoub removed an artificial heart from a patient who had had it implanted in his abdomen for fifteen months, attached by wires to a power pack on a trolley, while waiting for a heart transplant. The operation, a combined heart transplant, kidney transplant and removal of the artificial heart, was filmed. "Look at the absolute beauty of biology compared with the crude nature of technology," murmured the surgeon as he pulled out the old artificial heart, like God hauling up a wrecked and embedded submarine tangled in seaweed that had been lying rusting on the seabed.

The biventricular assist device is an artificial computerized heart which can be used temporarily, while a patient is awaiting transplant. It achieved national fame in April 2000, when it helped save the life of a child called Sally Slater, in sudden and immediate need of a heart. She is only the second child to have successfully used an artificial heart in Britain. A few months later in Oxford Peter Houghton, aged sixty-two, was successfully given a battery-operated Jarvik 2000, the first permanent electric internal artificial heart. He plugs himself into portable batteries through a socket in the back of his head.

As for surgery itself, one future lies in robotics. This makes splitting the chest, that great medical leap, that great invasion, redundant. "The reason we make incisions is that we have big hands," says Dr. Randall Wolff, director of minimally invasive cardiac surgery at Ohio State University. Now tiny computerized robot arms, controlled by surgeons nowhere near the patient, who watch on screens as they work, go in through little holes punched between the ribs, as they do elsewhere for laparoscopy and arthroscopy operations. (I've had both, and I can tell you it is fascinating watching your own operation on a screen as it takes place under local anesthetic, watching as a Captain Hook robot arm pulls your cartilage this way and that and a Captain Sawtooth arm comes in and nibbles away the torn section, leaving a cloud of white bits like a snowstorm underwater. I had a sense of big fish trying to eat a white reef, and making a big mess of it. Inside is very like underwater. Captain Underwatercameraman watches silently. The silence is eerie. Just the heavy breathing of the blood-pressure cuff on your arm, ebbing and flowing. And that was just on my knee . . .) The small section of the heart to be worked on is immobilized by a local device called a stabilizer so that the heart/lung machine is not needed. This method is so far done for front-of-heart single-blocked artery patients and for slipping in a pacemaker; getting to the sides and back of the heart is another question. The surgery is at what one doctor called the "Model T" stage. The two robots in Britain are called, rather sweetly, Zeus and da Vinci.

New surgical methods and possibilities are developing as I write. Alongside, an equally fast-developing school of thought believes that surgery, however brilliant, is not the answer. It is not the engine of Descartes's machine that needs a service; it is the more ancient idea of the heart-soul that needs recognition and attention, and the original artificial division between body and soul.

I haven't mentioned the human heart transplant yet. This, the most extraordinary and extraordinarily attention-grabbing bit of surgery mankind has achieved, is the moment when the lump of flesh and the home of the soul really come up against each other's claims to the name of heart. If, before we go there, you would like to see exactly what else the heart has been, and thus to understand quite how outrageous an achievement it was, I suggest you detour via Chambers Two, Three and Four: Religion, Art and Love. Otherwise, read on . . .

5

"THE LORD WILL GIVE YOU A NEW HEART": FROM JEREMIAH TO CHRISTIAAN BARNARD

By the early 1960s the anatomical heart was no longer an unexplored country. As Christiaan Barnard (d. 2001) put it, the heart was now "open to the sight of man, just as it was open to his touch on the operating table." And when a heart was dead or dying, "there was only one total solution: cut out the heart and replace it with a mechanical pump, or transplant the normal heart of a human being who had died from some other disease or accident." In the human imagination—certainly in Barnard's—the transplant was the final miracle.

First, a word of reason. The vast majority of patients having heart surgery have coronary artery bypass grafts or balloon angioplasties. Serious though these procedures are, heart transplantation is something else. It is a complex process, hugely expensive (the operation alone costs about U.S. $125,000); immunosuppressive drugs need to be taken for life; there is a severe shortage of donor hearts; and the physical and psychological burdens on the extremely ill transplantee are so huge as to be matched only by the natural but voyeuristic interest we all still have in the phenomenon. That said, it has good operative results and fair medium-term survival rates.

Transplantation as a viable technique depended not only on all the usual requirements of advanced surgery, but also on a way of dealing with the problem of rejection. The sixteenth-century Bolognese Gaspare Tagliocozzi (*taglio* means "I cut," *cozzi* is halfway between penises and mussels—nice name for a surgeon) described "the force and power of individuality" encountered when trying to rebuild noses which had been cut off as a punishment: they wouldn't take skin from a second party, and he theorized that the body recognized anything alien as an enemy, and sought to destroy it, which is a pretty fair

Christiaan Barnard. © *Corbis*

description of what the immune system does. Rejection of an organ is certain unless the donor is the recipient's identical twin. (Blood is a tissue, not an organ, so the match doesn't have to be so exact; organs are made of various kinds of tissues, each with its matching requirements.)

There are two ways of dealing with rejection. You can mute the response system with antirejection drugs, such as cyclosporine, which was discovered in 1969 in a lump of Norwegian earth, and was revolutionary at the time, though it has now been partially replaced by Nizoral, which is much cheaper. Steroids were vital but are not needed so much now (they contributed to the problem of atherosclerosis and had other side effects).

The other method is to make the new organ less foreign: in March 2000 the existence of five cloned piglets in Virginia was announced, steps on the way to "pharming" organs for human transplant. The next step is to switch off their pig-gene alpha 1–3 gal transferase and insert another gene, to be switched on at the moment of surgery, which would prevent clotting. It's all experimental until more is known about the possibilities of pig disease crossing into the human population: bovine spongiform encephalopathy (BSE) and Creutzfeldt-Jakob Disease (CJD) cast long shadows here. If successful, it will also help ease the fact that there are currently about twenty potential recipients for each donated organ.

In 1967, when Barnard performed the first human heart transplant, not only was rejection still a big issue ("There is today no problem in the actual transplantation," he wrote. "The difficulty is in how to maintain the existence of a foreign organ in a body without it being rejected."); there was also the great spiritual and intellectual leap to be made, to imagine it either possible or desirable to take a bit of someone and put it inside someone else. A Scottish surgeon, John Hunter,* had

---

*John Hunter had heart disease himself: when suffering an attack of angina he would look in the mirror to record his appearance as part of his description of symptoms. He has been diag-

transplanted a human tooth into a cockerel's comb in the late eighteenth century, and testicles from one chicken into another.

But the heart was not a tooth, or a chicken's testicle. Much of the prevailing culture in the 1960s, only a few hundred years after the physical workings of the heart had been deciphered, still considered the heart to be the home of the soul. We often hear of surgeons playing God; here we can give the biblical reference: Jeremiah 24:7—"And I will give them a heart," and Ezekiel 11:19—"I will take the stony heart out of their flesh and will give them a heart of flesh."

Barnard said that transplant couldn't be any worse than keeping hearts in jars of formaldehyde on a laboratory bench: a striking image but not one very sympathetic to the less tangible qualities of the heart. It is not surprising that the first heart transplant took place in a country which had fewer rules than elsewhere about what doctors could or could not do, and was anyway a pariah to much of the world—what more could South Africa under apartheid do to upset the world's opinion of it? Barnard's ideal recipient, he said, would be "a Bantu with cardiomyopathy," because that would give him "a young man with a good body who has only one defect: heart disease." But he was forbidden from operating on a black man because, his chief said, "overseas they will say we are experimenting on non-whites."

By 1967 Barnard had transplanted forty-eight dog hearts and had grafted an extra head onto a dog too, because it had been done in the Soviet Union. His patient for the first human transplant, far from being a fit young black man, was fifty-three-year-old Louis Washkansky, with a seven-year history of heart attacks and, without a transplant, only a few weeks to live.

"This heart," wrote Barnard, "was beyond the reach of medicine or surgery. It bore the waste of a battlefield, strewn with many separate deaths . . . a monstrous and insensitive jellyfish somehow lodged in a human chest." At the time he commented: "I've never seen such massive destruction—are you sure

---

nosed, 200 years later, as a typical type-A personality: low self-esteem, high consciousness of time pressure, aggressive and ridiculously hardworking. He tore his Achilles' tendon while dancing and was once nearly killed wrestling with a bull. He knew that his hot temper contributed to his angina attacks, once saying, "My life is in the hands of any rascal who chooses to tease and annoy me." He died of a heart attack after having been contradicted during a free and frank exchange of opinions at St. George's Hospital in London; his coronary arteries were found to be, in his own description of another postmortem, "from their origin to many of their ramifications upon the heart . . . one piece of bone."

CHRISTIAAN BARNARD

Christiaan Barnard was intensely competitive: in his autobiography he constantly links his medical success back to his defeat in a school running race by a boy who was four years older than him. He never got over it. Like Hunter, he would score pretty high on a type-A personality test. His life story is a long—and riveting—tale of walking barefoot to school; of working or studying twenty hours a day; of vanity, brilliance, tenacity, audacity, sentimentality, selfishness and an everspringing sense of the melodramatic.

Consider this passage about a blue baby whose life he failed to save (his younger brother Abraham had died of a similar defective valve):

> A boy who might have grown into a man if I had been a better doctor . . . came to me, defective. He came, asking for a new heart . . . I could not give it to him; modern medicine had no means for this. But it did not absolve me . . . we were guilty. My home . . . was inside the heart of that dead child, somewhere within its chambers where the great vessels were transposed, where a valve was malformed. Wherever that heart failed, there was the seat of my existence, the centre of my life. For as I stood outside that boy's death chamber, so I stood outside myself.

The heart as the center of one's being is a concept we are accustomed to; somebody else's heart too, when we are in love. Here, though, the surgeon is being strictly godly: living, like Jesus, inside the heart as a house (see page 197 for more on this); being responsible for life and death, seeing in the flaws of a human heart his own identity and purpose. The biblical terms— "chamber" and "seat"—emphasize it. That Barnard fell in love with the hearts he worked with is not to be doubted; there was also a strong religious element to it.

this man's still alive?" The fact that Washkansky *was* still alive made him a kind of hero to Barnard, "because he struggled to live long enough to be there when we arrived. The man with a heart like a ruined battlefield had refused to surrender, fighting on and on until the moment came when I walked in to say he had a chance to live with a heart transplant."

When they opened him,

> Louis Washkansky's heart came into full view—rolling in a rhythm of its own like a separate and angry sea, yellow from the storms of half a century, yet streaked with blue currents from its depths—blue veins drifting across the heaving waste and ruin of a ravaged heart. On the right, the purple atrium slid back and forth with each contraction—struggling as would a monstrous fish tied to the shoreline of the yellow sea. The split chest-cage hung open, motionless as sundered rock. Separate and alone within the hush of its dark cavity, the great heart twisted on itself as though seeking some exit, only to return with a sudden shudder as the left ventricle once more—how many million times had it happened?—sought to expel its own private lake of blood, its scarred and ruined muscles closing in a sudden spasm, then collapsing in a moment of exhaustion, a moment seized by the upper atrium to send down still more blood into the unemptied lake below where the life of Louis Washkansky lay trapped, beyond the reach of knife or prayer. So it went, rolling and heaving, one beat after another, like a boxer about to collapse in the ring, fighting on, throwing out punches without strength . . . we had arrived in time to see . . . the dying of a fighting heart.

The power of Barnard's language in describing Washkansky's heart is almost shocking: part biblical, part Joseph Conrad. The images he evokes are ancient, strong and thoroughly religious: the heart in the sea, the heart as a separate person (the boxer); the heart as a "ruin" (formerly a house), the "sundered rock" and "dark cavity" recalling the cleft in the rock of the Psalms and the wounds of Christ; the heart imprisoned: "tied to the shoreline."

The heart of Denise Darvall, the young brain-dead* car-crash victim whose family had allowed her heart to be given up, was still beating away.

---

*Brain death is when all brain activity has ceased forever, but the heart is still beating either naturally or artificially. Your brain can die and your heart can live on. But if your heart dies, you need a replacement, or you die. In most countries a brain-dead person is legally dead; but the first heart transplant in Japan took place only in 1999, because until 1998 the heart had to die for the person to be dead; this is still the case in some Islamic countries.

Soon, I knew [wrote Barnard], the tragedy would begin. The heart would find its life fluid returning from lungs which no longer breathed the oxygen of life. It would begin to struggle against its own death, reacting at first as if meeting only a small inconvenience. Unaware of what was happening, it would simply pump more excitedly—expecting some relief. Yet this would never come, and it would fall back in the first wave of confusion and fatigue. This would lead to thrashing for survival—as against strangulation. The ventricular peaks would shoot up in wild flight, and their intermediate planes would begin to jumble against one another like the sudden crashing of cars on a freight-train. The heart's beautiful symmetry would then be reduced to an erratic green line of wild jerks, struggling along until it entered the final isoelectric phase resembling a sawtooth—jagged lines of the heart seeking to rise like a dying bird, fluttering upward, only to fall once again onto its flat plane of death. [For more on the flying heart see page 274.]

Barnard's brother Marius, helping with the operation, said: "We're killing a heart."

From their patient's point of view, they should of course take the heart while it was alive, but they couldn't. "Why? What intermingling of mythology and ritual prevented us from touching a beating heart in a body which had been declared clinically dead? If this was forbidden we should not even be making the transplant." But they could not touch the heart until it had stopped beating. They waited fifteen minutes, and then a little longer.

Darvall's heart was small—Barnard realized that it looked small to him because he so rarely saw a normal healthy heart. Taken out, it was tiny, limp and blue. Perfused, it became "beautifully pink and firm." (There is a sexuality here. In everyday life we only see blood perfusing flesh, the limp growing firm and the pale turning pink, in erections and blushing.) Barnard had to cut the blood vessels on the bias, to give a large enough circumference to match up with Washkansky's: "similar to matching two halves of a sleeve while fitting a jacket"—images which recall Alexis Carrell and his lacemaking lessons. He left the corona of vessels at the top of the heart as a kind of lid of the pumpkin (see page 247 for more on the heart as a fruit). The hole when he removed Washkansky's heart was immense.

Even as he was performing the operation, Barnard decided to do it differently: rather than one big lid, he would make two small ones, one for each atrium, bearing the appropriate blood vessels, so that he wouldn't have to cut through the atrial septum; also it would be easier that way to fit Denise Darvall's little heart onto Washkansky's big lid. Her heart looked even tinier in the big cavity: women's hearts are in any case 20 percent smaller than men's, and Washkansky's disease had swollen out a cavity twice the normal size.

The operation completed (it had included a blood spillage all over the floor, an occluded artery blocking the circulation, a snipped coronary sinus—luckily in the dispensable heart—and an air bubble in the line to the pulmonary artery), Barnard and the team stood back: the new heart went into ventricular fibrillation. What was usually a sign of imminent death was here a sign of potential new life. The electric shock, administered to stop the heart so that it had a chance to begin to beat again in rhythm with itself, was strong enough to arch Washkansky's back. They waited—it seemed forever. Then—the contraction of the atria, and the contraction of the ventricles in response, and again, and again: "little by little it began to roll with the lovely rhythm of life."

After that, Barnard telephoned the medical superintendent of the hospital and told him what they had done.

Washkansky survived for eighteen days before dying of pneumonia. A hundred more heart transplants were performed in the next year; two thirds of the patients were dead within three months. Before cyclosporine, as Roy Porter points out in his admirable history of medicine, these operations were of more use to researchers than to the patients. Cases such as the child Laura Davies, who underwent a barrage of surgery including transplants and retransplants before she died in 1992; teenager Benito Agrelo, who was taken back to hospital in handcuffs when he decided he'd rather die than carry on with what were to him agonizing side effects of posttransplant medicine; and "Baby Fae," as she was known, who in 1984 was given a baboon's heart which lasted for a couple of weeks, show that the human guinea pig vs. human dignity debate is still alive and well. Though the heart transplant has been widely accepted as a useful procedure, it has never had an easy ride.

TRANSPLANT SURGERY NOW

To qualify for a heart transplant today you need to be in generally good health but with severe and otherwise untreatable congestive heart failure or primary disease of the heart muscle. If you have cancer, diabetes or any infection you can't have a transplant, because the immunosuppressives would render you unprotectable from your condition. To qualify as a transplant, a heart should come from someone under forty-five who has died of hemorrhage or brain injury, and is free of communicable disease. Blood type, immune response antigens and antibodies must be matched as closely as possible. The quicker the heart gets to the recipient the better: within three hours is good.

The recipient is put on antibiotics and immunosuppressives in preparation. Then they are anesthetized, their chest is opened, and they are connected up to the heart/lung machine. The pericardium is opened and the heart removed, leaving the atrial back wall to which the new heart will be connected. The recipient's pulmonary artery and aorta are severed close to the heart, to be joined up to the equivalent vessels in the donor's heart. The process takes up to ten hours, the transplant itself takes about one hour. The patient should be walking in two days, discharged in two weeks and good as new in three months. They will need to take immunosuppressives for the rest of their life (the follow-up drugs cost about U.S. $6,000 per annum, and undermine the immune system), and they will be monitored.

Eighty-five percent of recipients now live more than a year; 65 percent more than five years. Recent research has claimed that there is no benefit to be had from heart transplants except for the very sickest: apart from those at death's door, people die at just the same rate as they would if they had not had the operation.

So much for the history and the stark facts. Let's look now at direct experience. Claire Sylvia, an intelligent, good-looking, Jewish-American dancer, choreographer and teacher found, in her late forties, that she had primary pulmonary hypertension, a weakening of the blood vessels in the lungs which increases pressure in the lungs and leads to right-side heart failure. It's not curable, and sufferers usually die within three to five years—unless they have a heart/lung transplant. Which she did. Ms. Sylvia wrote a book—*A Change of Heart*—which offers an interesting account of the whole process, including the personal experience which makes her story even more unusual: her belief that she took on character traits of the boy whose heart she carries.

Ms. Sylvia meditates, thinks of herself as "open" and is not ashamed to write of "the healing energy of the universe" and suchlike: terms easy to mock yet which deal with areas that conventional wisdom often seems afraid to approach. She once took snake venom for her condition and ended up unconscious on the floor. She is aware that her story could sound like "a parody of New Age psychobabble." And she is funny: she cracks a joke about her operation having become so run of the mill that Hallmark probably makes "So you're having a transplant!" cards.

While she was being evaluated for her transplant, she was told by a nurse that "a transplant is a mixed blessing. To some extent, you'll just be exchanging one set of problems for another." Her response was: "At least I'd be alive to have a set of problems." The hospital was interested in her outlook and character: "To be blunt," she writes, "they saw themselves as guardians of a precious gift that was in exceedingly short supply, and they weren't about to waste that gift on anyone who wasn't going to take excellent care of it." The coronary arteries of transplanted hearts are particularly vulnerable to plaque formation, and atherosclerosis can quickly start up again in a transplantee who doesn't maintain good habits. Sylvia felt that the hospital was looking for conscientious, obedient, positive-thinking people.

Before her transplant, in 1988, she had rebirth dreams: a baby was cut by a glowing knife but not hurt; the operation had been safely completed but she had to drink four glasses of milk a day; she was pregnant, transparent, and the fetus had her mother's face. She felt she was "carrying the embryo that would give birth to my new life." In her dream life (as throughout history) the new heart was a pure and direct symbol of rebirth and resurrection: her own resurrection.

The donor from whom her new organs were harvested (she, like many of us on first hearing it, was shocked by this use of the word) was an eighteen-year-old-boy who had died in a motorcycle accident. His heart, still alive though the rest of him was dead, now had to survive the opening up of the cavity in which it lived and the dismantling of the compact arrangement of organs around it: his liver and kidneys (and corneas) were also being transplanted, and would suffer if the heart panicked. Before it is stopped with a potassium solution, the heart could start to fibrillate, at any stage. An anesthetist is present—slightly alarming, given the donor is dead; but anesthesia is given not only to prevent pain, but to suppress unconscious physiological reactions, such as changes in heart rate or blood pressure, which might make the surgery difficult or impossible. Although the donor feels no pain, some part of him will respond like the living creature he is—if it didn't, the body would not be so useful to surgeons and recipients. This is as discomfiting territory now as it was to Barnard's team in 1967. How can an organ be alive in a dead body? But this is what transplant surgery is based on.

Once removed, the heart and lungs, bloodless, are put in a saline solution (I can't picture this without remembering the washing of the heart), in sterile bags, on ice at 4°C, in a picnic cooler, and transported—by plane as often as not (the winged heart, heading to the next life).

Claire Sylvia reports her transplant coordinator's reaction to entering the operating theater:

> Gail was greeted by an astonishing sight: a living, breathing human being, a woman she knew personally, whose chest cavity was not only open but completely empty. In the space formerly occupied by her heart and lungs there was nothing at all. "I couldn't believe it," she told me later. "Nobody could. Although we were all wearing masks, I could see the look of amazement on everyone's face. Except for Dr. Baldwin, none of us, not even the surgeons, had ever seen anything like this."

"His heart is in his body, and it shall never fall away therefrom," it says in the Book of the Dead. There are many ways of being heartless: St. Anthony's miser (see page 212), the lost ancient Egyptian, the man without love, the transplant pair. Sherwin Nuland, himself a surgeon, wrote in his account of watching a heart transplant operation: "The wonder of a beating heart is minor compared to the incomprehensibility of no heart at all."

"Then as calmly as if he were putting a child to bed, Dr. Baldwin lowered the new heart and lungs into my chest until they were exactly where he wanted them." Then follows the trimming of tissues and vessels, then the positioning of the organs (first the lungs and then the heart, if both are being done). The surgeons connect the pulmonary arteries and sew the atrium of the new heart to the back atrium wall. The stitches must be strong (remember, the pressure of blood leaving the systemic heart would shoot water six feet in the air) and the fit snug and tight.

An empty heart looks strange and dead: overcooked macaroni and bits of dead squid, flaccid like a forgotten whoopee cushion, a pouch, just an empty thing. To see it fill up with blood is to understand that those ancients who believed that blood is life were right, even though they could never see this magical, heavenly proof. The heart rises back to life like bread rising, like a soufflé coming up, like a sea creature, a jellyfish ballooning as it pulses through the ocean. It fills up with life, heat, blood—and then it kicks off into its ancient, eternal rhythm: *ba-dum, ba-dum,* rolling in its cave. Gabriel comes to mind, filling Muhammad's heart with divine radiance. And every heart that you ever heard of being filled with anything: love, fear, courage.

The brain does not start the newly placed heart: the sinus node self-starts it. The heart is its own captain here. If it fails to do so, it is restarted with electricity through paddle-shaped electrodes. Sometimes a pacemaker is attached, which will keep the beat on the strait and narrow, like a good tight rhythm section in a band.

"My new heart and lungs, which had been pale and white because of preservative fluids and lack of blood, quickly took on a healthy pink glow," wrote Sylvia. Her surgeon attached a wire in case she might need a pacemaker later, wired shut the sternum, and stapled up the chest. "I knew none of this, of course. While all this was going on I was far away in a remote and mysterious place."

As we've seen, for every available and suitable donor heart, there are twenty or more recipients waiting. In Britain only 1 percent of organs from hospital deaths are suitable for transplant. While in Virginia pigs are being prepared for cloning organs, in China the organs of executed criminals are routinely removed for medical purposes; and an American doctor, Barry Jacobs, set up the International Kidney Exchange Inc. to import third-world kidneys for U.S. customers (you need only one healthy kidney, so selling the other may seem a good idea if you are penniless). The buying and selling of blood, sperm, eggs, womb time, babies are already common—but why stop there? The idea has become moot that we could sell our organs before we die, payment in advance, which would mean that at least we, rather than our descendants, would get the financial benefit, as capitalism gets its hands even on the giving and saving of life. But selling your heart may seem uncomfortably close to selling your soul. (If you don't like the idea, get youself an organ donor registration card.)

But there are interesting ramifications: could the company you've sold your heart to come around and tell you off for smoking and drinking cream liqueurs, thus risking their investment? What if you sold your heart to several different companies? You could make a packet, and you'd be dead by the time they found out . . . But more realistically, if doctors are looking for healthy hearts from victims aged less than forty-five who died from brain injury or hemorrhage—well, how can we guarantee that our heart will be of any use to them? You sell your heart, die, and then your heart is rejected anyway . . . I'd rather chance it with my heart being weighed and judged by the Egyptian gods (see page 113). Robert Moss, who had a heart transplant in August 2000, had a different decision to make when he lent his old heart, pickled in formaldehyde, to an exhibition at the Science Museum in London, in hope of encouraging potential donors.

THE PSYCHOLOGICAL IMPLICATIONS

The psychological aspects of heart surgery fall into two camps. First, as Huang Ti, the Yellow Emperor, observed, "When the minds of the people are closed and wisdom is locked out they remain tied to disease." Herodotus knew that "you ought not to attempt to cure the body without the soul," and Harvey, more specifically, wrote: "A mental disturbance provoking pain, excessive joy, hope or anxiety extends to the heart, where it affects temper and rate." The health of your heart affects your emotions; your emotions affect the health of your heart. This is the logical and sensible school of cardiac psychology, which recognizes that habits and what's called "life choices" so affect a disease that clearly the patients' minds as well as their organs must be addressed.

(There are many interesting theories about when and how the division between body and soul came about—the lapse into a nonholistic attitude that is the single greatest weakness of modern Western medicine. Some blame Plato, others say it happened when rationalists wanted papal permission to dissect human cadavers and they were given it on the understanding that they would investigate only the body, leaving the emotions, the spirit, the conscience and the thoughts to men of religion . . . so they did. And so did everybody else in Europe, for generations. Some blame the Cartesians, who rejected the idea that the heart had emotional qualities; some blame the religious who clung to their mystic heart in the face of all that science could have told them if they'd been listening.)

The second camp is the ancient, wild, attractive and probably utterly fallacious notion that organs carry within them spiritual (psychological, if you like) qualities. An old folktale concerns a doctor who, seeking to prove his skill, takes out his own heart. Unfortunately it is eaten during the night, and he is supplied instead with a hog's heart, which he puts in, only to find that he has an uncontrollable urge to rootle in the ground. Some years after Harvey published *De Motu Cordis,* Dr. Richard Lower ran blood from one animal into the veins of another (not unlike the cross-circulation technique briefly tried in the 1950s to make heart surgery possible). Samuel Pepys heard of this and immediately wondered what would happen if an English archbishop were to be filled up with the blood of a Quaker. "It may be of mighty use to a man's health for the mending of bad blood by borrowing from a better body," he mused. A German surgeon suggested that blood transfusions might be useful to make couples get on better: by sharing blood perhaps they would be more likely to share tastes and moods. The argument got rather tetchy, and in 1688 the French Chamber of Deputies banned all transfusions. Then, in January 2000, I turned on the television and heard Lenny Henry making jokes about someone who received a pig's heart getting a job hunting truffles. Nothing changes.

In this second camp, the old argument that beset anatomy for centuries is still going on: do we stick with the knowledge of the ancients, or do we only trust our own eyes? In an interesting turnaround, scientific, rational, mechanistic Western medicine is now taking the part of the respected elder statesman and everything "nonscientific" that of the revolutionary young pioneer: here we are talking about everything from homeopathy to Rolfing via truly ancient physical disciplines such as yoga, a startling range of New Age bollocks and the outer reaches of scientific potentials such as energy cardiology. The role of the heart in this flourishing area of disagreement is pleasantly illustrative, particularly the heart as bearer of spiritual qualities and of identity as manifested in personal attributes and preferences, especially in the field of transplantation.

WHO AM I?

Heart transplantees, we are told over and over, often feel the presence of their donor. A woman formerly terrified of water had a great desire to go swimming and sailing after her transplant: her donor was a sailor who had died in a boating accident. A born-again Christian woke up swearing and cursing after receiving the heart of a biker. (The biker's mother was in the hospital, and recognized her son's vocabulary.) Another suddenly took to bananas and puddings, and reproached his donor for ruining his dance rhythms and undermining his skill at horseshoes. "Of course he's different," said his wife. "There are genes and energy in him from somebody else's body. Those things affect you." There is a story about an eight-year-old girl who received the heart of a ten-year-old who had been murdered: the girl had dreadful nightmares, and in the end told the police exactly what had happened and who had committed the crime; on the basis of her information they made an arrest and got a conviction. Surgery short of transplant can also have an effect: in 1999 Reverend Arthur Cornwall, of Cape Town, South Africa, sued surgeons for removing his soul during a heart operation. Since the operation, he claimed, his sermons had been "shoddy and uninspired." Boxing writer F. X. Toole said: "I didn't have the heart for it [rejection of his writing]. The reason I didn't have the heart for it is I didn't have my soul. It took open-heart surgery to give me my soul back; it gave me the heart to put up with rejection."

In 1996 the *Daily Mail* published an article about a heart/lung transplantee who ran a race against the man who had been given his old heart (this is called domino transplantation and is quite rare). "How does it feel?" asked the journalist. One domino transplantee, in the rare position of having both given and accepted a heart, gave the answer that she could still "sense my heart, wherever it is. I think it's because the energy that was my heart is still in me and connected with the stuff that is my heart in another body."

"How do you feel?" transplantees are asked: the Palestinian who got the Israeli soldier's heart, the Muslim who got a Roman Catholic heart, the men who get women's hearts. (Recently the family of a white donor would only let the heart go to a white recipient "because it is what he would have wanted." So how might a recipient feel about getting a racist heart?) The question really is: do you feel changed? The Christianity which has shaped Western society has long sought to transform the heart. However conscious we are or aren't of this, we *expect* a change of heart to mean a change of heart. Even if the heart is not the seat of the soul, it has been its given address for so long that we cannot just let squatters come and go without wondering . . . are you still you?

The question, put nakedly, is "Does changing the heart mean changing the personality?" In 1992 a group of Austrian researchers (Bunzel, Schmidl-Mohl, Grundbock and Wollenek) asked just this of forty-seven transplant patients: 79 percent denied the notion, ridiculed the question and said their personalities had not changed at all, which the researchers described as "massive defense and denial reactions." For example, men who had received women's hearts joked about "turning lesbian" or "turning gay"; said they hadn't changed, of course not, they'd asked their wives if they'd changed and they'd agreed (but why had they asked, if not because they thought they might have?).

This level of denial is backed up by other research: in the early 1980s Dr. François Mai interviewed twenty heart transplantees, of whom eighteen denied having any feelings about their new heart or the donor. This kind of depersonalization and repression—comments such as "it's just a pump" and "I never think about it"—can be a good protection if it helps patients to avoid feelings that would be unbearable at the time. But it doesn't prove anything either way—perhaps they were repressing their feelings, but perhaps they really did have no feelings, or perhaps they didn't want to be thought loopy or labeled as having a psychiatric problem, or perhaps they didn't want to put off potential donors with spooky tales. The famous Dr. Cooley showed a used-car dealer his old heart, in a jar of formaldehyde. "Doesn't it make you feel a little odd looking at your heart? Don't you have some sort of emotional tie to it?" he asked. "I've owned a lot of cars in my life," replied the perfectly Cartesian car dealer. "Not one of them did I develop an emotional attachment to." (It is unusual for a patient to be more Cartesian than his surgeon.)

Fifteen percent of the Austrian group said that they had been changed, but only because they had been through a life-threatening event, not by the organ itself. Six percent (three patients) reported a "distinct change of personality due to their new hearts." One felt he was calmer; one now liked fast cars and loud music, and said: "I have thoughts now that I never had before." The third—who had been divorced and remarried—called himself "we" rather than "I," and said, "Actually my wife and I could get married in church now. Because I'm no longer the one she originally married. I'll write to the pope . . ."

Families join in the identity crisis: "My father is Tyrolean," said one transplant recipient, "and my two sisters were born in Tyrol. But I was born in Vienna. In the transplantation I got the heart of a Tyrolean. Since then my sisters have been saying, now you are finally one of us."

These incorporation fantasies [as the Austrian researchers call them] forced them to change feelings and reactions and accept those of the donor . . . there seem to be severe problems regarding graft incorporation, which are based on the age-old idea of the heart as a centre that houses feelings and forms the personality. Even though we live in a high-tech age, we cannot get rid of the notion . . . of the heart . . . as the focus of love, source of personality and emotions . . . and its loss makes the patients and their relatives afraid of losing personality.

This is a perfect example of how science and its capabilities can outstrip the emotional capacity of human beings to deal with its developments. H. Rudiger, in *Die Metaphor vom Herzen in der Literatur,* wrote:

It is much harder to change or abandon an age-old idea deeply rooted in religion, art and poetry and stifled by conventions, than to understand intellectually the anatomical and physiological conditions for the transplantation of organs. And even when we realise how the exchange of an organ is feasible, for a long time we will not believe that this is the very same heart that houses feelings and forms the personality. Such a double-tracked coexistence of believing and knowledge belongs to . . . an epoch that has not yet succeeded in bridging over "heart" and "intellect." We are prisoners of our ancestors' pictorial imagination.

Part of the problem is that "the patient has to sustain a massive narcissistic insult" because "the heart as a vital organ is the key part of the symbolic self." If your heart fails you, *you* are failing you; if your heart is replaceable, it is a terrific blow to the self-esteem. This fact interferes with the psychological integration of the heart, and psychological rejection—psychic xenophobia, Sherwin Nuland calls it—can be associated with physical rejection. One patient, for example, feared becoming suicidal after learning that his donor was a suicide. Robert Moss said he did not think about having someone else's heart inside him for fear of rejection. One said: "The heart is rejecting me." Many referred to the heart as a separate entity: *the* heart, not *my* heart. Heart transplantees sometimes refer to themselves as "transplants"—"I am a transplant"—almost as if they were their heart. Or someone else's heart.

Gaining life at the expense of someone else's death—a death one is eagerly awaiting as the end of one's problems—makes people feel guilty. As Claire Sylvia put it: "Imagine: a hospital has agreed, at least in principle, to rip the heart and lungs out of your body and replace them with the heart and lungs of somebody who has just died. And for this you're being congratulated?"

(Another transplantee was less troubled by the news: "The nurses and every-body were almost cheering. The whole place was apeshit . . . I started getting chest pain, so they loaded me up with Demerol, and I was flying. It was a big party.")

"The depths of our gratitude," Sylvia wrote, "met the dark places in our souls during the long, complicated healing process." She uses traditional heart language here: where are the depths of gratitude exactly? And the dark places of the soul? Where would they meet, if any Desert Father or medieval mystic or seventeenth-century poet had imagined their meeting? Where both have always lived: in the organ she had just had replaced. Of course, attitudes differ—another transplantee felt that "If I have to spend the rest of my life preoccupied with staying alive, what's the point of living?" Another said: "I seem to have more of a reason to be afraid [of death] now than when I was sick, because I was given this great gift from someone who lost her life. I owe it to her to keep living."

God told Jeremiah that humanity had one heart, that there was no differ-ence between a man's and a woman's. Culturally, that notion did not stick, and many transplantees are curious about the sex and sexuality of their donor. They fear, expect or notice changes in their own sexual behavior, with "many" of the Austrian sample believing that "the heart has made all the difference." (Dr. Lawrence Cohen at Yale said that they "sometimes think they can extend the fact that they now have a young heart into many other spheres of their lives . . . it's as if their heart was their total life and body. The fact that their liver . . . and brain . . . and legs might be fifty is irrelevant—they have the heart of a young person.") Despite the side effects of the drugs—weight gain from steroids, hairiness and acne due to cyclosporine—women seemed less worried by receiving a man's heart than vice versa. One man would not have a woman's heart; one wanted only the heart of someone as good-natured as himself. One man undoubtedly changed: he became utterly convinced that he had been given the heart of a hen.

After her heart/lung transplant Claire Sylvia set up a therapy group for transplantees. They all felt that their identities had been affected, even changed (although, of course, these were the ones who were more likely to seek therapy in the first place). They had all experienced their new heart as something "other" with which some form of communication was taking place. Some became obsessed with the donor's identity and angry that they couldn't know it (most hospitals withhold the names of donor families and recipients to protect both from potential emotional fallout). Many felt claustrophobia immediately after the operation: one felt that "He wants to come out. I could feel his force, holding my fists, running his course." One, a skeptical and down-to-earth person, spoke of a catfight between two spirits, an image which came to her during a rejection crisis. She felt the donor—a woman—didn't want her to have the heart. She spoke to her heart, telling it: "You were somebody else's heart, but now you're mine."

One woman dreamed of traveling through her blood vessels: "This was my way of getting away from all those needles and tubes in the hospital. Nobody else could go there. When I reached my heart it was red and pulsating, soft and beautiful. It's a great feeling when you're in there and you know it's you, and that your heart is really working."

One transplantee talked to his heart: before a biopsy he would say to it, "Remember, now, we have to cooperate. If we fight, it will kill both of us." (My father, not a transplantee but a bypass veteran, speaks to his heart too. He visits it by visualizing going down, starting at the old Holborn Station in London, with two ancient Egyptian statues outside the entrance. He goes down the single escalator to the Central Line, along to the end of the platform, then through a hatch which leads down to the engine room of the ship on which he served during the Second World War. Here he congratulates the engine on all its good work, admires its smooth running and adjures it keep it up. This is all part of the same process as the relaxation response, meditation, the Sufi zikr, rosaries, *nosce te ipsum* and every other kind of union and communion with self and maker. The heart as an engine is a common postindustrial image: Denton Cooley's used car salesman, Sir William Osler's typical atherosclerosis sufferer who has an engine always going at "full speed ahead"; Robert Moss's description of his new heart as "a reconditioned engine." As far back as the seventeenth century Helkiah Crooke wrote of man's curiosity about "what manner of engine this is . . . this watch of his life.")

One white transplantee received the heart of a New York teenager whom he "assumed" was black. He had grown up racially prejudiced, and found that that fell away. He developed a crush on one of the black nurses and started listening to news items about African countries. He didn't want to know about his donor: "Sometimes I think about this person whose heart I have, but I put it out of my mind because it scares me. I sometimes picture the doctors standing over his body, waiting for that moment to take his heart, and a couple of hours later putting it in me. I won't go so far as to say that two people exist in me, but I have been changed. It might be different if I had received a new kidney, but the heart has spiritual, psychological and emotional attachments. I believe my donor's spirit is still around, and in that sense he's still alive." (But it doesn't do to underestimate the kidney: a Grand Dragon of the Ku Klux Klan received the kidney of a black donor, and went out and joined the National Association for the Advancement of Colored People.)

Another, convinced that her donor had been a young mother, saw terrifying visions which kept her awake at night. Fortunes were spent on this patient's surgery, medicine and physical aftercare; nothing was available to deal with her psychological needs.

As Castelnuovo-Tedesco put it, "the new organ is not psychologically inert." It has not always been recognized that the transplant process can be as psychological as it is physical; the resultant stress, combined with medication and organic brain symptoms, may result in psychiatric symptoms after surgery in as many as 50 percent of transplantees. In the past the body was simply bullied into accepting the new organ; now the process is more diplomatic as the body is persuaded that the new heart is not the enemy. Part of that is trying to make the link between the old idea of the spiritual heart and

---

This is an apocryphal, spooky story that I have heard from several different sources:

Late one rainy night, a man and his wife were arguing in the car on the way home. They fell into angry silence, and the only sound was the windshield wipers swishing and clicking. Then there was a terrible crash: he died; she lived. Years later she finally met the man who had received her husband's heart. She touched his chest and whispered—"I love you." The recipient started to laugh and said that his heart felt lighter—it had always felt heavy before. They talked about changes in his tastes and character, and then he told her, "Ever since the transplant, I've been bothered by the clicking of the windshield wipers on my car. I don't suppose you know what that's about?"

modern learning about what is surgically possible. As Sherwin Nuland put it: "No discovery of cellular biology will reduce by a single line of poetry the mystical faith that in some way this leaping thing within our chests is the central capital from which our lives are governed."

LIVING WITH A NEW HEART

Waking up after her transplant, Claire Sylvia wondered if the ECG could read how frightened she was. She was convinced that the new heart was deeper inside her than the old, and worried constantly about rejection: how did that manifest itself? She imagined the heart "breaking free of its stitches and popping right out." She felt, also, that she was frozen: "Maybe God planned it that way as a form of protection: if we express strong emotions too soon after surgery, the stitches could break." She wanted to thank the donor's family, "from my heart, as it were." And she wanted a beer—though she didn't like beer. She wondered for a moment, as you might, whether her donor had liked beer, whether "my new heart had reached me with its own set of tastes and preferences. It was a fascinating idea, and for a moment or two I rolled it around in my mind. Then I let it go."

Depression is common after heart surgery and transplants, as it is after surviving any trauma. After cardiac surgery people can be relieved, delirious, confused, depressed, paranoid. This depression has been compared to that of concentration camp survivors: it stems from a sense of guilt that you lived because someone else died. Sylvia suffered this, and she suffered a very particular identity crisis.

As a dancer, choreographer and teacher, she says, she was very aware of her body and its connections to her mind and spirit. "And now certain parts of that body—big major important parts—had been taken away and replaced with someone else's . . . Who was this 'else'? And how did he, or it, fit into me? I had always known who I was, but who was I now?" She felt as vulnerable and responsible as she had when she was pregnant. Those dreams came back to her. Her new heart and lungs were a new life inside her, "whose parameters were still unclear." (Pregnancy in the heart is not a new idea—see page 156.)

Two things stand out here: first, the sexuality of the images—both the act of sex, when part of a man fits inside a woman, and impregnation, with a new life emerging inside her as a result. And second, that this is the question asked by the ancient Greeks: where does the identity live? Claire Sylvia knew—in the heart which wasn't solely hers—not that she had lost her own identity, but that something else was in her as well. In science-fictionland, say you had a brain transplant, say it were possible: would you expect to get the donor's memories? Thoughts? Opinions? Knowledge? So what, if anything, do heart transplantees get free with their new heart?

One of my father's heart surgeons used to say, with nice self-deprecation: "I'm just the plumber." Perhaps surgeons have to think of flesh as nothing but material in order to be able to cut and stitch it. Maybe this is the innate problem with reconciling material and spiritual forms of medicine. One cardiologist I wrote to felt obliged to put the word "spiritual" in inverted commas, like that, as if it were in quarantine. When Claire Sylvia tried to talk to her surgeon about her feelings, he said: "Don't even think about your head. Act normal." She replied that for her it was normal to think about her head. "Although he had performed this difficult operation and has done it brilliantly, he seemed to have no idea what it was like to be on the receiving end. What troubled me even more was that he didn't seem to be interested in finding out." Another transplant patient reported being told to stop thinking with his pump. And a Yale School of Medicine cardiology professor said: "There is something about the mentality of a cardiac surgeon—he *does* play God."

Physically, Sylvia says, the transplant was easy—too easy, given the immensity of what had happened. But "emotionally, being reborn was painful and terribly difficult . . . It would have been easier . . . and more natural to die." The time table of necessity and recovery was based around the physical needs: no sex for six weeks, no driving for six weeks. Emotional recovery lagged. When one of Sylvia's two ex-husbands arrived unexpectedly, she realized a) that she'd forgotten about him, and b) that for the first time her new heart was feeling her feelings, and feeling them, she felt, more strongly than her old one had. Maybe her old one had been so weakened; "maybe this new heart could withstand more emotion."

And now to the strange bit of her story. She found she wanted chicken nuggets, sweets with peanuts and green peppers. She found herself admiring shorter, rounder, blonder women, where before she had admired tall dark slender ones. Being propositioned by a lesbian made her wonder what signals she was giving out. She dreamed of marrying a woman, and didn't know how to dress any more. She wanted to wear green and blue, rather than the red and hot pink she had liked before. She became more assertive, more aggressive, more confident. Like the Austrian transplantees, she wondered if having a male heart might affect her sexually. For the first time in her life, she did not feel incomplete without a relationship with a man; indeed, she found herself pushing men away. She occasionally wondered if her male heart might be jealous. "In some intangible way my sense of I had become a kind of 'We' . . . at times it almost felt as if a second soul were inhabiting my body."

Five months after the transplant, she dreamed of a young man called Tim L—, of breathing him into herself. She had dreams from his perspective: she was crossing something, choosing to go on rather than back. Another transplantee had a similar dream: he saw himself dead and then emerging into the light again. "His dream, like mine, seemed to have been experienced from the perspective of the donor's heart, a wandering entity that suddenly found itself in an unfamiliar world." (Her daughter, meanwhile, would greet this kind of thing with: "Why do you say that, O spiritual one?")

Physically, she felt like the man in the joke: "Doctor, after the operation will I be able to play the violin?" "I guarantee it," says the doctor. "That's wonderful, because I never could before." She was energetic to the point of restlessness: staying up later, making younger friends, younger flirts. She saw a headline in a tabloid: WOMAN GETS NEW HEART, GOES SEX CRAZY. Her migraines stopped—but they often fade with age anyway. She no longer minded humidity, her low blood sugar problem vanished. She was no longer cold all the time. She sweated more and had to get a stronger deodorant. And she was aware that this could simply be because she was alive and well again; or because she had almost died and been reborn; it could be due to the drugs, or to aging, rather than to the character of the boy whose heart she now had.

Also, "the pace of my heart seemed to be turned up a notch. A new energy all its own, with an intensity and drive I could barely keep up with." She felt as if she had a new, permanent, internal dance partner, and thought how shocking it must have been for Tim's heart to wake up in the body of a middle-aged woman. (She was, though she doesn't mention it, old enough to be her heart's mother.) "Was I crazy, or were my dreams and my changes suggesting that the human heart was more than a mechanical pump?" If so, they were only going back to what was believed for thousands of years, before scientific rationalism wiped the slate clean and—who knows?—perhaps threw out the odd invisible baby with the bathwater. New learning about the heart's complexity is advancing every day.

Claire Sylvia tracked down her donor's family through an obituary. His name was the name she had dreamed. She came to believe that the Tim in her was giving her these dreams and leading her to his family.

"What do I say?" she wondered. "'Hello, Mom and Dad, I'm partly your son'?" She genuinely thought that she was bringing a part of Tim back to them. (The hospitals have a point: anyone might be upset by the arrival out of the blue of someone claiming to be their dead child, reincarnated—but only partially.)

And what about her own emotional motives? She was delighted to hear that Tim had several brothers and sisters—she had problems with her own mother, and wanted to be taken in as the prodigal daughter, though she could well have been the same age as Tim's mother, or older.

As it was, they were well matched. She met most of the family, they showed her his baby shoes. His mother hugged her: grieving for her son, Claire Sylvia breathing with his lungs and living through his heart. "I wondered if my heart could stand it. What if my heart couldn't take it anymore, and I died right now?"

Tim's grandmother called her "part of the family." They had a press cutting about her. They showed her where he had the accident, and his grave. He was Catholic but she put a stone on it in the Jewish way. His mother had baked a cake with WELCOME on it: chocolate—his favorite. Claire Sylvia calls her "the mother of my heart." Later the father said to journalists: "His spirit is still there in those parts she received."

Oh—and he'd had chicken nuggets under his jacket when he died. He loved green peppers. He was incredibly energetic. He had a short blond girlfriend.

In the end, this story did become a can of worms. They went on a television chat show, the audience said they all needed brain transplants and the guest surgeon said the heart was just a stupid pump, everyone felt very attacked, and people began to doubt one another's motives. There were painful divergences. No one likes to be thought a kook, and having very strange experiences tends to make one doubt *everything*.

And what does the story tell us? That the human mind and emotional heart react in extraordinary ways to something as overwhelming as a heart transplant? Or is there (as they say) a "scientific explanation"? I don't mean the kind of science that by the end of chapter 4 has you thinking "yes, reincarnation sounds really sensible put like that." When explanations offered include psychometry, telepathy, clairvoyance and morphic resonance, it's time for the rational cavalry to come galloping in. I mean the kind of science which has always been the best kind—which balances what it sees with what it knows, and isn't afraid of either. There are after all more things in heaven and earth, Horatio (oh Reason), than are dreamed of in thy philosophy, and questions about the connections between mind and body, soul and matter, have been going on for thousands of years. Why stop now? I took a brief and entirely lay tour around some of the latest theories of the nature of the heart, and it seems that the heart is a more intelligent and complicated organ than we have thought.

Cellular memory—the theory that individual cells can remember—is the first stop. On the one hand, decades after having an immunization jab our bodies still "remember" that particular antigen. On the other, we have the undoubtedly effective technique of "Rolfing," which involves deep tissue massage to release early memories that are—somehow—"stored" in the body. Well-publicized experiments have been done with leucocytes by the U.S. Army Intelligence and Security Command, and Cleve Backster: cells scraped from the inside of the cheek and taken miles away responded to stimuli (a violent film, for example) given two days later to the person from whom they had been taken. (The reactions were measured by a kind of ECG and by a recording polygraph.) Would this work if the donor were dead? If so it's an interesting addition to the transplant identity questions. But at some stage—about here—it gets metaphysical, and rather too weird, and sadly beyond my remit. However—the ninth-century Chinese *Yu-Yang Miscellany* offers the following story:

> A man of Chin-Chou broke his shin bone. Chang Ch'i-Cheng gave him a medicinal wine to drink, pierced his flesh, removed a chip of bone and applied a salve. The patient recovered, but three years later his leg was aching again. Chang said, "That is because the bone I took out is cold." They looked for it and it was still under the bed. They washed it in an infusion, wrapped it in silk floss, and put it away, whereupon the pain stopped.

Li Shi-Chen, the great sixteenth-century Chinese pharmacologist, added, "Such is the responsiveness of *qi*; who says that dry bones are without consciousness?"

We know now that consciousness is not all in the mind: brain and body communicate through short chains of amino acids—neuropeptides and receptors. Human emotions are triggered by neuropeptides attaching themselves to receptors, which stimulates an electrical change in neurons. Peptides—"bits of brain"—exist throughout the body, including in the heart and stomach, and communicate not only with the brain (including the thalamus and the pituitary gland) but with the immune system, the hypothalamus and the pineal gland, which between them cover most bases of memory, emotions, learning and energy levels. Neurotransmitters found in the brain have also been found in the heart, suggesting communication between the two beyond the neurological connections already identified. A school of thought now suggests that the heart has as much influence over the brain as the brain has over the heart: in 1987 doctors at the National Institute of Mental Health reported that the heart asks the brain, neurohormonally, for updates, rather than just taking the brain's instructions.

A Change of Heart quotes a number of scientists who have different ideas on this subject, one of whom, Bruce Lipton, a former Stanford research scientist, writes:

> A transplanted heart comes with the donor's unique set of self receptors, which differ, naturally, from those of the recipient. As a result, the recipient now possesses cells which respond to two different "identities." Not every recipient will sense that a set of cells within their body is now responding to a second signal. But . . . as more and more transplants are performed, I think we'll see a growing number of people reporting these experiences.

Dr. Andrew Armour, professor of physiology and biophysics in the faculty of medicine at the University of Halifax, Nova Scotia, points out that experiments with dogs show that the intrinsic cardiac neurons which transplanted hearts bring with them retain their functional capacity to suppress and augment cardiac variables. You don't just get the pump, you get an important part of the nervous system too.

Rollin McCraty, research director of the HeartMath Institute in Boulder Creek, California, quotes Dr. Armour, saying: "It now appears that the heart has its own intrinsic nervous system . . . 'the little brain in the heart.'" He also mentions Dr. Ming-Hei Huang, a Harvard Medical School researcher who in 1995 discovered a new kind of cell in the heart.

These Intrinsic Cardiac Adrenergic cells seemed to synthesise and release catecholamines—a group name for a bunch of different chemicals, like dopamine, which used to be thought of as exclusive to the brain. ICA cells have magnetic properties, which suggest that the heart can respond to and interact with magnetic fields. A similar type of magnetic cell can be found in the brain. There may well be an electromagnetic connection between the heart and the brain, and the discovery of these new cells seems to support that possibility.

Gary E. Shwartz and Linda G. Russek, of the Human Energy Systems Laboratory at the University of Arizona, are innovators of a most attractive theory which they call "energy cardiology or cardio-energetics." They have published research which they say shows that the heart and brain communicate with each other "both energetically and physiologically." "The heart's electrocardiograms," they say, "can be registered in our brain waves. Moreover, loving people can register, in their brain waves, the electrocardiograms of other people's hearts." Shwartz and Russek write perfect Aristotelianism crossed with modern knowledge:

> Metaphorically the heart is the sun, the pulsing, energetic center of our biophysical solar system, and the brain is the earth . . . one implication of the energy cardiology/cardio-energetic revolution is the radical idea that energetically, the brain revolves around the heart, not the other way around.

One person who has made this area his life's work is Dr. Paul Pearsall, author of *The Heart's Code: The True Stories of Organ Transplant Patients and What They Reveal about Where We Store Our Memories*. This book claims that "the heart, not the brain, is the very essence of our being" and that "western medicine is only now catching up with what indigenous peoples have known for years"; that "the heart thinks, feels, remembers, loves and hates. It communicates the information and memory stored throughout its life to every cell in the human body . . ." Dr. Pearsall also points out that the science on which he bases his ideas is extremely new, that "professionals may have differing opinions about the implications of this research" and that "many of the theories presented here are not yet substantiated."

> Anybody who receives a new heart is getting a big ball of subtle energy . . . Ancient cultures have known about subtle energy throughout history, and have

viewed it as the vital force of all creation. Chinese call it Chi, the Japanese call it Ki, in Hawaii it's known as mana . . . the spirit of life itself, and the place where memories are stored . . . something keeps tugging at our hearts and drawing us back to the energy that brings us life, unites us in love, and leaves our physical body when we die. Physicists call this energy "the fifth force."

There is something charmingly old-fashioned in this: it sounds suspiciously like *pneuma,* the pre-Aristotelian world soul, drawn in through the nose and concocted in the ventricles, or like the "vital energy" that Louis Galvani thought he could find in the piles of frogs' legs that eventually led to the understanding of electricity, and the *rooh* of Islamic medicine.

> I don't have much doubt about cellular memory [Pearsall continues, but] why do some people have these experiences and not others? . . . the individuals who feel these changes are unusually aware of their own bodies. They're often artists, painters or poets—creative people, in other words, who are introspective and paying attention.

Or, it could be argued, overimaginative types who should get out more.

It is easy to mock a man who says that his heart told him he could connect with and influence the x-ray machine using "information-containing energy," less easy to mock anyone who has survived cancer, or the methods to which they ascribe their survival. Pearsall puts it down, at least in part, to the fact that he has learned to communicate with his heart, which he sees as the mediator of all the energy in the body. The heart, he says, pumps nutrients to every cell in our bodies, and therefore by definition is pumping "patterns of energy" containing the information that tells the cells how to be themselves. The heart, he says, has a code, related to this subtle energy, and recorded in every cell of the body, as an "informational template of the soul." It can communicate with its own body, and with other hearts, and store memories in its cells. "Is what we refer to as the soul at least in part a set of info-energetic cellular memories, a kind of cellular soul program that is constantly being modified during the soul's brief stay in the physical body?"

> As a cancer and bone marrow transplant survivor who has held a beating heart in his hand and felt its amazing spiritual essence, and who has not only read about but observed and taken part in experiments on invisible subtle en-

ergy, I have little doubt that the heart is the major energy center of my body and conveyor of a code that represents my soul . . . As a scientist, however, my brain demands more evidence, and that evidence is now emerging.

I won't attempt a full explanation of Dr. Pearsall's theories here, but they start like this: all systems are constantly exchanging mutually influential energy and being affected by the exchange; energy and information are the same thing; stored info-energy makes up cellular memories. All living things are by their nature manifestations of energy that know—remember—what they are and how they function. Our heart, by nature of its immense power, its millions of cells throbbing in unison and its central location in our body, is the central organ that constantly pulsates info-energy from, between and to all other organs and cells . . . every cell becomes a holographic or complete representation of our energetic heart. (Compare this description with Harvey's in *De Motu Cordis* on page 34.)

Pearsall is hopelessly and deliciously biased in favor of the heart—like Christiaan Barnard, he seems almost in love with it. One of the problems with acknowledging the glories of the heart, for him, is that the "arrogant brain" greets with "incredulous anger and dismissive mockery" the idea that it might not have sole charge of emotion, memory, contemplation and thinking.

"The brain has had things pretty much its own way for the past couple of centuries," writes Pearsall. "Unfortunately the brain has created an . . . often soulless world that contributes to failing hearts, weak immune systems, and malignant cells." While he acknowledges that it is the brain that worked out how to transplant hearts in the first place, he sees it as controlling, blaming, narcissistic, immature, whining, paranoid; it invents little versions of itself—computers, mobile phones—and damages the heart by exposing it to constant stress in the search for success. He longs for a warmer, slower, less high-tech world in which the heart can be heard, because this brain world is killing us (and it is the brain, he says, which holds us up from being willing to consider his propositions).

Shwartz and Russek say that "Pearsall takes such metaphors [the heart as the sun] and weaves a vision that is not only possible, but desirable." This desirability may be the key—we still want our hearts to be special. The system which these scientists propose is one many people would be happy to have proven, because it matches exactly what they have always "known in our hearts" (and we all know what we mean by that) to be "true." Loosely, the brain is associated with reason, self-advancement, self-protection, individuality, and the heart is the, well, heart of a network of subtle energies and connecting love. The brain is clever, the heart is wise; the brain is quick and knowledgeable, the heart is full of ancient love. (For Pearsall, the heart seems to have taken over what has most recently been assigned by science to the left brain.) The brain is the fox, and the heart is the hedgehog. (The fox in the story knows many things; the hedgehog knows one big thing. The fox runs round and round in circles snapping at the hedgehog, which he wants to eat; the hedgehog rolls up into a ball and waits.) The brain is *logos*—rational knowledge; the heart is *mythos*—intuitive knowledge. These are primary symbols, but while a brain approach to life has little room for the heart, a heart approach necessarily includes and welcomes the brain: inclusion, union, is the heart's job.

Unfortunately, my understanding of biophysics and psychoneuro-immunology is not up to telling you whether this is likely to be the nature of the future, or whether it's codswallop. Pearsall rather elegantly advises that we be skeptical about skepticism (moderation in all things, as the Delphic Oracle said); all I can do is be enchanted by the report that at the Princeton Engineering Anomalies Research Program, which studies the "interaction of human consciousness with sensitive physical devices and systems," couples of scientists "connected heart-to-heart in a love bond" have stronger "energy-connection effects" than other pairs of researchers. "L" energy, as they call this "fifth force," is vitally concerned with the surrender of individuality for the benefit of the group. Says Pearsall: "It appears that 'L' energy relates to being able to transcend our xenophobic proneness to cellular separateness as well as remembering our substantive and relational natures . . ." Or, as the Beatles put it, "All you need is love."

Cutting swiftly back to the physical heart, and the rational scientific route through this half-charted territory, I asked a noted London cardiologist about all this. He acknowledged that it's "easy to

> **DR. PEARSALL'S TIPS FOR GETTING IN TUNE WITH "L" ENERGY:**
>
> - Be patient
> - Be connected
> - Be pleasant
> - Be humble
> - Be gentle

PATANJALI'S FIVE CAUSES OF SUFFERING

- **Ignorance,** the failure to discriminate between the permanent and the impermanent, the pure and the impure, bliss and suffering, the Self and the non-Self.
- **Egoism,** the limiting sense of "I," results from the individual's intellect attributing the power of consciousness to itself.
- **Attachment,** clinging to pleasure.
- **Aversion,** clinging to pain.
- **The fear of death,** a spontaneous feeling, deeply rooted in us all, no matter how learned we may be.

fall over the edge" in these areas "of such interesting research," and confirmed my suspicion. "He's probably talking about love," he said, and wondered, had I read the Sufi poets?

As the alternative is considering the role of intrinsic cardiac parasympathetic postganglionic efferent neurons, I have no choice but to make my excuses and leave. And what have I learned? That whoever called the heart "nothing but a stupid pump" was probably wrong, that Dean Martin was right (Relax-Ay-Voo!) and that I look forward to future developments.

CHAMBER TWO

THE
RELIGIOUS HEART

1

A WORD ON SACRIFICE
AND THE AFTERLIFE

When I tell people I've been writing a history of the heart, the response is always a gesture to the left of the chest, and the question: "The organ, or the, er . . . ?" The answer is both. We might suppose that the physical heart is one thing and the spiritual/emotional heart is another, but the connection between the two is constant, in religion as much as in love. Every religion—that of the ancient Egyptians, of the Aztecs, Christianity, Islam, Buddhism, Hinduism and more—uses both the image and the actuality of the physical heart to represent emotional and spiritual qualities.

GODS AND SUFFERING

No religion springs unique and fully formed into the world. Jesus, whose crowned and radiant heart is so familiar in the West, followed a long line of ancient gods born on or around December 25, often of virgin mothers in a cave or underground chamber, who gave great benefits to mankind, died violently at the hands of evil, came back from the dead and took the part of man in heaven, and were celebrated on earth by devoted followers in ritualized meals, particularly in midwinter and at the spring equinox.

Gods who fulfill these criteria include Mithras, Dionysus, Adonis, Tammuz, Attis, Osiris and others. Their suffering took various forms: for Osiris, it was fratricide; for Persephone, rape; Christ, the crucifixion (after which he was, according to Matthew, "three days in the heart of the earth"); Dionysus, kidnapping and dismemberment by Titans; Odin, hanging on the World Ash. Adonis, Tammuz and Attis were all killed by a wild boar.

With their return they produced, or they became, a crop: Osiris's cycle of rebirth brought the fertilizing inundation of the Nile, necessary for crops to grow; Persephone's return revoked the famine her mother Demeter had visited upon the earth; Christ's heart is the storehouse of the world, and his flesh and blood are the bread and the wine; pomegranate trees sprang up where the blood of Dionysus fell; Odin learned the secret of runic wisdom from the tree he died on; anemones and violets grew from the spilled blood of Adonis and Attis. Tammuz, Persephone, Jesus, Dionysus and Mithras, among others, all die each year and are reborn in the spring. The name Ishtar, goddess of both fertility and chastity and wife of Tammuz, whom she rescued from the underworld, is the origin of the word "Easter," the Christian celebration of Christ's coming back to life, via the Norse goddess Eostre. Bethlehem was a shrine of Tammuz. Krishna was born of a virgin; so was Buddha Sakyamuni.

SACRIFICE

Sacrifice—whether human, animal or cucumber (not unheard of, when there was nothing better to offer)—reenacts these original acts of violence. The idea is that the catharsis of sacrifice will keep people safe by restoring order or heading off incipient disorder; it might guarantee crops or prevent crop failure. A sacrifice can be a bribe or an exchange of gifts, either of which can create a moment of union with the gods. Man is attempting to take control over life and death, hastening the process of moving on. The slaughter of the first born was a preemptive act of gratitude: if you give God the first, he'll give you lots more later.

Pier Paolo Pasolini's film *Medea* opens with a horribly fascinating scene of ancient human sacrifice, in which a boy is killed and dismembered and his parts distributed to the populace, who smear his blood on their crops and bury their share of him in their field. The part we see buried is the heart: the best, strongest, most efficacious part. There is a biblical undertone here: Jeremiah 32:41 reads, "I will plant them in this land assuredly, with my whole heart." Later, Medea sacrifices her brother and dismembers him so that she can elope with Jason. Then, when Jason betrays her, she sacrifices their sons.

And what is the significance of the heart in all this? The heart is the choicest bit of flesh; it is the link between flesh and soul and God, it is king of the body, the potent seed. Dionysus was reborn from the heart that his father Zeus snatched from the Titans' cooking pot. All sacrifice goes back to the myth of the god/king, slain in order that his people might thrive (for more on this, see J. G. Frazer's *The Golden Bough*). Christ is unusual in this tradition because he is God and man at the same time: both the sacrifice and he to whom sacrifice is made. All sacrificial cultures (with the honorable exception of the Aztecs, who were themselves sacrificed) have been working through history toward avoiding actual slaughter. It's a long journey from the stories of Bata and Medea to Christina Rossetti's Victorian hymn, "In the Bleak Mid Winter":

> What can I give him,
> Poor as I am?
> If I were a shepherd
> I would bring a lamb
> If I were a Wise Man
> I would do my part,
> Yet what I can I give him,
> Give my heart.

The earliest surviving written records are Mesopotamian: here is how a Mesopotamian priest would exorcise a demon, using the words with which the god Ea taught his son Marduk.

> Go, my son
> Take a white kid of Tammuz,
> Lay it down facing the sick man and
> Take out its heart and
> Place it in the hand of that man;
> Perform the incantation of Eridu,
> The kid whose heart thou hast taken out
> Is Li'i food with which thou shalt make atonement for the man . . .

The white kid is an archetypal virginal animal, whose innocence is given in exchange for the life of the beseecher.

> The kid is a substitute for mankind.
> He hath given the kid for his life,
> He hath given the head of the kid for the head of the man,
> He hath given the neck of the kid for the neck of the man,

He hath given the breast [heart] of the kid
For the breast [heart] of the man,

continues the priest, preempting Christ, the lamb of God, who taketh away the sin of the world.

Sacrifice was not a cheap or easy practice. Sacrifices have to be bought or caught or selected. Often human sacrifices could have been sold as slaves if they weren't to be killed. In many places at many times, sacrificees believed in the system and were happy to go. It's worth remembering that life in this world was not always the be-all and end-all that it is now in the West.

Now that most people in the West have little knowledge of God, we worship instead a never-ending series of sacrificial hypersexualized godlets known as celebrities, whom we both adore and torment, and plenty of whom die under the cosh of public "interest," wielded by the sacrifice-priests of the press. In the Christian tradition these people are both human and godlike. In the Christian tradition we both sacrifice *to* them: all that money and attention, all the special clothing and ritual consumption of inebriants, all those feastlike parties, which devotees witness through the media, and we sacrifice them: all those suicides and drink-and-drug deaths, all those female film stars who have to starve themselves to be thin enough to work, all that plastic surgery—literally they put themselves on the slab, under the knife, for our love. I write this the morning Paula Yates died: a famous, beautiful drug-eaten woman, wife to "rock gods," who read in a newspaper one morning, when very pregnant, that she ought to abort her child for the good of the world.

The difference is that these godlets have no afterlife, and the only way they come back to life is when the Public Eye opens another canful: there's always another yappy blonde who wants to make it on TV. This may be one reason why celebrities who survive the drug stage frequently find God: often God is the only way out. And religion is often good for addicts: strict rules, no question about what you have to do, something external laying down the law and letting you off a degree of personal responsibility. God, if you believe in Him, can be just as strict a master as heroin. Religion can still be the opium of the people.

IT IS often forgotten that Islam, Christianity and Judaism all share the same God and that only later developments—disputes over the comparative importance of prophets and the exact parentage of one in particular—divided them. Islamic and European ideas of the heart are reassuringly similar: hardly surprising, as they are branches of the same tree. The common root is ancient Egypt.

In the Memphis creation myth, Ptah thought of the world in his heart, and created it by naming it. A 700 B.C. inscription records a version supposedly copied from "a wish of the ancestors." It is strangely familiar: Ptah's heart thought of each thing as he created it, and his tongue repeated what had been thought of. His heart is the spirit, his tongue the word. His body is the universe. The myth contains within it roots of Christianity and Judaism and Islam, of microcosm and macrocosm, and of the power of the word in magic and in reality: "In the beginning was the word, and the word was with God, and the word was God." Everything that the nonphysical heart is to us now, it was to the ancient Egyptians then. All that has changed is the niceties, the decorations—and our anatomical knowledge.

THE WORDS

The hieroglyph for heart, used in both *ib* and *haty,* looks like a little heart with cut-off blood vessels or ears at each corner and a small neck—or crown—at the top. One theory suggests that it is based on a canopic jar, as there was a taboo on representing the organ itself. However, hearts were not put into canopic jars and the hieroglyph looks exactly like a heart, so this is probably a misreading. The hieroglyph is a very familiar shape, precursor of winged hearts down the ages (see page 279).

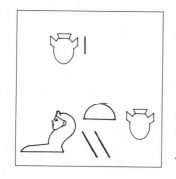

Sadly, *haty* can't be connected to the word "heart," which is from the Sanskrit *hrid*, via the Latin *cor* and Greek *kardia*. The word *haty* still exists in Coptic, meaning poitrine or chest.

Ib has been further confused by the word *eeb*, meaning dance, and the occasional punning use of a dancing figure hieroglyph to

The hieroglyphs for *ib* and *haty.*

represent a heart. The Egyptologist Gaston Maspero fancifully connected the two: some say that the hieroglyph for the heart is a dancing figure, and lead from this into the theory that the ancient Egyptians believed that a dancing woman creates a baby out of her menstrual blood, rather as butter is churned from milk, the blood coming down from the heart for this purpose. In this way the heart is literally the mother, which connects with "my mother, my heart" in the Book of the Dead. But *eeb*, though it sounds like *ib*, is not now thought to be connected to it, and the theory of the dancing mother heart though a lovely idea is not provable.

However, here is part of an Ifa divination song, from the Yoruba of Nigeria:

Slender menstrual flow,
We sought you in vain
You refused to come back.
But you grew hands and feet
And turned into a baby.
You, offspring of blood,
We saw you no more.
You did not return.
But you grew hands and feet, and turned into a baby.

One thing we didn't inherit, which would have made my job a lot easier is having two words for heart. Hieroglyphics depict both *ib* and *haty*. Very loosely, *haty* represented the physical heart, and *ib* the spiritual, emotional heart-soul. This distinction survived in the language until the end of the Egyptian civilization, even to the last Ptolemy, though the difference between the two often escapes the reader completely. Modern English has only the one word, though we have tried to divide the physical organ off from the emotional/spiritual core far more energetically than the Egyptians ever did.

The *ib*, the heart-soul, was immortal, and it was of ultimate importance for the Egyptians. Khepri, the self-created god, lived there, as did human individuality and the god in man. And when an ancient Egyptian died, the heart which had kept him physically alive came into its own.

When a corpse was mummified, many of the internal organs were put into separate canopic jars for preservation. The heart, however, had to remain inside the mummified body because it had a vital role to play in a person's continued existence after death. When someone died, they proceeded to the Hall of Two Truths. Here, before Osiris and a panel of other gods, the heart was weighed in scales against the feather of truth, emblem of the Goddess Maat. If your heart was not there to be weighed, there was no way for you to be judged worthy of eternal life, and you could not get to heaven. Having your heart in the right place was very, very important.

The complex, poetic process of judgement was governed by the Book of the Dead, a collection of spells and prayers, magic and religion, intended to ensure eternal life. It developed over a long period, with many versions and many translations of the many versions. You could buy a scroll of it and have your name inserted. According to this book, forty-two specific sins had to be denied, each to a specific god. Here are some of them:

- Wide-of-stride who comes from On, I have not done evil.
- Shadow-eater who comes from the cave, I have not stolen.
- Lion twins who come from heaven, I have not trimmed the measure.
- Cave-dweller who comes from the west, I have not sulked.
- Bastet who comes from the shrine, I have not winked.
- Backward-faced one who comes from the pit, I have not copulated with a boy.
- Dark one who comes from darkness, I have not reviled.
- Peace-bringer who comes from Sais, I have not been aggressive.
- Many-faced who comes from Djefet, I have not had a hasty heart.
- High-of-head who comes from the cave, I have not wanted more than I had.

And further sins too have to be denied:

I have not mistreated cattle.
I have not sinned in the Place of Truth.
I have not known what should not be known.
I have not done any harm.
I did not begin a day by exacting more than my due.
My name did not reach the barque of the mighty ruler.

I have not blasphemed a god.

I have not robbed the poor.

I have not caused pain.

I have not caused tears.

I have not deleted the loaves of the gods.

I have not eaten the cakes of the dead.

I have not taken milk from the mouth of children.

I have not held back water in its season.

I have not dammed a flowing stream.

I have not quenched a needed fire.

I am pure, I am pure, I am pure, I am pure!

I am pure as is pure the great heron in Hnes.

I am truly the nose of the Lord of Breath

Who sustains all the people . . .

THE PSYCHOSTASIA OF HUNEFER IN THE HALL OF TWO TRUTHS

Hunefer was an overseer at the palace of the nineteenth-dynasty Pharaoh Seti I (c. 1370 B.C.), a royal scribe and superintendent of cattle. Here we see jackal-headed Anubis, the first embalmer, taking him by the hand to lead him to the scales, and Horus leading him to Osiris. Ammit stands frustrated under the scales, and Thoth records the proceedings. Above, Hunefer kneels by a table of offerings before a panel of fourteen divine judges.

© The Art Archive /British Museum / Jacueline Hyde

Whether or not you were deemed pure was up to your heart. As it was weighed—the jackal-headed god Anubis did the weighing, and Thoth, the ibis-headed inventor of writing and history, recorded the result—the heart told the gods whether or not you had been good. To persuade it to offer a good report of you, a scarab made of green stone, basalt or haematite would be laid on the breast above the heart, or on the chest above it (see picture on page 6). Chapter XXXB from the Book of the Dead, pleading with the heart, would be either inscribed on the scarab or recited over it:

O my heart [*ib*] of my mother,
O my heart [*haty*] of my mother,
O my heart of my being,
Do not rise up against me as witness,
Do not oppose me in the tribunal,
Do not rebel against me before the guardians of the scales.
You are my *ka* [vital force, personality] within my body,
The Khnum [the creator of bodies] who prospers my limbs.
Go to the good place prepared for us,
Do not make my name stink before them,
The magistrates who put people in their places!
If it's good for us it is good for the judge,
It pleases him who renders judgment,
Do not invent lies before the god,
Before the great god, the lord of the west [Osiris],
Lo, your uprightness brings vindication!

Your heart, here representing your conscience, could speak against you, and you—the rest of you—might appeal to it for mercy as if it were a separate individual: it could save you or condemn you to death. The Middle Kingdom poem *The Dialogue of a Man and His Soul* is the story of a man who wants to die but his soul won't let him.

The heart was often referred to in the third person, as a friend; you could take counsel with it: "Come to me, my heart, so I can talk to you, and so you can answer my words. You may be able to explain to me what is happening across the land." It could even separate from your body, as did the heart of poor Sinuhe, the servant of Princess Nefru: when he returned from many years of self-imposed exile and was unexpectedly greeted with loving kindness, ointment and clean sheets by his old employers, "I did not know myself before him, while this god greeted me pleasantly. I was like a man seized by darkness. My *ba* [soul] was gone, my limbs trembled; my heart [*haty*] was not in my body, I did not know life from death." The meaning is clear. Your heart not being in your body is dire.

This separation is another reason for the constant declaration in funeral texts that "My heart is mine." Sometimes they read: "His heart is his, his heart does not say what he has done" (which slightly gives the game away. If I were Osiris I should want to take that heart to one side and have a word). There was a sort of institutionalized self-aggrandizement: in their inscriptions the ancient Egyptians aimed to persuade themselves, posterity and the gods of their virtues. Rather than confess their sins and seek forgiveness, they deny them forcefully and cast a spell in their hearts to stop the truth from getting out. In the end, when they are being weighed against a feather, they clearly need all the help they can get, including a magic prayer to shut up the heart, the better self. Perhaps it was just a very pragmatic approach to judgment. The prayer was found, according to some versions, by Prince Hordjedef under the feet of a statue of the god Thoth at his city of Hermopolis Magna, inscribed on a slab of quartzite, in the god's own writing.

The heart was always portrayed as faithful, and the scales evenly balanced, in the hope of inspiring a favorable judgment. Thoth answered: "Behold, I hold to be right the name of Osiris [insert name here]; and his heart, also, hath appeared upon the scales, and it hath not been found to be evil." All dead Egyptians were referred to as Osiris, to associate them with the god's resurrection. This is a simple imitation of God which we'll see later in Islam and Christianity. The entire ritual of mummification was an imitation of the death and resurrection of Osiris, that the dead might be given back their powers and abilities in the afterlife.

After the heart-weighing, Horus leads the deceased to Osiris, and though we are never shown Osiris's response, it is generally assumed that the virtuous dead will then proceed to his domains and live happily for eternity as a god. If you are found guilty, on the other hand, Ammit, the Eater of the Dead, with "the forepart of a crocodile, the hindquarters of a hippopotamus, and the middle part of a lion," will eat your heart there and then.

The weighing of the heart reappears in the Christian and Islamic ideas of Judgment Day. Take the thirteenth-century tympanum of the cathedral at

Detail of the tympanum of the cathedral at Bourges with scales, chalice, demons and damned souls. © *Scala*

Bourges: a beautiful angel, St. Michael, holds a pair of scales, weighing on one hand a chalice (see page 187 for the heart/cup connection) containing the good actions of the happy-looking child whose head the angel is caressing; on the other a nasty little bat-eared demon is desperately trying to trim the measure (one of the sins that had to be denied by the heart in the Book of the Dead). Standing around are various bigger demons, some with extra faces on their bellies, one with a winged bottom and breasts in the shape of dog-heads. They are busy pitching damned souls into a gaping cauldron over the fires of hell. Similar scenes are displayed at Chartres, Le Mans and Amiens, where the lamb lies in one pan and a wicked-looking head on the other. Sometimes—in the portal at Conques, for example—the devil is there in person, putting his finger on the scales like a crooked grocer. The image of the scales was not official church teaching, though it was used by St. Augustine, the Church Fathers and St. John Chrysostom. It first appeared in the Middle East and came from there to Europe, and on into everyday modern usage: lightheartedness and heavy-heartedness may no longer be quite so closely associated with sin and guilt, but the image persists.

After your heart has vouched for your virtue, it is washed with cool water and Anubis gives it back to you (remember Bata). Horus, in the Osiris myth, brought cool water from Elephantine to wash the god's heart. Water is a straightforward image: it is thirst-quenching, life-giving, refreshing, cleansing. It is also an ancient symbol of returning to the womb or to the primordial waters out of which, in almost every culture, the earth itself was born. In Egypt it echoed the flooding of the Nile, which revitalized the

A DIGRESSION: ITRY-SENU

I saw a human heart in the British Museum. It looked like the strange brown things you see in shop windows in Chinatown: like dried seaweed, like very very old bananas. It was a shriveled-up, dark-brown pouch, flattened, with some desiccated pipes here and there, lying in a nineteenth-century glass cabinet along with some lungs and a womb with a tumor, all of which it closely resembled. Faded labels in brown, dried-up nineteenth-century handwriting lay beside each.

In the 1820s Augustus Bozzi Granville, M.D., an eclectic, energetic and rather bossy gentleman, acquired the mummy of a woman, Itry-Senu, from Sir Archibald Edmonstone, a young patient newly returned from Egypt, who was keeping her at his house in Wimpole Street, having bought her at the Kings' Tombs in Alexandria. Granville took her apart, bit by careful bit, to see what medicine could discover.

Dr. Granville sought to prove his theories about the role of wax in mummification by making candles from substances found in the mummy, and burning them at the Royal Society. In the 1870s, when he gave Itry-Senu to the British Museum, he also gave some "specimens of recent mummies," arms and legs of stillborn infants "prepared by myself with wax according to the Egyptian method" fifty years earlier. To his annoyance, the British Museum was reluctant to display them, preferring to keep them, "as some funny gentleman appertaining to the museum once said to me," in a *museum clausum*.

country. Proffering devotion to God, Egyptians would say, "My heart is on your water," meaning "loyal to you." Bringing the boatless to shore was seen as a much-admired good act (see page 301 for how the image of the heart at sea has survived). Jeremiah also reflects the importance of washing: "O Jerusalem, wash thine heart from wickedness, that thou mayest be saved"; as do the Psalms: "Wash me thoroughly from my iniquitie, and cleanse me from my contrite heart . . . create in me a clean heart." Modern Christianity's tidy little version of the plunge into water is water on the forehead in baptism; it correlates with the water which flowed from Christ's wound at the crucifixion.

Weighed and washed, the heart waits till Isis calls the dead back to life, as she reanimated her son Horus and her brother/husband Osiris. For the dead to be reanimated, it is vital that their heart is not lost or hurt. Also, you will need it so that you can remember your life. This is another reason for having a heart scarab: as a spare. This comes from Chapter XXVI of the Book of the Dead (from the Papyrus of Ani):

> May my heart [*ib*] be with me in the house of hearts!
>
> May my heart be with me in the house of hearts!
>
> May my heart be with me, and may it rest there, or I shall not eat of the cakes of Osiris on the eastern side of the Lake of Flowers, neither shall I have a boat wherein to go down the Nile, nor another wherein to go up, nor shall I be able to sail down the Nile with thee.
>
> May my mouth be given to me that I may speak therewith, and my two legs to walk therewith . . .
>
> I understand with my heart, I have gained the mastery over my heart, I have gained mastery over my legs, I have gained the power to do whatsoever my *ka* pleaseth.
>
> My soul shall not be fettered to my body at the gates of the underworld; but I shall enter in peace and I shall come forth in peace.

A different translation recalls (or foreshadows) the Nina Simone song in which she enjoys having her arms, her legs, her heart, her voice, her eyes, her nose, her liver, "I got life . . .":

> My heart is mine in the house of hearts
> My heart is mine in the house of hearts
> My heart is for me
> I understand with my heart and my heart is for me
> I possess my two arms
> I possess my two legs
> I can do what my *ka* desires.

Another danger is that a demon might take your heart from you. Again, powerful words protect you. These are from the Papyrus of Nu:

Hail, thou Lion God! I am the flowerbush! . . .

Let not this heart [*haty*] be carried away from me by the fighting gods in Annu.

Hail, thou who dost wind bandages around Osiris and who hast seen Set!

Hail, thou who returnest after smiting and destroying him before the mighty ones!

This my heart [*ib*] sitteth and weepeth for itself before Osiris, it hath made supplication for me . . .

2

SACRED CHRISTIAN HEARTS—
WOUNDED, BROKEN
AND FLAMING

The Sacred Heart of Jesus, perhaps the most familiar religious heart, grew out of many ancient cults and ideas: it has as many manifestations as it has roots, and complex relations to the heart in other religions. It can represent gratitude, love, gratitude for love, repentance for former neglect of love, compassion for Christ's suffering, strengthening of love and purification of love in order to unite with the love of Jesus and the passing on of love, our own and God's.

Because the physical heart is an empty thing which is filled with something else—blood—it easy to imagine the metaphorical heart being filled with spiritual qualities. The heart, when filled, is fat and compact: the spiritual qualities can thus become visible, attainable. Things flow in and out of it, and it moves of its own accord, which only makes it more like us. Sexually, it is energetic as a man (full like an erection, spurting like an orgasm) and receptive as a woman. Everything about the image speaks of the mysterious made accessible. The simple way in which access was provided was—through a hole.

Physically, a heart does not break. As we have seen, it fails, it suffocates for lack of oxygen, it becomes old and flabby and incapable, it turns to stone—but it does not break. It's a muscle. But spiritually and emotionally, the broken or wounded heart is one of the most striking images in human history. In romantic love, Cupid shoots his wicked arrow into the heart, and humans fall in love with each other. In Christianity, Longinus the Roman speared Jesus through the heart on the cross, and the love of God poured out over humanity. Jesus' wounded heart and the wounded heart of the lover are closely related: both are at their most effective when wounded, because the wound lets love in and out. Paradoxically, wholeness is incomplete because it

The Sacred Heart of Jesus, by P. M. Ruiz: a flaming, blossoming,
pierced and adored depiction, typical of nineteenth-century
Mexico. © *The Art Archive / Pinacoteca Verreinel, Mexico City / Dagli Orti*

offers finality and completion, while human existence is more properly a continuing process.

Jesus' heart evolved out of the Old Testament, which evolved from the ancient Egyptian heart-soul. The word "heart" is used 858 times in the King
James version of the Bible, and in the Hebrew *lev*—which is sometimes translated into English as "soul"—appears 1,024 times. In the Old Testament the
job of the heart is to love God, to hold the law and to be steadfast under the
trials God puts it through; in so doing it covers much of the moral and emotional repertoire of the modern Western heart, expressed in terms from the

extreme morality of Jeremiah to the fabulous poetry in the Psalms and the Song of Songs.

Above all, the heart is where man and God meet. So the heart of Jesus, who is God and man at the same time, is a point of multiple union. Just as the heart was for the Greeks and the Egyptians the place where the physical and the emotional and the spiritual meet, so Christ's crucifixion is the moment when human physicality and the divine omnipotence collide most dramatically. And there, the center of all these dualities, the meeting place of the meeting places, is Christ's heart, full of love, which is going to make things better for humanity. From this heart, in the Gospel, flow blood and water, physical manifestations of love, to feed and cleanse and redeem the human race. Longinus opened a direct and permanent channel to an ancient, fertile idea—the heart of God, full of the love of God—and he linked it forever with Cupid, the "blind bow-boy's" crazy sexual love, with alarming results on both sides.

The spiritual and emotional importance of the Christian heart was defined by St. Augustine of Hippo in the fifth century. His language took the heart imagery of ancient Egypt, as filtered through the Bible, and made it the language of individual devotion, replete with words from the root *cor:* accord, discord, concord, record, cordial and many more. He demonstrated how, as well as reading the images in the Bible, Christians could use them in their own prayers and writings, and how the individual's heart related to God's heart—through the imitation of its suffering. The next stage was the gradual seeping out of the imagery from moments of mystical communion into everyday life, and here too Augustine played his part. He spoke of the heart in elevated language: of God's words stuck fast in his heart, of his heart needing purification, of the torments his heart suffered in mental pregnancy; he used the contrast between heart and mind that we are so used to today. And his heart had both mystic and everyday duties: the everyday merging into the mystical.

THE WOUNDS OF CHRIST

Fascination with the heart of Jesus came to a head in the seventeenth century. It was reached, in a charmingly literal segue, through the wound. St. Bernard, the "Honeysweet Doctor," gave this description of Christ on the cross: "Take heed and see his head inclyned to salve the, his mouthe to kysse the, his arms I-spred to be-clyp the, his hondes I-thrilled to yeve the, his syde opened to love the . . ." Christ crucified, open-armed to embrace the believer, openhearted, literally, through the wound.

Immediately after Christ's death the Church Fathers had acknowledged the importance of the wound in the side as the gate from which the blood and water of the Eucharist and baptism flowed. St. Gregory the Great compared it to the cleft in the Canticle: "O my dove, that art in the clefts of the rock, in the secret places of the stairs." St. Anselm wrote: "What sweetness is in his pierced side! That wound has given us a glimpse of the treasure house of His goodness, that is to say, the love of His Heart for us." St. Francis of Assisi's desire to share in the Passion of Christ led him to be stigmatized in 1224, and the five wounds of Christ's Passion—in each hand, each foot and the side—began to be venerated.

The wounds were known as the "wells" (echoing Isaiah's "Ye shall draw waters of joy out of the Saviour's fountains"), or doors, of salvation, and they became favored objects of contemplation. The wound in Christ's side was the door to Christ's heart and the love within it, through which Christians gain everlasting life; therefore it was called the "well of everlasting life."

By contemplating the wounds and the Passion the devotee would start to feel for Christ, and thus to feel like Christ; the contemplation of a physical object would lead to an awareness of its spiritual meaning and connotations and, ultimately, to connection with God. Saintly relics served much the same purpose, and other religions have similar rituals.

St. Augustine opens his *Confessions* with: "Our heart is restless till it rests in you." He adopted Plotinus's neo-Platonist belief that the human soul has degenerated since entering the flesh, and that what it needs and longs for is perfect union, with itself and with God, purged of all material distractions. This idea pervades human history and human nature, and is frequently held to be the fruit of contemplation or meditation, and to take place in the heart.

Augustine recommended that the man in search of this union should "Go into yourself." The Delphic Oracle said much the same when it advised inquirers to "know thyself." In the Orthodox Church, this was represented by the idea of uniting the mind and the heart: "All your inner disorder is due to . . . the mind and the heart each going their own way," wrote the Russian St. Theophan Zatvornik, "the Recluse," the great nineteenth-century upholder of the Orthodox Fathers.

You must unite the mind with the heart; then the tumult of your thoughts will cease, and you will acquire a rudder to guide the ship of your soul . . . how can this union be achieved? Make it your habit to pray with the mind in the heart: "Lord Jesus Christ, have mercy on me." And this . . . when it becomes grafted to your heart, will . . . unite your mind to your heart, it will quell the turbulence of your thoughts, and it will give you power to govern the movements of your soul.

And how do you find your heart, to put your mind there? "Where sadness, joy, anger and other emotions are felt, here is the heart. Stand here with attention." First there is prayer of the body—saying the words, going through the motions; then there is prayer of the mind, when you are concentrating; then, when you are doing, concentrating *and* feeling, you reach true prayer, prayer of the heart "so that the mind understands and the heart feels what the mind is thinking."

The heart's wounds were a particularly popular focus for prayer and devotion. The wound could be prayed to directly: one hymn begins: "*salve plaga lateris nostri redemptoris*" (hail the wound in the side of our redeemer). Even the lance which caused the wound was honored in fourteenth- and fifteenth-century prayers: "And for the like delful knife, that through thine heart gan wende, help me that sinful am in life and give me the bliss without end." And for oaths, the wounds are not entirely defunct yet: piratical villains and Barbara Cartland heroes still cry "Zounds!"—from "God's wounds"—at moments of stress. (Personally I prefer Smollett's "Oddsheartikins!")

Various indulgences (32,755 years of pardon—not to be sniffed at) were offered for particular prayers to the wounds of Christ. Henry VI (1422–68) had a picture of the wounds for his dining table, so that he could contemplate them as he ate. As an image, the wounds separated themselves from the body to become objects which could be viewed independently. They appeared as an elongated diamond-shape, or like conch shells, frilly edged, floating on clouds borne aloft by angels, or spitting blood. They illuminated manuscripts, jewelry, furniture and became part of the *arma christi,* passion shield or sacred blazons, in which the images of the two little hands, two little feet and the heart were arranged like heraldic images.

A late fifteenth-century English prayer roll (used like a prayer book, or as a talisman, or wrapped around a woman in labor to reduce her pain) shows

THE BOOK OF THE HEART

the wound in the side floating on a glorious blue and gold cloud; below it is the heart pierced by a nail (said to be life-size), which then also pierces the two feet, flanked by two more nails each piercing a disembodied hand and surrounded by the crown of thorns, which entwines the nails like a bower. The benefits of contemplating these wounds and the nails are listed alongside, and are considerable:

> Pope Innocent hath granted to every man and woman that berith upon them ye length of these nails seying daily v Pater nosters v Ave Marias and 1 Credo shall have vij giftes. The first is that he shal not dye no soden deth. The second is he shal not be slayne with no sword ne smyte. The iij is he shal not be poysoned. The iiij is his enemys shal not overcome hym. The v is he shall have sufficient goodes to his lyves ende. The vj is he shal not dye withowte all the sacramentes of holy church. The vij is he shall be defended from evell.

The disembodied wounds, it has to be said, look like vaginas. When pictured next to the nails, with their rounded heads, the sexual imagery becomes unavoidable. This may not have been a problem at the time: the heavy sexuality of this kind of image allowed base instincts to be channeled toward a higher purpose. A passionate relationship with Christ, like a passionate relationship with another human, would have its physical side. Nuns after all were his brides. Hence too the swooning and holy orgasms of Sts. Teresa and Catherine of Siena. When Christ invited Doubting Thomas to "reach hither thy hand, and thrust it into my side; and be not faithless, but believing," it was an invitation to love and faith, a consummation.

The wound was seen as a haven to which sinners, like the dove in the clefts of the rock, could retreat—an image echoed in a number of hymns: "Rock of Ages cleft for me, let me hide myself in thee" and "Jesu, lover of my soul, let me to thy bosom fly." In her tenth revelation the Anchoress Julian of Norwich was shown "with sweet the rejoicing . . . His Blessed Heart cleft in twain"; within, she saw "a feyer and delectable place, and large jnow for alle mankynde that shall be savyd and rest in pees and love." The wound not only shelters the sinner, but also, like a mother, feeds and cleans him, with the flowing blood and water. The wound is fertile, full of love; it leads to heaven, it bleeds.

But the wound did not open the gate only to heaven. On Judgment Day Christ would show his wounds both to the elect (as a pledge of his love for

The Incredulity of St. Thomas, by the seventeenth-century painter Bernardo Strozzi.
© *Museo de Arte, Puerto Rico / Bridgeman Art Library*

them) and to sinners (as a reproach). The very image which can take you to heaven can cast you down into hell too. Christ saves humanity by interceding on our behalf on the Day of Judgment, and redeeming our failings with his blood. This is not a million miles away from the role of the ancient Egyptians' hearts, which spoke for them before the god who had come back to life (Osiris);

Pages from a German devotional booklet, made of ivory, showing Christ alongside His disembodied wound, the crown of thorns and the bucket and sponge for putting vinegar in His wound (c. 1340).
© V&A Picture Library

in Christianity Christ became human and came back to life, in order to speak on behalf of man before his own divine father.

Taken literally, as it often has been, all this makes for bloody spectacle. A medieval preacher, John Mirk, urged his congregation to repentance with the tale of a sick man who refused to make confession to a vision of the bleeding wounded Christ, who in response drew "out of hys wounde yn hys syde his hond full of blod," and "cast the blod ynto hys face, and therwyth anon thys seke man cryed and sayd 'Alas! Alas! I am dampnest for ay!' and so deyd."

It is easy to miss the fact that in all the pictures and images, the wound in Jesus' side is on the right, whereas the heart is (generally, but see page 42) on the left. This doesn't seem to have made the slightest bit of difference.

THE EMBLEM TRADITION

The many roles played by the heart in the Bible made keeping track of the complex relationship between man's heart and God's heart a considerable challenge. By the seventeenth century, Emblem Series—sets of edifying illustrations and complementary texts—were being published as an aid to contemplation. Heart Emblem Series emerged as specific guides to the duties and capacities of the Christian heart. In Bacon's words, "Embleme deduceth conceptions intellectuall to images sensible, and that which is sensible more forcibly strikes the memory and is more easily imprinted than that which is intellectuall"; a picture speaks a thousand words, especially if you can't read. In the Rosicrucian *Emblemata Sacra* of Daniel Cramer, published in 1616, number 15 is "I meditate": a human heart sits on a desk with an hourglass and a book; in the sky behind night and day pass by unnoticed. Through contemplation and familiarity,

Cramer's emblem *Meditor*: I meditate.
© *The British Library 95.a.22*

the heart of the reader (or looker)
learns the lessons alongside the hero
heart. The meditating heart speaks
to God on behalf of the individual.
God strengthens it: he is its strength;
it trusts him. "In the remembrance of
Allah hearts shall find rest," says the
Qu'ran; this is the same balm for an open
heart. (Remember—re-member—means to
put back together dismembered parts. A curative, healing
process.)

These "images sensible" were hugely popular across Europe and survived
into the nineteenth century—just. They dealt mostly with love (*Emblemata
Amatoria*), morality (*Emblemata Moralia*) and Christian religious processes
(*Emblemata Sacra*). Two stories emerged to illuminate the heart: in one the
heart, representing the human soul, becomes the proactive hero of a religious
and intellectual comic strip, suffering and winning and surrendering and being rescued. "Thou has prooved mine heart, thou hast visited me in the night,
thou hast tried me," it says in the Psalms, and the emblematists set out to show
every trial. This is, loosely, the story of the Old Testament heart. In the other,
the New Testament heart is a passive recipient of God's attention: it becomes
like a house that Jesus makes ready to live in (see page 197 for more on this).
Between the two, they offer a contemporary roundup of heart imagery, some
prebiblical and some still in use today: the broken heart, the flaming heart, the
heart with wings, hearts and roses, alongside images which now seem arcane,
though they are deep within our language and our assumptions about our
own natures: the heart as a book, a house, a mirror, a tree, a fruit, a plowed
field, a musical instrument.

THE WOUNDED HEART OF MAN

As Christ's heart is wounded, so too must the Christian's be. Daniel
Cramer's Emblems offered a sort of *Pilgrim's Progress*, starring the anthro-

Cramer's emblem *Sanor*: I am healed. "When he burns, he cures; he heals, when he wounds." The sword cuts, and God pours on balm.
© *The British Library 95.a.22*

pomorphic heart in forty cross-referring situations, showing the sheer variety of ways in which the heart of man can be wounded. It is bashed on an anvil by the hand of God to make it soft; a sword cuts it open and God's hand pours in balm: "for he hath torn, and he will heal us." It is tossed on a storm at sea—but it's all right, because later it is seen sprouting a cross atop a firm rock with the sea harmless below: "The wise man builds his house upon a rock." It is crucified, a fat little sacrifice on a fat little crucifix, and that's all right too, because later it is absolved, and on the cross instead is a parchment on which God is writing the fact. In Emblem 23 God writes the name IESU on the heart with a sharp quill, and in 24 he puts it in a furnace to try it. Within each of these trials is the seed of its cure: this is a heart quality which recurs in Islam.

The heart thus imitates the suffering of Christ, and is tried by God in every way that can be found in the Bible. The heart learns its lessons, and in the end it is gathered to heaven in a golden crown (Emblem 28), albeit with a scythe and spade stuck through it.*

There is another wound that is most alarming to modern eyes: the heart can be circumcised. But according to Jeremiah, God is quite clear: "Circumcise yourselves to the Lord, and take away the foreskins of your heart, ye men of Judah and inhabitants of Jerusalem: lest my furie come forth like fire." When Pharaoh hardened his heart, which happened all the time while the Jews were in Egypt, it was the direct opposite of the softening, wounding circumcision. Circumcision of the flesh is a physical token of the covenant be-

---

*It's possible the spade is a mistake: *spade* in Italian means swords, plural of *spada*, and is used to described the seven blades which pierced the Immaculate Heart of Mary (see page 133), representing her seven sorrows.

tween God and Abraham; the soul of the uncircumcised was cut off from God's people. Circumcision of the heart was a dedication of the soul to match the dedication of the flesh: the heart, once again, was a person's very self. This circumcision also later became connected with the idea of the written-on heart: the engraving of God's law in the heart, and what St. Augustine called "the temptations which I have cut off and thrust away from my heart." God transformed you, into your most inner self. As the seventeenth-century emblematist Christopher Harvey wrote in his *Schola Cordis (The School of the Heart)*:

> Consider then my crosse, my nails and spear
> And let that thought
> Cut razorlike thine heart
> When thou dost heare
> How deare I bought
> Thy freedom from the power of sinne
> And that distress which thou wast in.

Another point: by claiming even men's penises, God was claiming all their masculine potency; in the case of his womenfolk he was more likely to answer their prayers for a child: Sarah, Rebecca, Rachel, Hannah, Samson's anonymous mother and of course Mary all bore children as a direct result of him putting something inside them. Zeus fathered children all over the place; so did Jahweh, in his way.

Another version of the heart's foreskin was the caul, a metaphorical version of the pericardium. In *Pilgrim's Progress* Christian's wife hardened her heart against accompanying her husband on his odyssey; when she realized how wrong she had been "the caul of her heart" was "rent in sunder," thus allowing

The Circumcision of the Heart, from Christopher Harvey's *Schola Cordis.* © *The British Library 11623.a.4*

for regeneration. This is a nice rebirth image too, because the anatomical caul, the sac in which the fetus exists before birth, has to break for the baby to emerge.

There is in fact a condition in which an inflamed and stiffened pericardium needs to be lanced (see page 43).

THE SACRED HEART

So who would not want to live in Jesus' heart, that fair and delectable place, in peace and love? After the Reformation the devotion to the wounds receded; but meanwhile the Sacred Heart of Jesus was increasingly venerated. As an image, the heart of Christ did much to bring together the Old and New Testaments, developing as it did Old Testament imagery. The body of Christ on the cross represents both the Church as an institution and a physical church, built in the shape of the cross, Jesus' heart at the juncture of nave and transept, where God (at the altar) and the congregation (in the nave) meet.

Sts. Anselm and Bernard of Clairvaux declared their love for Jesus' heart. Bernard's follower Gilbert of Holland, a monk at Swineshead in Lincolnshire, had this to say, quoting the canticle: "Give thyself up to the love of this heart, thou hast wounded my heart, O my beloved." This wounded heart shows the vehemence of his love:

> O heart that has deigned, so sweet art thou, to manifest thyself in beatings like to those of our hearts that we might give thee love for love! . . . Shall we not call that soul blessed which pierces with the darts of its love the very Heart of our Lord Jesus Christ? *Vulnerasti cor meum, Vulnerasti cor meum.* Weary not of wounding thy beloved, O faithful spouse! Let thy acts of love be as darts to pierce him. Happy shalt thou be if thy arrows be firm fixed in his heart, if his heart be the object of thy love, if thy gaze be ever centred on him. Sweet wound, whence cometh all our strength!

A chain reaction develops: the touch, the wound, the connection, the love, the ecstasy, the salvation. Many were shocked when the film director Derek Jarman fell for St. Sebastian and his phallic darts and when Madonna (the pop star, not his mother) suggested that Jesus was sexy; but it's been there all along in spadefuls, and nowhere more so than in the sweet piercings and palpitations of the wounded heart.

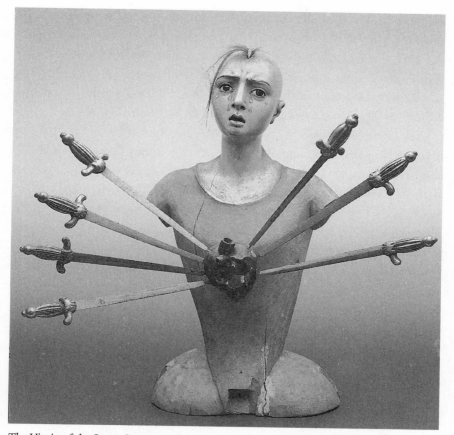

The Virgin of the Seven Sorrows, a seventeenth-century southern Italian woodcarving showing Mary's sorrows as blades through her heart. She would probably have had a wig originally. © *Musées Royaux d'Art et d'Histoire, Bruxelles*

THE IMMACULATE HEART OF MARY

The other great wounded Christian heart is Mary's. The image arose when Simeon told her, "Yea, a sword shall pierce through thine own soul also," referring to the terrible pain that she would suffer when her son came to be killed and through knowing all her life that this was going to happen. The seven dolors of Mary—Simeon's prophesy, the flight into Egypt, the loss of the Holy Child, meeting her son on the way to Calvary, his crucifixion, the taking down from the cross and his entombment—are often represented by the image of her heart with seven swords radiating from it like a halo or an aureole.

The heart is wreathed in roses (see page 240) where Jesus' wears thorns, because Mary is the "Rose without Thorns," and it burns with maternal love. The devotion to what came to be called her Immaculate Heart grew up alongside the devotion to her son's heart in the seventeenth century and, in 1944, August 22 was designated its feast day. Mary's heart offered a route to the heart of Jesus. St. Francis de Sales showed his gentler side in his *Treatise on the Love of God,* where he explains the perfection of Mary's heart by the fact that love is always "in itself calm, agreeable and peaceable: it only becomes impetuous and has recourse to violent attacks when it meets with opposition and resistance. When it finds no obstacle . . . it . . . conquers without violence."

"It is evident that no impetuous motion ever disturbed the heart of the Blessed Virgin," he writes, presumably urging Christian women to bear those seven swords through the heart, the death of an only child, without complaint. Like the poor, women exist to be squashed on earth in return for a promise of rewards in heaven: *stabat mater dolorosa.* Stabat. Stay. Like an obedient dog. Mary does often carry a handkerchief.

St. John Eudes, campaigner for the Sacred Heart of Jesus, took Mary as his mystical spouse by giving everything that he had to her, and wrote a book about her heart that took him twenty years. When he'd finished, he died. The curious St. Marguerite-Marie Alacoque (see page 150) taught her novices to see Mary's heart as a storehouse of inexhaustible love with power over the heart of her son.

Visions of the Virgin have frequently favored her heart. She appeared to a dying woman, Estelle Faguette, at Pellevoisin, near Bourges, France, in 1876, surrounded by roses and raindrops, and showed her a marble *ex voto* slab: it depicted a golden heart in flames with a crown of roses pierced by a sword and a scapular with a scarlet sacred heart motif. She scattered raindrops from her hands, each with the name of a grace written in it. Estelle lived another fifty years, making scapulars like the one Mary had shown her, and in 1900 visited Pope Leo XIII, who consecrated mankind to Mary's heart and ordered the promotion of Estelle's scapular. The walls of her chapel at Pellevoisin are covered in white marble *exvoti,* each bearing the scarlet heart. In 1832 a Parisian priest, Father Desgenettes, saw his sinful and fun-loving neighbors (of whom only 700 out of 27,000 ever took communion) burst spontaneously into cries of one of her names, "Refuge of Sinners," when he decided to obey a mystic voice that told him to consecrate his church to the Immaculate Heart of Mary.

THE BROKEN HEART

The broken heart is a great paradox because it is both good and bad. Clearly it is painful, destructive: it kills you. In *The Pentamerone* by Basile, poor Renza dies of a broken heart on hearing her lover kissing another: "So deep was the anguish she felt, that when her spirits hastened to succour her heart . . . the rush of blood was so great that, suffocating her, it made her breathe her last." This is the broken heart of glamorous modern romantic usage. The heart which in antiquity was broken by Cupid's arrow merely in the process of falling in love is now broken at the end of love, shattered by one terrible event—betrayal, usually. It can never be mended, not if it is to retain its credibility. Jesus' heart, once pierced, remains broken in sorrow for our sins, in a state of suspended animation, always wounded, never healing; always healing, never healed. For it must remain open: it's the gate of heaven, the well of everlasting life.

Georges Bataille put it like this: "Human beings are never united with each other except through tears and wounds." Damien Hirst said: "I love holes . . . like holes in the head for eyes or like the holes bored into the skulls of living

Venus stands on the heart, surrounded by hearts being tortured and damaged in a variety of ways, while a man kneels before her. Is it religious or erotic? Or both? From a fourteenth-century German woodcut by Meister Casper. © *Wellcome Library, London*

people in the middle ages to let the evil out. You've got to find some way to let the ideas come in from outside."

And Oscar Wilde, in "The Ballad of Reading Gaol," wrote:

Ah! Happy those whose hearts can break
And peace of pardon win!
How else may man make straight his plan
And cleanse his soul from Sin?
How else but through a broken heart
May Lord Christ enter in?

Above all, the wounded or broken heart allows what is outside to enter in and what is within to go out into the world. It is a form of sacrifice: death and destruction allow—are necessary for—new growth. The prison guards, burying a hanged man,

... think a murderer's heart would taint
Each simple seed they sow.
It is not true! God's kindly earth
Is kindlier than men know ...
Out of his mouth a red, red rose!
Out of his heart a white!
For who can say by what strange way,
Christ brings His will to light ...

In the same way the nightingale's heart's blood feeds the rose as the nightingale dies (see page 245). Wilde, his old life over, came out of jail to a new life of a sort. Redemption is possible, rebirth is the proper order; eggs are broken, omelets are made.

Of course it is about sex. The heart here is female. "Heart" was common Tudor slang for vagina. This makes sense, because before William Harvey discovered the macho anatomical truth of its pumping and spurting (he compared it to a gun), 1,500 years of Galenic theory had been describing the heart as an organ which attracts rather than expels, a suction pump rather than an ejaculator. So Cupid's arrow, the phallus, wounds the heart; the wound is a vagina, which admits love; the lord (Lord Jesus or Lord Rochester or Lord Byron, whoever) enters in. The orgasm is the *petit mort,* the death caused by the wound, the ineffable sweetness of the darts piercing Jesus' heart and causing him unspeakable satisfaction. The lady, according to Richard Duke, "hugs the dart that wounded her, and dies." Seed is sewn; love and babies and rose bushes and sheaves of wheat are conceived. In the seventeenth century Sir John Harington described a faithless wife whose husband knows that "strangers lodge their arrows in thy quiver," and Rochester could write of his "dart of love . . . which nature still directed with such art/that it through every cunt reached every heart."

St. Augustine's first heartbreak was giving up his concubine: when she was "torn . . . from his side," his heart, "which clung to her, was broken and wounded and dripping blood," but he had to give her up for God. After his conversion, God "had shot through our hearts with your charity, and we carried about with us your words like arrows fixed deep in our flesh." Once again, new growth comes from destruction. In a *ghazal* by the fourteenth-century Persian sufi Hafiz,

> The tulip, following close behind the feet of spring, her scarlet chalice rears;
> There Ferhad for the love of Shirin pined, dying the desert red with his
>   heart's tears.

Which takes us right back to Dionysus and Bata.

Many songwriters claim that only love can break a heart (Neil Young, Burt Bacharach and Hal David among them), but Jeremiah knew better: "Mine heart within me is broken because of the prophets: all my bones shake: I am like a drunken man, and like a man whom wine hath overcome, because of the Lord, and because of the words of his holiness." According to the Psalms, reproach can break a heart. A broken heart almost always has God lurking about somewhere, and the best of modern broken hearts do not forget this debt.

One of the great moments of crossover between religious and worldly love is when Al Green—who after a misspent youth culminating in a jealous lover throwing a pan of boiling grits on him and then shooting herself, became a preacher—sings so melodiously, "How can you mend a broken heart?" Seven of the eight notes of the opening phrase are the same, with only the penultimate one—the "ken" of broken—lifting, and then only by a single tone before sinking back down to the original, the immobilization of grief from which the brokenhearted (in the modern, emotional sense) see no escape. Sung by him, this song carries the evangelical undertone: only God loves you forever. Only God can heal the broken heart. When Al the lover sings:

> How can you mend a broken heart?
> How can you stop the rain from falling down?
> How can you stop the sun from shining?
> What makes the world go 'round?
> How can you mend this broken man?
> How can a loser ever win?
> Somebody, help me mend my broken heart,
> and let me live again,

Al the preacher knows that "The Lord is nigh unto them that are of a broken heart," that "He healeth the broken in heart, and bindeth up their wounds." Al the believer, meanwhile, breaks out at the end into his beautiful wailing extemporization: "I've got a feeling that I want to *live again* . . ." And if he is to live again, the broken heart is part of the process. Generally we understand that though we may welcome wounds we have a responsibility to protect our hearts from heartbreak; only at the very worst times should we submit to it. Juliet called for it only when her heart (her treasure chest, recalling St. Anthony—see page 212) was empty and useless: "O break, my heart!—poor bankrupt, break at once." Only the cruelest lover will carry on breaking a heart, as Rumi (d. 1273), the greatest Sufi poet, knew:

> This that is tormented and very tired,
> Tortured with restraints like a madman,
> This heart
> Still you keep breaking the shell
> to get the taste of its kernel!

Hafiz's hardest of images has the same vicious physicality:

> Each curling lock of your luxuriant hair
> Breaks into barbed hooks to catch my heart,
> My broken heart is wounded everywhere
> And crimson drops from countless punctures start.

Which recalls the twelfth-century Persian Anvari:

> Close to me came the Sun of Loveliness at night
> Tall as a cypress, a face like the radiant moon
> Thousands of souls aflame through his ruby lips
> Thousands of hearts caught in the snare of his tresses.

And, older still, from an ancient Egyptian poem: "Her brow a snare of willow/And I the wild goose!"

A wounded, ill-treated heart can go one of two ways: either it scars up and becomes hard and unfeeling, or the spiritual wound can become a semipermanent, creative source of education, communication and sensitivity, linking sex and knowledge again, and recalling Adam and Eve.

In modern usage, if the wounded heart actually breaks, then you die, or "some part of you" or "something inside" dies: a postcoital peace descends, the relief of knowing that it is all over. In one sense, as George Bernard Shaw said, "when your heart is broken . . . it is the end of happiness and the beginning of peace." Dying, in this school of thought, is not the worst that can happen: Wilde's Happy Prince, the gold-clad and jewel-encrusted statue who gave his wealth to the poor he looked out over, had a heart of lead which in the end broke with sorrow. The heart, together with the body of the swallow that had distributed the prince's largesse, was thrown on the town dump. An angel, instructed to bring to God the two most precious things in the town, flew down for them, and the prince went to sit with God, and the bird was to sing in Paradise forevermore.

Which is all very well when the heart is broken by the wickedness of the world. When it is broken by a lover, who cares for heaven?

My Heart
Thou sent'st to me a hart was sound,
I tooke it to be thine;
But when I saw it had a wound,
I knew that hart was myne.
A bountie of a stronge conceit,
To send myne owne to mee,
And send it in a worse estate
Then when it came to thee.

The hart I sent thee had no stayne,
It was entyre and sound;
But thou hast sent it back again
Sicke of a deadly wound.
Oh heavens, how wouldst thou use a hart
That should rebellyous bee,
Since thou hast slayne myne with a dart
That so much honorde thee!

JOHN DONNE

Och ochon! And it is not hunger
Want of food, of drink or of sleep,
That has caused me to be pale and wan,
But 'tis the love of a young man has plainly wasted me.
'Tis early in the morning I saw the youth
Mounted on horseback going the road;
He did not draw near me or speak a word to me,
And on returning home I wept my fill.
When I go to the Well of Loneliness
I sit down to make lamentation,
When I see the world and see not my lad,
Who had the shadow of amber mantling in his cheeks.
Yon is the Sunday I gave you love,
The very Sunday before Easter Sunday,
When I was on my knees reading the Passion
My two eyes were constantly giving you love.
My mother told me not to speak to you,
Today nor tomorrow nor on Sunday,—
It was a bad time she gave me for my choice,
'Twas shutting the door after the theft.
O little mother give myself to him,
And give all that you have in the world to him,
Go yourself asking alms
And come not West or East to seek me.
My heart is as black as a sloe,
Or as black as coal that would be in a forge,
Or as the sole of a shoe on white halls,

And sure you have wasted my life and health.
You have taken East and you have taken West from me
You have taken the path before me and the path behind me,
You have taken the moon and you have taken the sun from me,
And great is my fear that you have taken God from me!

From *Cumha Chroidhe Chailin*, taken down in Irish from a recitation in Cork in 1900, and translated by Pádraic Pearse

So is there any comfort? Hardly, according to W. H. Auden:

The nightingales are sobbing in
The orchards of our mothers,
And hearts that we broke long ago
Have long been breaking others;
Tears are round, the sea is deep:
Roll them overboard and sleep.

THE FLAMING HEART

There is another form of the ever-damaged heart. Before we thought up anything more complicated to worship, we worshipped the sun, and fire. How could we not? They gave us light and warmth; grew and cooked our food; they were versions of each other and we were entirely dependent on them. In classical poetry love was identified with flames and with the heart. The ideas of light (enlightenment, wisdom) and warmth (love, verging on suffering if overdone) combine in the image of flame to represent the basis of devout religion, in particular in Christianity and Islam.

And sacrifices were burned. Many a passionate lover, of God or human love object, has considered himself a burnt offering in the flames of love. When the Orthodox Fathers defined the feelings the heart should experience during the prayer of the heart, they mentioned: 1) soreness, penitential compunction (from *pungere,* to pierce or puncture); 2) *umilenie*: warm tenderness; compunction combined with responsive loving joy; and 3) spiritual warmth, the burning of the spirit, the flame of grace, related also to Divine Light.

The Adoration of the Heart of Mary, seated in Majesty. An eighteenth-century French painting: note the flames. © *Musées Royaux d'Art et d'Histoire, Bruxelles*

The flaming heart is the emblem of St. Augustine: his heart burned with love for Jesus. Here, from his *Confessions,* is Augustine's experience of going into himself in search of union with God:

> With you as my guide I entered into my innermost citadel . . . and with my soul's eye, such as it was, saw above that same eye of my soul the immutable light higher than my mind—not the light of everyday, obvious to everyone, nor a larger version of the same kind . . . it was utterly different from all our kinds of light . . .

THE EYE OF THE HEART

In the Song of Songs we are told: "I sleep, and my heart watcheth." How could the heart watch, unless it had an eye? St. Augustine saw God's light with the eye of his soul, and at the Last Supper St. John, resting with his head on Christ's breast with his eyes closed, saw more deeply than the other disciples because his heart was watching as it lay against Jesus' heart. The eye of the heart sees most clearly, and it never sleeps (in Emblems it tends to a disconcerting, baleful expression). Because of this John was particularly beloved by Jesus.

P. C. Van Der Hooft's emblem: *The Eye of the Heart.*
© *The British Library 11556.bbb.32*

The heart's eye was most poetically revealed in Sufism, the mystical branch of Islam. In Islam the heart is where the spirit lives in the body; it is the final refuge of the soul, and the channel of communication between man and God; it is where God lives in humanity. "Within man there is a fleshy morsel, and when it is corrupt the body is corrupt, and when it is sound the body is sound. Truly it is the *qalb*—the heart," said Muhammad. Though Muhammad called it a "fleshy morsel," al-Ghazzali points out that

In truth it does not belong to the visible world but to the invisible, and has come to into this world as a traveller visits a foreign country for the sake of merchandise, and will presently return to its native land. It is the knowledge of this entity and its attributes which is the key to the knowledge of God.

The Islamic heart is the essence of self, of control, of perception and interpretation. The heart distinguishes human beings from animals. It is material and nonmaterial, and leads the entire person toward God and truth.

Sufis depend on insight and divine inspiration, an allegorical approach to Islam the key to which is in Surah 6 of the Qur'an: "The eyes of the head comprehendeth Him not . . . In the matter of comprehending God, the eye of the heart has been bestowed by God." The eye of the heart in Islam sees via poetic imagery—often its own image. In only the second Surah of the Qur'an we are told that Allah has sealed hearts of disbelievers and put a covering over their eyes. "They perceive not, they believe not," "deaf, dumb and blind, they return not." Compare this with Isaiah 6:10: "Make the heart of this people fat, and make their ears heavy, and shut their eyes: lest they see with their eyes, and heare with their ears, and understand with their heart . . ."

Augustine, in his vision, learned that "The person who knows the truth knows it, and he who knows it knows eternity. Love knows it. Eternal truth and true love and beloved eternity: you are my God." He trembled with love and awe, and when God cried from far away, "Now, I am who I am," Augustine heard him "in the way one hears within the heart, and all doubt left me."

His usage was a backbone of the Emblem tradition; nowhere more so than in the flaming heart. Going into yourself, you need a torch to see by; for purging, union and transformation you need the alchemical properties of heat. Passion burns you up (as the ancients knew: see page 287 for the romantic aspects of flaming desire).

Daniel Cramer's heart series shows some of the variety of flaming hearts. In "I love" the hand of God appears from behind a little cloud to sprinkle incense on the heart as it burns sacrificially on a fire. In "I am illuminated" God puts a lantern on top of the heart. In number 7, "I am constant," winds blow up the fire in the heart, which perches bravely on an altar. In number 8, "I breathe," God sprinkles incense on the heart's flames: the perfumes of prayer again, as the heart is sacrificed—devoted—to God. In Christopher Harvey's series Jesus brings his lantern into the heart to frighten away the nasty vices, and of course the fixed-up house of the heart (see page 197) needs heat and warmth and illumination; likewise the eye that heart sometimes bears (see below) needs light to see, read and admit wisdom.

Allah, like Christ to Christians, is the Light: "the Light of the heavens and the earth. The similitude of His light is as a niche wherein is a lamp. The lamp is a glass. The glass is as it were a shining star . . . the lamp is found in houses which Allah has allowed to be exalted and that his name shall be remembered therein . . ." This passage from the Qur'an has much in common with the Christian Emblem of Christ holding high his lantern in the heart of the devout. "The seat of the animal soul is the heart," wrote al-Ghazzali. "It may be compared to a lamp carried about within a cottage, the light of which falls upon the walls wherever it goes. The heart is the wick of this lamp, and when the supply is cut off for any reason, the lamp dies."

In Islam too the heat can become overtly sacrificial, a form of the creative wound, as when the phoenix rises from the ashes. As Hafiz wrote:

> My heart, sad hermit, stains the cloister floor
> With drops of blood, the sweat of anguish dire;
> Ah, wash me clean, and o'er my body pour
> Love's generous wine! The worshippers of Fire
> Have bowed them down and magnified my name
> For in my heart there burns a living flame
> Which pierces death's impenetrable door.

St. Philip of the Joyful Heart, who believed above all in Christian cheerfulness ("A joyous heart is more easily made perfect than one which is cast down"), died when his heart burned with the heat of a thousand fires; usually, though, the flaming heart burns without destroying, like the Burning Bush of the Old Testament. During the fifth century St. Brendan visited a monastery where the lamps were lit each evening by a mysterious flaming arrow; their oil never burned down and their wicks left no ashes: their light, he was told, was spiritual, not physical. So should a heart burn for God.

3

THE EMOTIONAL HEARTS
OF NUNS

For some medieval Christians, the heart image became literal: Christ's heart was open to them, so they went in. To others, the imitation of Christ and the biblical maxim that he "lives within" his followers meant that he would come into theirs. To make these visits more comfortable, the heart became a house (see page 197). Many welcomed him on personal visits. Some swapped hearts with him. The medieval Sacred Heart of Jesus is close bosom friend of the repressed libido and a direct forefather of sentimental romance. The monogamous fidelity required of romantic heroes was not required of Christ. He loved all his brides, as we see, with all his heart: the fact that it was broken simply made access easier.

THE HEART IN VISIONS

From the twelfth century Christ became increasingly sociable. He first appeared to St. Gertrude of Helfta to admonish her for studying too hard. The kisses she received from him were "far surpassing in delight the most exquisite perfume or the sweetest honey," and when she recited the office of one of the saints, "each word she uttered appeared to dart like an arrow from her heart into the Sacred Heart of our Lord, penetrating it deeply and causing it unspeakable satisfaction." On another occasion he presented her with his heart. Not surprisingly, she "feared and wondered at his amazing goodness, thinking it unbecoming that the adorable heart which is the treasure house of the Divinity should assist her, a miserable creature . . ." Later he planted a tree in her heart and brought a band of holy virgins to sit on the nuns' altar. Not every appearance was so grand: when she asked him to intercede with the weather, he sent a thunderstorm for her cheek. He asked St. John to look after her, who placed her at the opening of Christ's divine heart "so that you may drink in the sweet consolations flowing from it."

Christ spoke to Gertrude gently, comparing his love to a mother's; then said, in a most unmotherly way, "I will pierce you in such a way that your wound will never be healed." Her health was not good, and he offered her "fresh merit" if she suffered a protracted death, promising to "dwell in your heart as a dove in its nest and at the same time I will cherish you in my bosom until your death." They discussed exactly what kind of chariot would take Gertrude away to Jesus when she died. And she had a vision of her death which was quite dazzling, most inappropriate for someone sworn to a humble life and absolutely understandable in someone desperate for love and attention. Gertrude, young and beautiful in gorgeous apparel, dies in Christ's arms with her head held to his heart. His garments are adorned with roses, and angels are all around in clouds of incense. Mary arrives to console her, and St. Michael offers to defend her. Toads, serpents and devils fall back in confusion. Patriarchs arrive, bearing verdant branches laden with good deeds, followed by prophets, with gold mirrors; St. John the Evangelist comes with a gold ring representing his fidelity, and all the other apostles, martyrs and confessors bearing golden palms and flowers, and holy widows offering good works in golden caskets. Holy Innocents send down bright rays of their spotless lives, and choirs of virgins bring gold-tipped roses. "As soon as the saint had been decorated with these flowers, her divine spouse bent down to her and she was united to Him so closely that she experienced inexpressible delight."

A number of nuns lived out these strange and passionate love stories. The Cistercian ecstatic Lukardis of Oberweimar "saw a golden ladder rising from her heart, whose summit reached the highest point of heaven, in whose summit she saw Christ her lover resting on the ladder and leaning down toward her, looking at her." The heart of the Dominican nun Adelheid Langmann became as bright as the sun when she saw the Christ child playing there; she compared it to a monstrance. Around 1206 Christ appeared to St. Lutgard of Aywières, a Benedictine nun, "crucified and bleeding. From the cross an arm broke away, embraced her, pressed her against His right side, and [she] placed her mouth on His wound. She drank in a sweetness so powerful that she was from that time stronger and more alert in the service of God."

Apropos this drinking: it was only when I looked at a painting by Frida

My Nurse and I, by Frida Kahlo (1937). © *Schalkwijk / Art Resource, New York*

Kahlo, *My Nurse and I* (1937), that I realized the missing link. How could the wound in Christ's chest, from which flows food and endless love, not be connected to the mother's breast, from which as babies we receive food, love, sweetness and joy, a feeling of safety, happiness and union? It is accepted now that the link of food, love and safety in their mother's arms is good for babies and their future happiness; I was also reminded of an ex-junkie friend, who told me, "Heroin was mother's love, that's all. It filled that hole." As the song by John Prine goes: "There's a hole in Daddy's arm where all the money goes"; once again it's the filling and the drinking up, the piercing and the wounding. Mother's milk is impersonated by the sacrament of blood, by wine and whiskey, by heroin. Take it, and sweet happiness floods in. St. Bernard of Clairvaux put it thus: "Embrace him whom you long for, make yourself drunk with this torrent of delight, and suck the honey and milk of consolation from the breast." The problem of course is that the cruel impersonators do not in the long run give you the life offered by the milk (and the sacrament, if you believe in it): they give you at best a temporary fake paradise followed by a hangover; at worst addiction and death. (The role of "a superior power" in the twelve-steps system of overcoming addiction to drugs and alcohol is just another example. But as Raymond Carver wrote: "I don't have a heart when it comes/To this booze thing. Sad, yes, Christ alone knows.") Milk, wine and heart's blood are connected in a *ghazal* by Hafiz:

> If for wine the cup-bearer pour forth my blood,
> As the milk from a mother's bosom flows,
> At his word let my heart yield its crimson flood.

St. Hedwig of Silesia waited longingly for the coming of the Lord like a rock star waiting for his dealer, or Bridget Jones waiting for the phone to ring, like Sylvia Plath waiting for Ted Hughes. Her servant Boguslaus spied on her devotions, and wrote that her

> heart was like a flame; she was unable to rest for the love of God whom she loved; she longed for the presence of her beloved, as the hart panteth after fountains of water . . . She continually awaited the coming of the consoler, so that on his arrival and knocking at the gate of the heart she could quickly open the door.

The eternal female passivity in the face of what we desire is only just—maybe—beginning to be shaken off. Waiting to be wanted; self-cloistering by passivity. Of course, God is very convenient here because he wants everybody.

Christ appeared frequently to the Dominican St. Catherine of Siena. On April 1, 1375, in the chapel of Santa Cristina in Pisa, she

> saw the Lord fixed to the cross coming towards me in a great light . . . from the scars of his most sacred wounds I saw five rays of blood coming down towards me, to my hands, my feet and my heart. Realising what was about to happen, I exclaimed, "Oh Lord God, I beg you,—do not let these scars show on the outside of my body!" As I said this, before the rays reached me their

colour changed from blood red to the colour of light, and in the form of pure light they arrived at the five points of my body, hands, feet and heart.*

This spiritual deflowering, the piercing of a virgin in the name of love, disconcerted the Franciscans, who felt that St. Francis, till then the only stigmatized person, was being usurped for political reasons by the Dominicans. Papal recognition of Catherine's stigmata was granted only in 1630. However, she had gone one further: Christ came to her with a heart in his hands, opened a matching wound in her chest and, recalling Ezekiel's promise that God's word would "take away the stony heart out of your flesh . . . and give you a heart of flesh," put the heart inside her. Alongside the spiritual improvement, this is a clear love swap, like Sir Philip Sidney's (see page 312): "My true love hath my heart and I have his." (St. Catherine was not the first saint to receive the holy transplant: the thirteenth-century Cistercian nun St. Mechtilde of Hackeborn had a similar exchange.)

This saintly heart swap begs the question: there are surely far stonier hearts than the hearts of saints—harder, less fertile, in far greater need of treatment? When people talk of arrogant doctors playing God, do they know that the first heart transplants took place in medieval mystical visions? Another question emerges: is imagining someone else's heart to be your heart, within your body, another way of consuming it, another quasi-sacramental ingestion? We shall see below how nuns managed to get God and his heart inside their own bodies, with interesting undercurrents of sex, conception and eating. A wounded heart is per se vulnerable; many forms of love can enter and leave. The young St. Teresa of Avila was pierced through the heart by an angel's burning golden arrow and spent her life and posterity carrying an overflowing cargo of heart symbolism: sex, conception, writing, wounding, burning, proxy phallicism . . .

ST. MARGUERITE-MARIE ALACOQUE

The Visitandine nun St. Marguerite-Marie Alacoque (1647–90) is often credited with the creation of the Sacred Heart as a cult; in fact she only propagated it, though with astonishing success. The Sacred Heart was already in place

---

*The crucifix is now in the church of St. Catherine in Fontebranda, near Siena.

across Europe both as idea and as artistic image. The custom of separate heart burial (see page 324) both reinforced the significance of the heart as an organ and made it popular as an image on monuments and churches from the tenth century onward. The heart symbol was used by Carthusian monks (in Cologne each monk's cell had a heart carved above the doorway); the idea and devotion was common to Benedictines, Dominicans, Cistercians and Franciscans as well. In *The Vision of William Concerning Piers Plowman* William Langland speaks of sins as "brode hoked arwes" in "Goddes Herte." During the religious challenges of the sixteenth and seventeenth centuries the Sacred Heart served as an emblem for English Catholics (a hidden-away and suffering organ fit in well with their own experiences). The Blazon of the Wounds was the badge used by the Pilgrimage of Grace, the Catholic rebellion against Henry VIII in 1536–37.

Marguerite-Marie was born at Lhautecour, near Autun, in July 1647. At the age of four she was sent to live with her godmother, where she developed a passionate love for Jesus and Mary; they appeared to her in a vision and lived, she believed, in the tabernacle of the local chapel. When she was eight her father died and her destitute mother sent her to a convent where, two years later, she decided to become a nun. The process was not immediate. Four years of illness, including paralysis, followed at her old home, now occupied by a cruel uncle; she only recovered, she believed, because she had consecrated her life to the Virgin Mary.

Her mother, too, was sick; she had erysipelas, a febrile skin inflammation—also known as "the rose," or St. Anthony's fire. Marguerite-Marie had to beg for food for both of them; she wept all night for her mother's pains, and prayed to Jesus to be her nurse. "He so

Exchanging of hearts: St. Marguerite-Marie Alacoque. © *Musées Royaux d'Art et d'Histoire, Bruxelles* mercifully heard my prayer that when I had returned home I found that the swelling on her face had burst, leaving a wound as big as the palm of the hand, and it gave forth a horrible stench." No one would treat this wound, so the child did, cutting away "bad flesh" each day. She concentrated on the Passion of Christ to give her strength and, by the end, had worked herself up to "so great a love for sufferings and humiliations that when her rough relatives raised their hands to strike her she was sorry when they forebore to do so." Her mother begged her to marry to save them both and otherwise she would die of grief; but Marguerite-Marie had promised herself to God. Torn, she spent sleepless nights praying in the woods and scourged herself. God was putting her through this pain, she believed, to purify her soul.

When she was sixteen her brother inherited the property, and life became easy; she began to "see company and to dress in order to please them," she wrote. "I committed great sins, for once I disguised myself at Carnival-time from a foolish desire to give pleasure." But then Jesus appeared to her covered in blood, as after his scourging. Full of contrition, she scourged herself, and tied chains round herself, and allowed knotted cords to embed themselves in her flesh, "to take vengeance on my flesh." But she continued to enjoy the frivolities she considered sinful. Hardly surprisingly, she soon became ill.

When two of her brothers died she gave up worldly pleasures. Now instead she paid poor children to learn the catechism from her, and visited the poor and afflicted. "I loathed the sight of sores. I forced myself to dress them and even to kiss them, in order to overcome myself . . . my divine master knew so well how to make up for my want of skill that these sores were soon healed even when they were very malignant."

Her family were still keen for her to marry; moreover, she suspected she would not make a good nun (her opinion of herself was always low) and was about to give up her vow of chastity when God spoke to her heart, saying that he would forsake her forever if she abandoned him now, whereupon her heart "became as unmoveable as a rock." Breaking her mother's heart instead, she redevoted herself to Mary, who said to her: "Fear nothing, you shall be my true daughter and I will always be your good mother." Marguerite-Marie loved Jesus too: "I used to bind my fingers tightly, and pierced them with needles to give him some drops of blood. I took the discipline every day in honour of his scourging." Her written confession was so long that the priest made her skip several pages at a time.

Marguerite-Marie entered a convent far from home, the Congregation of the Visitation at Paray-le-Monial, founded by St. Francis de Sales. "Religion is nothing else than a school of self-denial and mortification," he had written, which at once suited and fed Marguerite-Marie's particular neurosis. Its coat of arms was the Sacred Heart of Jesus and the Immaculate Heart of Mary, united. "The nuns . . . may . . . imitate the Heart of Jesus in meekness and humility, the base and foundation of their order," he wrote. At the age of twenty-three Marguerite told her family that she wanted them to forget her; she was going to forget the world. She never left the building again.

She was told to think of her soul as a blank canvas for God to paint on. For her, this meant first cleaning the canvas—which she did with such rigor that even the prophet of self-denial and mortification, St. Francis de Sales, who in life had promised to make a big racket in the cell of any nun who neglected sweetness and moderation in her bodily penances, came back from the dead to chide her. "It is obedience and not the practice of mortification which upholds this congregation," he said. "These words have remained ever engraved on my heart," she wrote (she had "Jesus" written there too). She didn't, however, according either to modern standards or contemporary ones, act upon them. Instead, she begged her novice mistress for "humiliations." One such involved eating cheese, which she hated so much that her brother had arranged with the convent that she should not ever have to eat it. She made such a drama of preparing to eat the cheese that the mistress said she was not worthy to eat it. So she prayed: "My divine master took pleasure in beholding divine love fighting against the repugnance of nature in his unworthy slave." In the end "I went on my knees before my mistress, begging her in pity to allow me to do what she has wished me to do."

This nasty Jesus came to her, telling her to give up a friendship, because he wanted no divided heart. When teaching the little girls, the Sisters of the Little Habit, she chastised them severely whenever they were guilty of "particular friendship." Marguerite-Marie was considered peculiar as a result of all this, and there was talk of sending her away: the convent wanted nuns to be like little violets in their humility, while she was blossoming like a rose in the rays of the sun with her flashy mortifications. "I cannot live for a moment without suffering," she said, putting broken crocks in her bed and ashes on her food. She "would have destroyed her body . . . if she had been allowed." On the day she made her final vows, she wrote a declaration of love for Jesus, in her own blood, signed "Sister Marguerite-Marie henceforth dead to the world."

In the liturgy of the Sacred Heart we hear: "If anyone is thirsty, let him come to me; whosoever believes in me, let him drink." Marguerite-Marie, in her confusion, fell for one of the great risks of the Sacred Heart: the risk of taking literally the allegory.

Influenced by St. Francis de Sales's attitude to food ("It is an infallible mark of a wayward, infamous, base, abject and degraded mind to think about food and drink before mealtime, much more so to . . . delight in recalling the sensual satisfaction we had in swallowing those bits of food") and by her experiences nursing her mother, she invented what Olivier Debroise called a "mysticism of the disgusting." The kisses to overcome her disgust at sores combined in her mind with the sanctity of Christ's wounds, the passion of the Passion and the school of religious masochism in which she lived, to produce a novel treatment for the sick: to cure her patients she again took up kissing their sores and ulcers, and in a perverse imitation of the Eucharist, she ate and drank their bodily secretions. She licked away the vomit of a nun with stomach cancer; she sucked pus from an abscess on a child's foot, and she referred to these peculiar sacraments as "delicacies." "She did many other penance no less revolting in nature," wrote Mother de Saumaise, who knew her for six years, "and she eagerly sought for them as soon as she learned that God had been offended." The rationale is plain: through her suffering, she can make it up to God for the grief other people have inflicted on him. The fact that she enjoyed doing so might, you might think, disqualify the suffering. To some this was a disgusting mockery performed by a neurotic; others considered it a step on the pathway to spiritual perfection.

On December 27, 1673, Marguerite-Marie saw the Sacred Heart for the first time, shining like the sun and transparent as glass, bearing the wound which it had received on the cross: it was encircled by a crown of thorns and there was a cross above it. Her job was to spread its glory; she had been chosen by the unkind and insecure Jesus she had concocted because she was "an abyss of unworthiness and ignorance . . . so that it may be seen that everything has been done by Me." Then she was struck with a terrible pain in her side, which lasted for weeks, especially on Fridays.

St. John of the Cross said of visions: "We may know their nature by their effects." Marguerite-Marie, as a result of her vision, increased her mortifications, wanted to confess to her fellow nuns "the great heap of rottenness that was in me," couldn't eat, couldn't talk, took to wearing a hair shirt and a girdle studded with iron spikes, ate only spoiled food and crumbs from the floor and so on. "She never allowed herself to indulge in any satisfaction of mind or body," wrote Mother de Saumaise.

"Next time, Jesus Christ, my sweet master, showed himself to me, shining with glory," wrote Marguerite-Marie. "His five wounds were brilliant like five suns, and flames burst forth on all sides from this sacred humanity, but especially from his adorable breast; and it opened and I beheld his most loving and most beloved Heart, which was the living fountain of these flames . . ."

He then complained that mankind was ungrateful and cold, and asked her to get up every Thursday night at eleven and remain prostrate on the floor with her face to the earth for an hour, in order to atone for all the sins of mankind and give consolation to his heart. Overwhelmed by this wonderful vision, she swooned. "I never felt any suffering so much as that of not suffering enough." So she carved his name across her chest and, when that healed, burned it on with a candle.

In her third vision Christ complained again and demanded a special festival of his heart to atone for the insults it had received; in return it would pour the influences of its love upon those who honored it. The idea was taken up by Père de la Colombière, a priest who had been sent to keep an eye on Marguerite-Marie's eccentricities, but who fell for them instead. She already had her pupils making little embroidered and painted hearts, like fliers, to hand round; de la Colombière took considerable pains to publicize the festival (the first Friday after the Octave of Corpus Christi) with printed pamphlets. Some of her fellow nuns, meanwhile, took to throwing holy water on her, thinking she was possessed by the devil.

In 1670 St. John Eudes obtained official permission "to celebrate solemnly every year on 31 August the feast of the Adorable Heart of our Lord Jesus Christ, with an octave, and . . . to keep the same Office the first Thursday of every month." On June 21, 1675, the first consecration of the Sacred Heart was given and St. Marguerite-Marie saw her dream come to pass (the Jesuits also soon saw the potential of the image), but God told her that she could not fulfill her duty until she died, which she was of course very happy to do, aged just forty-three, refusing to see her family, adjuring her novices to mortify themselves to atone for her sins. After death her face was so lovely that none of the nuns could bear to leave the room.

There is a shelf full of biographies, fading green and red clothbound volumes of Victorian devotion, in the same floriate language (ineffable sweetness on every page) and gold-embossed binding. Her sickness, her sufferings, her graces, her vocation. Pages of devotion. You feel sick quite quickly. One of her biographers, the Reverend Albert Barry, writes of her tribulations: "As flowers when they are crushed give forth a more delicious fragrance, so her virtues became more perfect in infirmity and more pleasing to the Sacred Heart of Jesus." She adds up to a package of young girl disorders, out of time and out of place: her childhood fraught with loss, her self-harm, self-obsession, self-starvation, her use of food for punishment, her grasping of self-hatred and holding it to her as a mystical masochistic love object, a gift for her sadistic, snitty mystic husband, an imaginary boyfriend who beats her up.

Physically demanding devotions have by no means disappeared. Every seven years the men of Guardia Sanframondi in southern Italy parade in penitence, wearing open-fronted white robes and white masks, beating themselves rhythmically on the chest with special mallets. On their chests appear livid red bruises, imitations of Christ's wound, recalling the burning, the compunction, all the suffering of the heart. Miracles cured those who prayed at Marguerite-Marie's tomb. Marseilles was saved from the plague because the bishop appeared barefoot with a rope around his neck and consecrated the city to the Sacred Heart. The promises her Christ made to those who put up a picture of his heart were very appealing, and the devotion took off.

THE CULT OF THE SACRED HEART

St. Alphonsus, in the eighteenth century, announced that there was no proof that the heart was the seat of all affection—indeed such an idea was contrary to science—but that the Sacred Heart should be venerated anyway, because of the Bible and the age-old tradition of the image, and despite all these mad nuns. Everyone loved the Sacred Heart, but many disputed the thinking behind the cult and the extremes to which it was taken. (Even Luther, who deplored it, had used the image: to "transform our heart," he wrote, "we must impress the example of the virgin in our heart . . . so that we too will become

Sacred Heart, by Pompeo Batoni (eighteenth-century Italian): Jesus offers his radiant suffering heart to mankind. © *Chiesa del Gesu, Roma/Scala*

pregnant with the Holy Spirit and receive Christ spiritually.") The heart continued its progress through the niceties of the Roman Catholic hierarchy; in 1756 the Polish bishops and the Archconfraternity of the Sacred Heart won approbation for the public liturgy of the Sacred Heart. Pius IX made the celebration of the feast of the Sacred Heart obligatory in 1856. In 1873 the Basilique du Voeu de la Nation au Sacré Coeur, better known simply as the Sacré Coeur, was planned, in order to restore France's weakened spiritual and moral health which, it was felt, had led to their defeat by Prussia in 1870. The church was built in Montmartre—the Martyrs' Mount—for added intensity, and finished only in 1919. Meanwhile in 1898 Pope Leo XIII dedicated the universe to the Sacred Heart of Jesus. Then in 1956 Pius XII added the twentieth-century qualification in the encyclical *Haurietis Aquas*, which declares specifically that the veneration of the Sacred Heart is not dependent on individual revelation but on the Bible and on tradition.

The universal reasons for devotion to the heart were put precisely by Cardinal Newman:

> My God, my saviour, I adore thy sacred heart, for that heart is the seat and source of all thy tenderest human affections for us sinners. It is the instrument and organ of thy love. It did beat for us. It yearned for us. It ached for us and for our salvation. It was on fire through zeal that the glory of God might be manifested in and by us. It is the channel through which has come to us all thy overflowing human affection, and thy divine charity towards us . . . in one inseparable mingled stream, through that sacred heart.

Did I say universal? Catholic missionaries in Rwanda at the end of the nineteenth century found that their picture of the Sacred Heart gave rise to rumors that they ate the hearts of their converts.

4

THE AZTECS

Possibly the oldest known three-dimensional representation of a heart is a man-shaped Olmec ceramic jar, some 4,000 years old, from Mexico. The heart, with two chambers and blood vessels sprouting from the top, makes his torso and belly; he sits on his legs mermaid-style and holds on to the vessels with his arms. His fat-mouthed head emerges where the aorta would be. It is the only one of its kind: perhaps it held sacrificial blood, or sacrificial hearts.

The Aztecs of Mexico, as every schoolboy knows, sacrificed human beings, tearing out their hearts on pyramids so that the sun, on which all life depended, could be nourished with the heart's blood. They did not invent either human sacrifice or the significance of the heart in those lands: 7,000-year-old skeletons found at Tehucan bear witness to the longevity of human sacrifice in Mexico. Five hundred years before the Aztecs, the Great Temple of the civilization of Tula, northwest of Mexico City, was ornamented with friezes showing coyotes, jaguars and eagles clutching blood-dripping hearts. The eagle is a representation of the sun; here it is feeding on hearts. The Caucas, farther south in Colombia, had a long tradition of heart-eating following human sacrifice; the neighboring Armas were also recorded offering human hearts to their gods. The Aztecs were the last heart-sacrificers of Central America, the pinnacle, the best recorded and the ones witnessed by Europeans; this is why we know most about them.

More precisely, they were recycling a vital energy, *tonalli,* "the warmth of the sun," which exists in the universe and in all living things, and which is squandered by human beings when they die and wasted on their difficult journey to Mictlan, the place of the dead. Regulating death—sacrifice—harnessed the *tonalli* and allowed it to be used for the benefit of the living instead. (Christian Duverger correlates this to splitting the atom to release atomic energy; the Aztecs split the body for the same end.) The sacrificial

Olmec ceramic jar in the form of an anthropomorphic heart (c. 1200–900 B.C.). *Private Collection*

dead, along with warriors killed during or after a battle, gave their energy to the sun: "they carried [the sun] to the middle of the sky, to its zenith, to its apogee." Women who died in childbirth brought it down in the evening, on a palanquin of green feathers, uttering war cries to make it happy. The House of the Sun was heaven: they would go there too, and after four years be transformed into hummingbirds and butterflies on earth, to sip nectar. The moral is, those who sacrifice themselves to the common good have a happy ending; those who don't end up alone and lost.

In 1251, when what is now Mexico was occupied by many tribes, the Culhuaque gave a heart to the Mexica Azteca for the altar of a new temple: "It was of excrement and whippoorwill feathers, wherefore the Mexica were much saddened." A much more fruitful heart awaited them not far down the line, according to the legend of the founding of Tenochtitlan, the ancient Aztec capital where Mexico City now stands. The Mexica leader Cuauhtlequetzqui (Bloody Eagle), searching for land for his tribe, defeated a famous magician called Copil and had his heart buried "in the place of the canes and the reed." He instructed the priest:

> In this place will be born and will grow the heart of Copil, and you, Tenuche, you will go and observe when there springs forth the *tenuchtli*, the red prickly pear, born from the heart of Copil; and you will note the precise moment at which on the top of this cactus there stands an eagle, holding tightly with its talons a half-erect snake, which the eagle mauls, trying to devour it, while the snake hisses and gasps. Thus will occur the omen that means that no-one in the world will ever destroy or erase the honour, the fame of Mexico Tenochtitlan.

Thus Mexico City is founded on a heart, a fruit heart at that (see page 246); the heart is also once again the house, the place to live and be safe. Centuries later, after the Spaniard Cortés had done his considerable best to destroy the honor of Tenochtitlan, a cathedral was built on the spot where Copil's heart was buried.

There were eighteen months in the Aztec year; each month had a feast, lasting its whole length. The rituals were complex, often beautiful, and devoted to particular gods. Games (sometimes to select who should die) and dancing induced exhaustion, and intoxicating drink and incenses, fasting and vigils stimulated the energy levels to the utmost degree, so that none should be wasted when death released it. These practices also stopped the victims from resisting their fate: though the mind knew and believed that to be sacrificed was an honor, the body by instinct rejects death. Rather than anesthesia, a hyperesthesia was induced.

The victim was held down, back arched, breast to the sky, over the *techcatl,* the sacrificial stone, by five priests. The sacrificial priest then sliced open the chest with the *tecpatl,* a flint knife, just beneath the rib cage. He took out the heart with his hand and offered it— and thus the *tonalli*—up to the sun. Up to six pints of blood would be spilled when the heart is taken out like this: it would spill on the ground, echoing rain and nourishing the sun.

The Sun was not the only god to accept hearts: so too did the Rain God, the Smoking Mirror God, the Humming Bird of the South, the Plumed Serpent, the Fire God, the God of War and the Corn Goddess. Coatlicue, mother of the Seed God Huitzilopochtli, wore a necklace of the bloody hearts of sacrifice victims (a three-meter basalt monolith representing her was found in 1790). According to

A sacrificed heart is offered to Quetzalcoatl on this pre-Toltec stele from Guatemala. © *Werner Forman Archive / Museum für Völkerkunde, Berlin*

some versions of the story, Huitzilopochtli killed his mother and ate her heart before starting on his enemies; more usually he saved her from her murderous daughter.

To give an idea of the complexity of the rituals, here is an account of the feast of Etzalqualiztli, recorded by the Franciscan Fray Bernardino de Sahagún, in his *Codex Fiorentino*. (He arrived in New Spain in 1529 and wrote twelve volumes covering every aspect of Aztec life, in Nahuatl and Spanish.) The purpose of this feast was to encourage rain.

On the feast day, after several days of complicated and precise ritual and fasting, everyone cooked beans and maize, and the pleasure girls and brave warriors danced all night in gangs from house to house with circles painted round their eyes, holding maize staves and demanding food.

> And when the sun arose, then the Fire Priest adorned himself. He put on his sleeveless jacket, over it he placed his netted cape, called the mist or the dew cape, adorned with crossed motmot feathers. Then he carried on his back the round paper rosette, and he went placing a pleated paper ornament on the nape of his neck. And his forehead was painted blue; besides he put iron pyrites on it . . . And with him he went grasping a paper incense bag, with shells attached, covered with seashells.

Other priests carried the mist rattle board, little gods molded of rubber and cones of incense with quetzal-feather tassels on their tips. "And when this was done, when the trumpets were played, thereupon was their placing in order upon the road. Then there was departing."

Now the remaining transgressors who had slipped up in the course of the ceremonies were led along, grasped, rolled, carried, pushed, abused and cast into puddles, "mingled in the mud," till they reached a place called Totecco, where all the accoutrements (rubber gods, paper ornaments, incense) were burned, and the transgressors were thrown into the water, and "if any tried to come up, they submerged him." Some drowned, and some were saved, and some escaped and ran away, and some were held upside down by their relatives so as to get rid of the water they had swallowed. Shell trumpets were blown, and the survivors went sick and shivering to their homes.

Then the priests adorned themselves: blue faces, pleated paper ornaments, seashell-adorned incense bags made of ocelot skin or of paper to represent

ocelot, the northern phalarope or the duck. The Fire Priest of the Temple of
Tlaloc put on his crown of heron and quetzal feathers and coated his face with
liquid rubber; he wore his mist jacket and his hair fell to his loins. He led them
all to the Temple of Tlaloc, where he scattered herbs, and spread out the green
and white mats, and set out four round green stones, and struck them with a
blue hook.

That night, to the sound of trumpets and reed pipes and conch shells and
the horizontal drum (which croaked and growled and droned), and with the
burning of the paper ornaments and the precious feathers, at midnight

> began the slaying. The captives went leading, they died. And when they died,
> thereupon died the impersonators of the Rain Gods. And when they slashed
> open the breasts of the victims . . . they seized his heart; they went to place it
> in a vessel painted blue, named the cloud vessel, which was painted with rub-
> ber on four sides, and its accoutrements were papers dotted with drops of liq-
> uid rubber, much rubber. They were covered with rubber. All this they did
> likewise to all the impersonators. All their hearts they continued casting
> there . . . all the bystanders, who had been watching continually, all went with
> their hand filled with artemesia flowers. They went thrusting them, they went
> lunging with them to and fro, they went fanning themselves . . . It was said that
> thus they frightened away the worms, that their children's eyes might not be-
> come wormy. Some put the flowers in their ears.

When everyone to be killed was killed, the cloud vessels full of hearts were
brought to the water's edge and loaded, with the priests and the offerings as
yet unburned, into a boat ornamented with rubber, and poled speedily with
blue-painted poles.

> And when they went to arrive in midwater . . . there they brought the boat
> in . . . thereupon trumpets were played. The Fire Priest arose in the prow of the
> boat. Then they gave him the cloud vessel, which went filled there with hearts.
> Thereupon he cast it in the midst of the water. It immediately was swallowed,
> it immediately pierced [the water]. And then the water foamed, kept surging,
> roared, crackled continually, crackled as it surged. Bits of foam formed.

Then there was dedication and scattering of sacrificial banners, going back
to land, washing off the blue, as dawn broke. Anyone who had run away dur-

ing the feast was ducked. "And when this was done, then there was a quick departure . . . Enough. Here ended the feast of Etzalqualiztli."

Not all sacrificial victims were tormented. For the festival of Tezcatlipoca, a man was chosen to impersonate the god for a year before being sacrificed, and he lived a life appropriate to a god. The list of his perfections goes on for several pages, starting with "of fair countenance, of good understanding, quick, of clean body, slender, reedlike, like a stout cane, like a stone column all over" and going through "smoothed, like a tomato" with straight hair, no pimples, with a forehead not shaped like a tomato or a bag, not swollen-cheeked, bulging-eyed, bent-nosed, large-toothed, rough-tongued, thick-lipped, bumpy-headed, bowl-lipped, bowl-toothed, twisted-necked, long-handed, of protruding or hatchet-shaped navel, of wrinkled or shrunken stomach, flabby or hatchet-shaped buttocks, and with no warts. "He was importuned, he was sighed for, there was bowing before him." He went about playing the flute, with eight servitors. He wore a stole of popcorn flowers, golden shell earrings, earplugs of turquoise, a seashell breast ornament, gold and turquoise bracelets all up his arms, golden bells on his legs and obsidian sandals with ocelot-skin ears: "Thus was arrayed he who died after one year."

Twenty days before the feast he took off his grandeur and "went fasting in black." He was given four wives. Later there were four days of feasting and dancing and singing, after which he went of his own accord up to the temple, breaking his flute and his whistle as he went. There he was killed, and his heart taken and raised up in dedication to the Sun. "And this betokened our life on earth. For he who rejoiced, who possessed riches, who sought, who esteemed, our lord's sweetness . . . thus ended in great misery . . . No one on earth went exhausting happiness, riches, wealth."

The heart which Aztecs offered up in dedication was not only a simple blood bag to feed the thirsty sun. Montezuma, when he knew Cortés was upon him, said, "My heart burns as though it has been washed in chillis." Nahuatl songs recorded soon after the conquest show hearts full of bravery, sorrow and love: "My heart knows how truly I weep for my friend, how truly as it lives on earth it cries aloud for thee, my friend, to God"; or "Truly I doubt in my heart if I really see you, dear friends"; or "I shall leave my songs in order that some time I may mingle the flowers of my heart with the children and the nobles."

The poet-king of Texcuco, Nezahualcoyotl (d. 1472), used the heart to mean the seat of his understanding. He wrote, in his mournful and carpe diem way (most of his poetry compares the lives of kings to flowers and green willow trees: so glorious, so soon to die): "I feel, when alone, that my heart is pleased but for a brief time, and that all pleasure soon passes." The Victorian translator D. G. Brinton translates *yollotl* variously as either "heart" or "soul." It is the same *yollotl* which is taken from the breast of the sacrifice victim. In Peru, when Pizarro was doing to the Incas what Cortés did to the Aztecs, Manco Inca and his last surviving warriors fled from Cuzco to the secret city of Vilcabamba in the high Andes, taking with them the *punchal,* the most important object of the Inca Empire: a gold representation of the rising sun which hid within its breast a doughy heart, made from the ashes of the hearts of the greatest Inca ancestors. (Ancestor worship was absolutely fundamental in this area: during the Chimu Empire [900–1465] dead kings had property rights. Their mummies remained in their palaces, with servants, and attended important ceremonies. Each new ruler had to build a new palace and a new fortune.)

AZTEC SACRIFICE, CHRISTIAN RITUAL

It is terribly easy to syncretize the bloody sacrificial Aztec heart with the Catholic Sacred Heart of Jesus. This, as an idea, arrived in the New World from Europe in the sixteenth century, though as an image probably not until 150 years later, when the specific image took off in Europe. All the same, when the Spanish monks talked of Christ's heart, and of men directing their hearts toward Christ, of hearts "full for God," and of Christ's blood and body "given up" and consumed, they were on familiar metaphorical ground. The ideas of self-sacrifice, redemption and communication with God were recognizable from the old religion and were associated with the heart. At the same time the startling and sometimes gory realism of Spanish religious paintings reflected the literal roles of the heart for the Aztecs. In 1649 there was a public auto-da-fé, a stake-burning of heretics, in Mexico City, not far from the old sacrificial pyramid of the Aztecs, which, as Nigel Davies observes in his excellent book *Human Sacrifice,* "might suggest that under the Spaniards sacrificial rites had hardly changed."

The Aztec Sun God drank the blood of his human sacrifices; Christians drink the blood of God, made human and sacrificed. The Aztec made effigies of their seed god, out of amaranth seeds and sacrificial human blood, which they then ate; Christians eat the body of God in a piece of bread. One of Christianity's greatest talents was incorporating religions which had come before it or stood in its way. As early as 1688 the rites of Huitzilopochtli were being compared to the Christian sacrament by Sor Juana Inés de la Cruz in her play *The Divine Narcissus.*

Seen in this light, Christianity does look disconcertingly like a religion of human sacrifice. Sacrifice means "made sacred"; the Aztec sacrificed man imitates—becomes—the god before dying; in Christianity God becomes man before dying. Though the Christian sacrifice was only done once, it was and is the central tenet; there is much about it that looks most peculiar to a purely rational mind. In 567 the Council of Tours had to forbid the arrangement of the host in the shape of a human body, and in 1215 Pope Innocent III declared that transubstantiation was a fact: the wafer *was* the flesh and the wine *was* the blood (not represented: *became*). During the early years of the Inquisition one of the horrendous crimes of which Jews were accused was torturing the consecrated wafer: the wafer was held to feel pain. A thirteenth-century mold that made communion wafers in the shape of the heart survives in Spain.

As well as the sacrifice of Jesus, there was martyrdom. It is easy to dismiss the practice of suttee by Indian widows as mad—like the actions of the inhabitants of Dahomey, who only 300 years ago fought for the right to be buried alive with their masters, or the inhabitants of ancient Ur who followed their king into his tomb as a sacred duty, performed the rituals and then drank poison from the gold cups found at each corpse's side thousands of years later—but how are the Christian martyrs different? From the firm faith and self-righteousness of the early Christian martyrs up to St. Marguerite-Marie Alacoque we see, alongside naked faith, an uncalled-for and masochistic glory in self-inflicted pain and death.

A key to any religion is that earthly life is not that important: man must become as God and, ideally, live forever: through sacrifice or being reborn. Only in the past couple of hundred years in the West has rationalism dictated that earthly life is sacred. Meanwhile the customs of past beliefs lurk all over everyday life even in the most "civilized" places. When we lift a glass and say "Cheers" or "Your health," we are just celebrating the raising of the chalice to God at the altar, and before that the raising of the cup of sacrificial blood.

5

THE HEART AS A
MAGIC OBJECT

We say "Bless you" when someone sneezes, because the soul jumps from the heart into the mouth for a moment, and we cover our mouths when we yawn, so the devil cannot jump in and get the soul out. Heart magic is powerful, but there is a very simple, everyday, physical aspect to it.

An animal's heart could serve much the same purpose as a voodoo doll or a manikin: hurt it, and your enemy is hurt. In 1929 George Lyman Kittredge could write that it was "even now a common practice to torment an enemy by sticking pins, needles, or thorns in an animal's heart and . . . roasting it or parching it in the chimney." He told of a Devonshire wizard who in 1842 sought to destroy a witch by piercing six bullocks' hearts, two with pins, four with nails. They were then melted, put into a barrel and rolled downhill. The witch died and her body, according to the records of the Devonshire Association, showed the marks. The pin-sticking is clearly an upended version of the pierced heart of Christ and the arrows of Cupid, but the way it is used invokes hatred and revenge instead of love and redemption.

If a witch uses a heart against you, you can use one against her too: in 1605 Sir Roger Wilbraham reported that one Mr. Harley was told by "a knowen witch . . . to burn the hart by rosting on a spitt and the witch wold come to the dore before the hart was rosted." This roasted heart would identify her: a pin-stuck heart could be used to destroy her and act as a counter-charm. Also in Devon, so the story goes, in the mid-nineteenth century, two witches called Paddy Goselin and Mary Ann Pyecraft put a curse on the cattle of a farmer to whom they owed money; Mother Sunshine, a neighboring white witch, recommended taking the heart of one of four bulls that died from the curse, sticking it with pins and hanging it in the chimney. Three more bullocks that had gone mad recovered, and no more fell sick. If your

WESTMINSTER CHARM

Found in the old millstream ditch under Great College Street, Westminster: a small corked jug containing hair, nail clippings and a piece of formerly red serge in the shape of a heart, stuck through with round-headed brass pins. Needles and red flannel crop up too as "tricks" in the southern states of America (the flannel represents the Holy Ghost): if someone tries to bring badness on you in this way, you turn it back on them by burning their trick or throwing it in water, so that they burn or drown. "Hands" or mojos, little bags of red flannel and black cloth filled with magic items such as bits of animals, "graveyard dirt" (from the top of the coffin, just above the breast of the corpse), moss, nails, and red pepper could be used in defense as well as attack. Often a piece of red flannel was put inside the little bag as well.

From the Suffolk and Essex Free Press, *January 3, 1883*

On December 30th a dairyman found between three and four pounds missing from his cashbox. His wife . . . confessed that a couple of women [strangers] had promised her that . . . for a few shillings they could convert any amount of gold to treble its value by Easter Sunday next, [if she let them] trace the planets upon the coins and then secrete them about the premises, but on no account were they to be touched before Easter Sunday, or the planets would . . . visit the house with affliction. The dairy man . . . forced from his wife the knowledge that the money was hanging in the chimney. There he found a semi-smoked heart, evidently that of a pig or a sheep. It was tightly encased in wrappings of scarlet and black material. A number of crosses and other emblems formed of projecting pins covered it completely on one side. On opening it, the cavity of the heart was found to contain several farthings, which had been brightened by some rough substance. It is believed the strangers . . . have absconded the richer by several pounds.

animals haven't died yet and you can't afford to sacrifice bullocks, a black cockerel's heart would do, or a toad's, or a piece of bacon or even red cloth cut in the shape of a heart and sprinkled with blood. You cook it, or hang it

Ornamental pin cushion, made by a wounded British soldier as occupational therapy at the turn of the twentieth century.

up the chimney, or rest it on the bar from which the pot hangs over the fire, or bury it under the house or the barn, and say your spell. Here's one from Devon: May each pin/Thus stuck in/This poor heart/In hers go/Who hurt me so/Till she departs.

This was all quite real: buried pin-stuck hearts have been unearthed all over Britain. Taunton Museum has two pigs' hearts found up a chimney; a bullock's heart stuck with whitethorn, pins and nails was found in a Dorset chimney in 1884; and even in 1908, as reported by *The Times,* a witch in London was piercing sheep's hearts.

In January 1827 Sir Walter Scott wrote in his diary: "Called on Skene [the watercolorist and, as it happens, my great-great-grandfather], to give him, for the Antiquarian Society, a heart, human apparently, stuck full of pins. It was found lying opposite to the threshold of an old tenement in [Dalkeith], a little below the surface; it is in perfect preservation." It turned out to be a calf's heart and is now in the Edinburgh Museum of Antiquities, mottled orangey brown, looking like a haggis with cloves stuck in it.

As this level of gore grew less acceptable in the nineteenth century, decent, law-abiding, heart-shaped kitchen pin cushions, made of velvet and merino, with ruching and beading, became popular. They tended to have a loop by which they could be hung up. Soldiers and sailors liked them too—either to make, sticking bead-headed pins in patterns during the long dull hours at sea, but more particularly as good-luck gifts. At sea or in the kitchen, these are simple anti-curse charms descended from more bloody magic. I have one made by a wounded soldier in the First World War as occupational therapy and sent home as a simple spell (though probably not acknowledged as such) to maintain love and loyalty. These tend to bear the same mass-produced embroidered poem ("Think of me, when the golden sun is sinking") which looks like a child's name tape.

SAFEKEEPING OF THE HEART

Sometimes a heart needs to be kept elsewhere for its own safety. An enchanter, in particular, can be almost invincible, if no one knows the secret of where his heart, or his soul, is kept. The idea starts, as do so many things, with Bata, and proceeds across to India, Persia and back into European legend and as far as New Zealand. In India, the missing heart is usually in a bird; or it could be in a necklace, in a box, in the heart of a fish, in a tank or in a pair of bees on top of a crystal pillar in a water tank (Bengal). It could be in a stone, in the head of a bird, in the head of a leveret, in the middle head of a seven-headed hydra (Rome); or in a board, or in the heart of a fox or in a mountain (Serbia); or in a golden cockchafer, or inside a golden clock, or inside a golden sheep, or inside a golden stag or in the ninety-ninth island (Hungary). A djinn in *The Arabian Nights* kept his souls "in the crop of a sparrow, and shut up the bird

---

TOBIAS AND THE ANGEL

The Bible is not above heart magic: Tobit, in exile in Egypt, had been blinded by sparrows' dung while sleeping outside (he could not sleep inside because he had secretly and illegally been burying the dead, and was therefore unclean). His niece Sara, meanwhile, had already buried seven husbands, none of whom had had the chance to lie with her because "a wicked spirit loveth her, which hurteth nobody but those who come unto her." Tobit sent his son Tobias on a journey to Rages in Media, accompanied by the angel Raphael in disguise. On the journey, as "the young man went down to wash himself, a fish leaped out of the river and would have devoured him." Raphael told Tobias to catch the fish. "Touching the heart and the liver," he said, "if a devil or an evil spirit trouble any, we must make a smoke thereof before the man or the woman, and the party shall be no more vexed"; the gall, in turn, healed blindness. Raphael then arranged for Tobias to marry Sara, and to burn the heart and liver of the fish on the ashes of perfume in the marriage chamber, and "the devil shall smell it and flee away." When Tobias heard this "he loved her, and his heart was effectually conjoined to her." All went according to plan, and on their return home he stroked his father's eyes with the gall, which cured his blindness.

---

in a box. The box I set in a casket, and enclosing this in seven other caskets and seven chests, laid the whole in an alabastrine coffer, which I buried within the marge of yon earth-circling sea." Ogres often kept their hearts in eggs. To destroy the villain, the hero needs to find out his secret (often it is revealed by the captive princess, who has been listening to sleep-talking or extracting confidences), then destroy the life token.

Witches steal human hearts for their own purposes and replace them with a heart of straw or stone. Tam Lin, the enchanted knight of Scots ballad, nearly suffered this fate. He was loved by the Fairy Queen, and when fair Janet won him back, the Queen cried:

> If I had kent what I ken this night
> If I had kent it yestreen,
> I wad hae taen out thy heart of flesh
> and put in a heart o' stane.

Here are some charms you may or may not want to try:

- Hildegarde of Bingen (1098–1179), mystic, musician and saint, writes in her *Subtleties* that the heart of a vulture, split in two and dried by fire and sun, worn in a belt of doeskin, will make you tremble when poison is near.
- If a child is born deformed, it is because someone had written its name in pins on a pin cushion; in which case you must steal the pin cushion, take out the pins and stick them instead in a calf's heart, which is to be buried in the churchyard.
- A bat's heart makes a lucky hand for a gambler.
- A heart (often a pigeon's) hung over the door would make a lover come to you; placed under the pillow it will bring back a faithless lover; pierced, it will punish him. Don't stab the heart (or the doll's heart) unless you want him to die. Kittredge reports a love charm, "a doll stuck about the heart with tintacks," found in a barn in Lincolnshire in 1867, which was probably intended to magic up a rendezvous.
- All sorts of objects, living and dead, can represent the heart of the lost love:

> It's not this candle alone I stick
> But [*insert name here*]'s heart I mean to prick . . .
> 'Tis not this blood I mean to burn
> But [*insert name here*]'s heart I wish to turn
> May he neither rest nor sleep
> Till he return to me to speak.

In Somerset they used an onion, and in Bombay, a nut; in Sicily, a lemon, and in Fiji, a plantain sucker, in the same way. In Genoa in 1928 a girl was found with a photograph of her untrue lover and a lamb's heart pierced with pins; she was going to bury them in the graveyard, in order to get him back. In the southern States, a white dove's heart, swallowed point downward, brings love. Quite how you make someone swallow it is another question. Easier to wear a little of your love's hair near to your heart for the same result.

- In Melanesia, the Etoro and Kaluli peoples divine whether or not someone is a witch by their hearts. It works on much the same principle as witch-ducking. Once the suspect has been killed, her heart is exhibited on a stake: a bright or yellow heart confirms that she was indeed a witch.

- Swallowing the heart of a black snake will make you ill-natured and long-winded but valiant; its blood, drunk warm with whiskey, makes you strong and hard-working.

- *Les Secrets Merveilleux de la Magie Naturelle et Cabalistique du Petit Albert*, a book "absolutely determined on making us rich," says Grillot de Givry, offers this talisman (see page 173): which is to be made on "virgin parchment on the day and hour of Jupiter, the scheme of the heavens wearing a fortunate aspect." Fortune, a lovely girl in a wisp of cloth, standing on a sphere, is accosted by a hand offering a heart and coming out of a cloud, with the word *reluctante* written upside down and *Eriam fortuna* (right way up) above and below respectively. The talisman should be fastened to your hat.

- Though Islamic law forbids the use of magic, Islam has its share of methods, *amalim*, somewhere between prayers and charms, for curing heart problems, both physical and emotional. *Amalim* involve fasting, special meals of greens, vinegar, salt and barley,

Talisman for making a fortune, from *Les Secrets Merveilleux de la Magie Naturelle et Cabalistique du Petit Albert* (1722).

writing the verses in saffron and placing them under the pillow, or carrying them with you. *Amalim* exist for steadfastness of heart, for light in the heart which protects from chaos, for captivating and winning the hearts of other people, and to make you love someone and to make that person love you.

- If the beautiful name of Allah (the Excellent) is recited a number of times and blown on a morsel before eating it, the heart will be strengthened.
- To acquire independence in the heart from materialism, recite the name of Allah the One and Only a thousand times.
- Aya 9:15 from the Qur'an, "To make strong your heart and to keep your feet firm thereby," is very effective. It should be written and worn as a *taweez* around the neck in such a manner that the *taweez* remains fixed where the heart is situated. A plaster may be used to prevent it from shifting. Also 13:10: "Who have believed and whose hearts are at ease in the remembrance of Allah. Verily in the remembrance of Allah do hearts find rest."

EATING THE HUMAN HEART FOR MAGIC AND POWER

The most effective way to use the heart for magic is to eat it. When Pythagoras wrote: *"Cor ne edito"* (Don't eat the heart), he gave rise to a number of interpretations. For instance, there's Philemon Holland's allegorical interpretation: don't eat your heart, as in "offend not thine own soule, nor hurt and consume it with pensive cares." In Chapter 125 of the Book of the Dead, eating your own heart is one of the sins you have to deny: according to Budge, eating your heart means losing your temper; other translators offer "useless remorse" or *"agir sans conscience."* There's consumption for rebirth, like Dionysus and Bata. There is allegorical consumption—each man eats the thing he loves: the kissing, the taking into the body, the tasting of the beloved, the heart-shaped cakes and boxes of chocolates, the oral sex. And there is cannibalism. Human history is full of tales of heart cannibalism.

This is very rarely a matter of nutrition. The meat is too strong for that. Eating the dead is perverse, and eating the heart is eating the essence of the dead; we deny death by incorporating the dead person into someone who is still alive. Eating the heart is eating life itself: in tribal societies this could make you strong, but it could also kill you. In provençal troubadour poetry eating the heart was a staple of tragic romance (see page 306 for more on this).

According to Juvenal, the ancient Egyptians ate human flesh and offered human sacrifice. In the very oldest of the Pyramid texts, a remnant perhaps from even older and more brutal times, there is talk of eating the hearts of enemies and of gods: of the deceased "who live on the hearts of the Gods," "content to live on the hearts because it is their magic power." In later sources the hearts of enemies are presented to the newly divine dead in the form of animals, partisans of Set; the hearts of these animals would be laid on the ground before the new Osiris, or thrown in a lake, to represent Osiris's victory over Set. At Medinet Habu, in Upper Egypt, warm cakes represent the hearts of the enemies. Whether real hearts were actually eaten then we may never know.

When Hannibal, a film about a cannibal serial killer, opened in 2001, its publicity slogan was: "This Valentine's Day, are you certain it's just you after your partner's heart?" Sid Ahmed Rezala, who was charged with murder in France in the summer of 2000, said: "If someone had done to my family what I am charged with doing, I would not have rested, I would have torn out his heart and eaten it." That same month Mike Tyson snarled at Lennox Lewis in the boxing ring: "I'm the most ruthless, brutal champion . . . I want to eat your heart . . . I want to rip his heart out and feed it to him."

During the Cultural Revolution in China, in the southwestern province of Guangxi, cannibalism was recognized and officially sanctioned as a punishment for "social dregs"—class enemies—in the name of the proletarian dictatorship. Victims were subjected to public "criticism," beaten to death, then dismembered. The liver was the most desired organ; the heart, as ever, the most symbolically rich. Zheng Yi, a veteran of Tiananmen Square, has written a book about it which I recommend to the strong of stomach; for the rest I offer only this quote, from Yi Wangsheng. This old man was eighty-six at the time of the interview, recalling the murder of a bandit's son in 1968.

> Yes, I killed him. No matter who asks the question, I have the same answer suggested to us by Chairman Mao. Fear nothing! Everyone supported us and what I killed was the enemy. Fear nothing! Will his ghost return and seek revenge? Ha! To engage in revolution, my heart is red. Didn't Chairman Mao say, "Kill or be killed"? If I live, you must die. Class struggle! I laid the first knife on him . . . I was not involved in cutting out his heart and liver . . . the heart was cut into finger-sized slices. People in the crowd struggled to get a piece. The people were so numerous I didn't even get a share.

Eating the heart of the enemy is an ancient practice, but usually it followed his death either in fair fight (because the heart represents his virtues and strengths, which the eater wishes to incorporate) or after a strictly ritualized sacrifice. Wherever human sacrifice involved dismemberment (rather than simply accompanying a king or potentate to the next life), the heart has been prized.

The great chef Brillat Savarin said that there is no great gap between *sabor,* to taste, and *saber,* to know. A baby puts everything in its mouth to find out what it is; we all learn by tasting—literally, metaphorically, emotionally. An Ibo saying has it: "Tales are the food of the ear." And the heart was then the seat of knowledge as well as love. Eating the heart gives you knowledge.

The core of African medicine lies in association: linking what the medicine has with what the patient needs. Usually it involves herbalism; but it is a quick leap to sorcery and witchcraft, from eating eyes to improve vision to eating the heart for courage and strength. Among the Yoruba, the king would eat the heart of his predecessor in order to take on his status. The Ashanti of Ghana would only eat the heart, and only young warriors who had not killed in battle could eat it because they needed a boost in valor. (When we encourage each other saying "Take heart!" are we suggesting taking our own hearts, or someone else's? U.S. soldiers in Vietnam consumed a different kind of heart, though perhaps with similar intent: a Purple Heart was an amphetamine, as well as a medal.)

In 1822 the heart of Sir Charles McCarthy, a British imperial administrator, was eaten after he unwisely underestimated the skill, size, nature and loyalty of the Ashanti armies. Believing that they were just waiting for a sign before deserting, he had his band play "God Save the King" on the banks of the Bonsu River, deep in the rain forest. The Ashanti musicians gave their reply, and a tuneful duel ensued before the real fight. (Each Ashanti division had its own identifiable drums and horns; the thousands of warriors invisible in the thick wet forest placed each other and communicated by the voices of their instruments. The warriors were wearing, as on special occasions, crimson thigh boots held up with cowrie shell suspenders.) McCarthy was wrong about the Ashanti, and paid the price.

In the Icelandic Volsunga saga, eating a dragon's heart makes you brave; in the Ynglinga saga, eating the heart of a ferocious animal makes you cruel, and dragon's heart blood can cure you if you are sick. Eating a magic bird's heart can make you rich (by spitting gold, or finding a coin under your pillow each morning). Depending on the bird in question, it could also make you king. According to a Spanish tale, a magic serpent's heart can kill giants. Often you can disenchant yourself by eating the enchanter's heart. Eating the heart of a jackal makes you lose your strength. A king of Arakan in Burma dedicated his whole life to Buddha's Eightfold Path of Compassion; but it was prophesied

he would die soon after his coronation. He put it off as long as he could, but then came a seer who told that not only could he be saved, but he could master invisi-

A twelfth-century Norwegian carving showing the Viking Sigurd roasting a dragon's heart while his companion, Regin, sleeps. Sigurd burns his finger, puts it to his mouth and tastes the dragon's blood, whereupon he understands the speech of the birds, who tell him that Regin is planning to betray him. © *Werner Forman Archive / Universitetets Oldsaksamling, Oslo*

bility, if he drank an elixir made from 2,000 white doves' hearts and 6,000 human hearts. So he did. It didn't work: he died. This may or may not be true.

But eating a heart can also get you pregnant. In "The Enchanted Hind," a story from Basile's *Pentamerone,* a barren queen conceives through smelling and eating a sea dragon's heart cooked by a virgin. But so potent was this heart that the virgin became pregnant too, as did the furniture, and a few days later "the big state bed produced a little bed, the big chest a little casket . . . and the chamber pot had a little chamber pot that was a joy to behold."

THE HEART
IN ART

Caritas—Divine Love offering her heart to God—by Giotto (c. 1305). © *Scala*

1

PINE CONES AND PEACHES,
MIRACLES, MEXICANS AND
MODERN ART, OR HOW THE
HEART GOT ITS SHAPE

Such an interesting thing as the heart frequently needed to be depicted: its physical reality, and the ideas that lived in it. Out of the sheer variety of the subject matter came an astonishing range of representations. The physical heart started out described as pine-cone shaped, which is more or less accurate, when it is contracted in death, and it ended up—well, it hasn't ended up yet. As for the metaphorical heart: it was a house, a book, a rose, a harp, a drum, a pomegranate, a bunch of grapes . . .

So how—during the years of increasing anatomical knowledge—did the heart end up with a broad scalloped top and a pointy bottom?

FROM THE PINE CONE TO THE VALENTINE HEART

For generations during Europe's Dark Ages, hearts were described but not drawn, and when they were drawn, either for scientific or allegorical purposes, they were drawn from description: pine-cone shaped. Pine-cone hearts can be seen in Situs figures and also in art: *Douz Regart* (Sweet Regard), a character in the French *Roman de la Poire* of about 1250, offers a pine-cone heart to the Fair Lady; Giotto's *Caritas* (see picture on page 180) in the Capella dell'Arena at Padua holds up her pine-cone heart to God for all the world as if she had just taken it from the fruit bowl in her other hand. It is large, and a tiny God in the corner reaches down with two tiny hands to take it from her. The over-large heart reappears in many works: it may have been meant to illustrate St. Augustine's idea that the heart grows with its love for God. The heart of San

Filipo Neri, St. Philip of the Joyful Heart, was much admired for its immensity after his death at the end of the sixteenth century—it broke some of his ribs. He once gave a sinful musician the penance of standing in the middle of the Corso in Rome and laughing: if anyone asked why, he was to say "Because I am a good Christian." In a fourteenth-century *Madonna with Caritas* by the Master of the Stefaneschi Altar, Caritas offers her pine-cone heart up to the infant Jesus, echoing later paintings of Jesus sitting with his pomegranate. The heart of Caritas often flamed like later sacred hearts; however, she tended to hold it by the fat end, what we think of as upside down, so the flames came from what would later become the pointy end. By 1360 a Caritas by Giovanni del Biondo shows her heart held by the pointy end, slightly scalloped and with the flames coming out of the aorta like a gas jet. How did this change come about?

The first hearts with indentations in the top appeared in the early fourteenth century in northern Italy. Pierre Vinken, a Dutch cardiologist who has written a wonderfully detailed book following the process, suggests that the first scalloped hearts appear on a necklace round the neck of Love's horse in Francesco da Barberino's *Documenti d'Amore* from the early 1300s and in an anatomical book by de Vigevano published in 1347. An *Amor* by Giotto of 1323 shows the blindfold boy himself with a string of conquered hearts strung about his torso like a bandit's Sam Browne: you have to look closely but I reckon they are indented. Just. Vinken thinks not. Barberino studied in Bologna, a center of anatomical study, so he would have been acquainted with developments in anatomy—including erroneous ones. Vinken connects the dent with the old question of the number of chambers in the physical heart. Ancient discussions of a smaller third chamber in the middle, between the two obvious ventricles, led, through confused translation, to phrases such as Galen's "*duos ventriculos, dextrum et sinistrum, et in medio fovum*," reappearing in Middle English as "two ventricles, right and left, and in the middle a ditch or pit." According to another description, from Mondino, the third chamber lay "in the thickness of the septum": would this mean inside the heart, or seen from the outside? Once a *fovea* or "concavity" is seen as a ditch, it is clearly open on one side, so it cannot be within the heart. Even if it is inside the heart, it is only natural to make a central indentation on the top of the heart to show that the chamber in the middle is smaller than those on either side. Scribes who copied and translated the texts on the whole knew nothing of anatomy, and would have had a job trying to reconcile all the descriptions. Imagine drawing a diagram from my description of the anatomical heart on page 39.

Moreover, ever since the earliest Greek observers the heart had always been considered to have two sides (hence the pores through the septum to unite the two systems). This was quietly reinforced by the biblical image of the two tablets of the law, written in the heart. The broken heart also has a role here: a heart split in two is a contrite heart, a heart ready to receive God's love, a compassionate heart. The heart's symbolic role wanted and needed the heart to be visibly dual. The dent achieved this. (However, the pine-cone heart persisted into the sixteenth century, and Vinken spotted it in Tibetan temple decorations of 1800.)

The first person to draw a heart that looked like the anatomical heart we know today was Leonardo da Vinci. More than fifty of his pages of drawings and notes (in mirror-writing) on the heart and cardiovascular system survive in the Queen's collection at Windsor—drawings of almost incredible delicacy, beauty and, in the end, accuracy.

Compare his drawings of an ox's heart, which has been dated to 1513, with the Situs figure from the 1513 edition of Johannes Peyligk's *Compendiosa capitis phisici declaratio,* Leipzig (see page 185). The purpose of the Situs figures, as their name suggests, was to show what was where inside the human body, and they were the end result of frequent copying; they were also printed, and continued to be reproduced for years before anyone got round to calling a halt or updating them. (The printing press was a great advance in Germany—these figures tended to be German—but in this curious way also a hindrance.) Even so, it is extraordinary to think that these two images were made in the same year.

Leonardo (like Verrocchio, Mantegna, Signorelli, Dürer and Michelangelo) watched dissections; he also performed them himself:

I have dissected more than ten human bodies, destroying all the various members and removing the minutest particles of flesh which surrounded these veins, without causing any effusion of blood . . . And as one single body did not suffice for so long a time, it was necessary to proceed by stages with so many bodies as would render my knowledge complete; this I repeated twice in order to achieve the differences. And though you should have a love for such things you may perhaps be deterred by natural repugnance, and if this does not prevent you, you may perhaps be deterred by passing the night hours in the company of these corpses, quartered and flayed and horrible to behold.

The corpses Leonardo took to bits would have been those of executed criminals, and though public dissection did take place, it is clear that Leonardo was working with a degree of secrecy, at night. His motives were both—and specifically—anatomical and spiritual. The artist, he held, would "reveal to men the origin of their . . . cause of existence. Division of the spiritual from the material parts."

So he studied the valves, stuck a sharp rod into a living heart to see by the movements of the end of the rod what the movements of the heart were, and explained these in terms of hydrodynamics and mechanics. He saw that the heart was four-chambered and muscular and that it was the source of all the blood vessels—in this he was ahead of Galen. (There is a rumor that he also

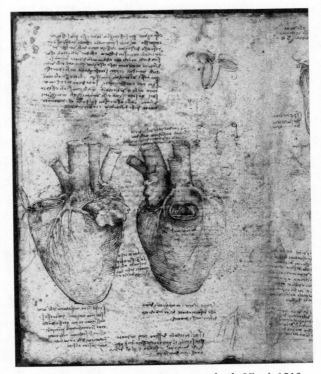

Two views of an ox's heart, by Leonardo da Vinci, 1513.
The Royal Collection. © 2001, Her Majesty Queen Elizabeth II

Peyligk's Situs figure, also 1513. The heart, labeled "cor," is sticking out to the left.
© *The British Library 740716*

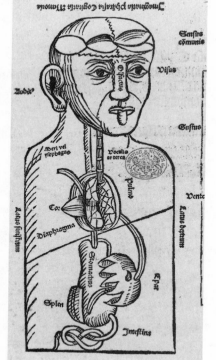

identified the circulation of the blood. He probably didn't.) His work was not a great influence at the time, though—it wasn't made public until the eighteenth century.

What happened was that the anatomical heart and the symbolic heart began to part ways. The anatomical indent was eventually dispelled along with the myth of the third chamber, but while Leonardo and Vesalius and Harvey et al. were investigating the appearance and actions of the real heart, a stylized heart developed alongside. This heart icon had a selective attitude to anatomy: Galen had spoken of the coronary arteries as "coursing around in a circle through the body of the heart"; the garland of thorns began to circle the symbolic heart. He spoke of the heart's base (in modern terms, the top—the base of the pine cone) being surrounded like a crown (*corona*); now this became an actual crown, worn on top or round the middle, a crown of thorns or flames, the crown of the King of Heaven. The chambers of the heart developed into the image of the heart as a house.

The bloody reality of Renaissance anatomy schools did not fit so well with the heart's seemingly bottomless supply of imagery for religion and love, so the flesh and the spirit made a little space between them. Not too much, because love and religion liked to be able to call on pain and blood; but enough. The Sacred Heart did not, despite exceptions, take off among Protestants as it did among Catholics. The sexuality, the blood and palpitating and proto-cannibalism were not suited to a religion whose formative urge was to separate the physical from the spiritual. Just as the wafer for Protestants was not *really* the body, and the wine was not *really* the blood, so the anatomical heart, where the physical and the spiritual meet, was not an appropriate religious emblem. This is not to say that the symbol died away—we know it didn't. It evolved into the pure, clean, simple, Protestant and ultimately secular heart, artificially removed from the southern European heart of blood and guts: neither anatomically correct nor religiously overpowering; a clean and graphic heart, shorn of aortas, crowns, thorns and any realism, to be found on playing cards and Valentines, bumper stickers and T-shirts, cartoons and sweeties.

And perhaps this, too, is one of the roots of modern Western life's feeling of detachment from itself and why holisticism has become so popular. The two images of the heart can represent mankind's internal division, an idea which leads back to Sufi, Buddhist, Hindu, Jewish and mystical Christian ideas of the heart as the place of union: where man meets God, and knows himself.

At times the pine-cone shape was tweaked at the bottom into a comma-shape, following the ancient advice that it bends slightly to the left. Sometimes it had ears: a pine cone with ears. For much of the Renaissance it was plump all over, peach-shaped, with a relatively flat bottom. The convex-sided scalloped heart, with its concomitant pointed end, has predominated since the sixteenth century; in the twentieth a straight-sided heart emerged. (The cockles of the heart, by the way, are the ventricles, from *cochleae cordis,* the snails of the heart, so-called for their shape.)

The two-dimensional shape that we think of as heart-shaped was in existence before it came to represent the heart. It is a version of a pitcher or jar, as in ancient Egypt; or the ivy leaf—*folium hederae,* or spade leaf—common in Roman, Byzantine and Coptic ornamentation, usually accompanied by tendrils and a stalk. The heart-shaped watermarks and printers' marks seen on papers and in books from the fourteenth century on are probably derived from this, though they too took on religious adaptations such as crowns and arrows. In Morocco silver talismans of a similar shape, probably derived from a spearhead or blade, and set with carnelians, were worn by warriors as an emblem of valor, hanging from their belts. (The heart has a long and interesting relationship with blades, from Cupid's arrows on, but it does not often appear as one.) In cards, Hearts are descended from cups; Spades—leaves—are what used to be heart-shaped (*spada* is the Italian for sword—back to blades again).

The red and stalkless Valentine heart first appeared in Byzantine art: it appears upside down in seventh-century mosaics in the martyrium church of St. Demetrios at Thessaloniki. Thereafter St. Demetrios is often represented in icons wearing a mantle ornamented with inverted hearts, probably based on an actual textile of the time. Here the shape probably has nothing to do with the heart itself, but we can tell they are not leaves because a contemporaneous set of enamel plaques of Constantine IX Monomachus shows both the heart-decorated cloth—on the emperor, his queen and two dancing girls—and a garden full of birds and some rather gorgeous leafy plants, and the leaves are nothing like the hearts. Moreover, in the Mani, the westernmost of the three long fingers at the tip of mainland Greece, the cult of Demeter, mother of Persephone, was very strong even after the coming of Christianity. She adapted into St. Demetria, a female saint listed in no hagiopedia that I have ever seen; in fact I suspect she only existed there, and not for very long, because in due course her femininity followed her pagan identity and she became St. Demetrios. Those two inconvenient habits dispatched, Demetrios remains patron of most of the tiny domed churches which pop out of that area's unlikely—and extremely infertile—landscape. It is tempting but ungovernably fanciful to see a link between the hearts of St. Demetrios's mantle and the pomegranate eaten by Persephone and held by Christ as a symbol of his Passion (see page 253) and to tie it up as a big fertility–heart connection.

WHY HEARTS ON PLAYING CARDS?

John Hall's *Emblems with Elegant Figures* includes a plate wherein Anima, the soul, holds up the heart to heaven. The text reads: "Inebriate my heart, O God, with the sober intemperance of thy love," and a chalice pours down—wine? blood? love?—to fill it. On page 203 a fifteenth-century nun is getting drunk with God in a divine cardiomorphic picnic. George Herbert put it like this:

> Who knows not love, let him assay
> And taste that juice, which on the cross a pike
> Did set again abroach, then let him say
> If ever he did taste the like.
> Love is the liquor sweet and most divine
> Which my God feels as blood; but I, as wine.

The chalice was the Holy Grail, held by Joseph of Arimathaea at the Crucifixion to catch Christ's blood as it poured from the wound in his side (in

Effusio Sanguinis, from San Casciano in Val di Pesa: a book cover showing directly the link between the heart and the cup. © *Scala*

reality, you may remember, blood in the left ventricle leaves with enough pressure to shoot water about six feet in the air). By association, as a blood holder, the grail became a kind of heart itself. The blood/wine/love pours to and from hearts and chalices, which is how the *copas* (cups) of the old Spanish card deck became the hearts we know now.

VOTIVE HEARTS

One of the main purposes of the depicted heart, whatever its shape, was to render the idea of sacrifice bloodless as society became civilized. Bread and wine replaced flesh and blood, representation replaced the reality, and the image of the heart could mean a million things, depending on how it was used.

For hundreds of years Christian sacrifice has been rendered safely bloodless through votive art: small representations of body parts which were (and are) bought cheaply and left in their thousands on altars across the Catholic

A calendar for 1863, showing a reliquary bust of Garibaldi, surrounded by votive hearts. The poem says "These are the candles and this is the saint," which the very anticlerical Garibaldi would have found amusing. © *Scala*

Votive hearts from Dr. Boyadjian's collection. © *Musées Royaux d'Art et d'Histoire, Bruxelles*

world as bribes and gifts to the saints and to Mary. They have three purposes: to request a cure, to prevent a problem in the first place, and to give thanks for a cure or prevention granted. Hearts are hugely popular, because they can symbolize any problem concerning any emotion traditionally represented by the heart: a crisis of faith, of love, of hope, of courage. A heart with a leg or an eye on it denotes a prayer both for the cure of the sick body part and for comfort through the sickness. At the same time it's an offering of devotion to God, a very simple sacrificial emblem. The Spanish name is *milagro*—miracle. Like the nuns imitating Jesus, they imitate in hope of becoming. When the prayer has been granted, the grateful recipient offers up a *retablo* or ex voto; perhaps a painting, often on tin or cheap cloth, of the miracle as it occurs, with an expression of thanks written on a banner or a cloud. "Votive," like devotion, is from the Latin *vovere*, to vow; in Roman times *devotio* also meant self-sacrifice: you might offer to sacrifice yourself so that, say, the emperor would recover from his illness. Caligula liked it, of course, and one Pacuvius sacrificed himself for Augustus.

In fifteenth-century Germany and Austria votive emblems could be polyvisceral: the heart still attached to the lungs, trachea, stomach or liver. This harks back to times when the viscera were read: the liver by the Babylonians, the whole caboodle by the Etruscans. St. Ansanus, one of the patrons of Siena, appears in paintings holding the curious bunch up by the trachea.

A Belgian-Armenian cardiologist, Dr. N. Boyadjian, collected heart-shaped ex votos for many years—they are part of his wonderful collection, the Musée du Coeur, at the Musées Royaux in Brussels, and well worth visiting (see this page). He has flat, elegant silver hearts from Italy, surrounded by filigree lace; fat, hollow copper ones from Belgium and France with doors in for putting a message or prayer inside; embroidered cloth hearts stuck with beads and stones from Portugal and Spain.

Alongside are curious heart objects made by nuns in the eighteenth and nineteenth centuries, declaring their dedication to the twin hearts of Christ and Mary: little paintings, embroidered heart-shaped frames for holy pictures, tiny ornamental sacred heart cushions or lockets or reliquaries made of velvet, fine straw, little pearls, dried or silk flowers, pleated satin, lace and wax, bits of mirror, their own hair. They are skillfully made, dedicated objects, reeking of devotion and long hours.

MEXICO

In votive form, and in wildly baroque religious art, the Sacred Heart image took off with remarkable success in the Hispanic New World. For many generations, the hugely mixed population of Mexico (Spanish, Indian, mestizo, black, Creole) had not only its share of illiteracy—which is mother to the power of images, and was seized on by evangelical colonialists, particularly ones with such an arsenal of imagery as Spanish Christianity had in the sixteenth century—but also more than its share of naturally available hallucinatory drugs. By the seventeenth century these drugs were promoting widespread belief in miracles; these soon became commonplace and even more powerful. A radiant heart appeared over the deathbed of any half-decent priest. Heart images went wild: sinners bathe in a pool of blood flowing from the wound; eucharistic wafers fall from the heart; Christ himself is in the chalice; lambs drink from a basin into which flows blood direct from a radiant wounded heart, wreathed in thorns and sprouting a vine; a wheatsheaf and a cross, with angels looking on.

During the nineteenth century votive paintings in Mexico were the work of local artists; later industrially produced objects, initially from Barcelona, began to take over. You lost the personal touch (a portrait of your healed self that looked like you) but they were cheaper (like, no doubt, the mass-produced Books of the Dead). Today in Latin America votive hearts are usually made of pressed tin, sometimes painted. The bleeding heart is still everywhere in Mexico. You can buy flags in Tijuana tourist shops bearing the fighting eagle and snake of Cuauhtlequetzqui, alongside straightforward votive hearts, alongside reproductions of what happened when the *milagros* were taken on by high art: the paintings of Frida Kahlo, the master and mistress of heart symbolism.

FRIDA KAHLO

Consider *Memory,* painted in 1937, when her husband, the painter Diego Rivera,* was having an affair with her sister. As usual it is a self-portrait; Kahlo stands helpless, weeping and without arms, one foot on land, one on a tiny boat in the sea; on either side of her a different set of clothes, a different identity, that she might wear. At her feet lies her enormous heart, pumping out blood from every vessel, which seeps away into the valley behind and into the sea: pain, and wasted love, lots of it. Where her heart should be is a clean and simple hole, transfixed by a long thin rod; on either end of the rod sits a tiny little winged cupid. They seem to be playing seesaw, heedless of her pain, swinging on the scales of judgment too, without a thought for the pain this causes her or of the danger to her of their playing in this hole while her heart, displaced, beats on. What clearer representation could there be of the effects of thoughtless infidelity? Frida in her martyrdom to romantic love uses the age-old Christian metaphors. In *The Remembrance of an Open Wound* she portrays herself with her skirt lifted up displaying a dripping vaginalike wound in her thigh, worthy of a medieval representation of the five wounds (see page 124); in several of her 1940 self-portraits she has a crown of thorns around her neck, drops of blood falling where it scratches her, both an ornament and a torture.

The strongest of her heart pictures is *The Two Fridas,* painted in the autumn of 1939, when she and Diego divorced. Frida sits with herself—her imaginary friend, her secret self, her own sister; she is both Spanish and Indian, the independent artist who would take money from no man and Diego's devoted high priestess. The Frida on the right, she said, represents the Frida that Diego loved; the one on the left, the one he no longer loved. Both their hearts are visible. The loved Frida's heart is whole and strong, sitting on an undamaged shirt front. The heart of Frida the unloved is cut open: the insides

---

*At the National Institute of Cardiology in Mexico City, by the way, there are two murals by Diego Rivera showing the history of cardiography, including portraits of Harvey, Withering and Heberden.

The Two Fridas, by Frida Kahlo, 1939. © *Artothek*

are visible and the shirt front—white and frilled like a wedding dress—is torn open too. From a portrait of Diego as a child held in the loved Frida's hand a long vein winds out through her heart to the unloved Frida's heart, and down to her lap, where she holds the open end in a pair of medical pincers—uselessly, because the blood is dripping out on to her virginal white skirt and mingling with the red flowers embroidered at its hem. The two Fridas are holding hands. Behind them is a stormy sky. In her diary Frida quoted a poem by Elias Nandino: "My blood is the miracle which runs in the vessels of the air from my heart to yours." Then she addressed it to Diego; here the image seems addressed to herself, her own strength, her own heart.

Frida Kahlo was a masochist in her own way: as a girl she had polio, and her father swore that she would be cured; as an older woman, when things

This nineteenth-century English valentine showing Cupid painting a heart-shaped portrait of a lady echoes the troubadours and the written-on heart, and foreshadows Frida Kahlo's *Self Portrait with Portrait of Dr. Juan Farill.* © *The Art Archive / Private Collection*

went bad with Diego she precipitated a health crisis (not difficult, as she suffered from a fused spine) and gained attention both from him and from doctors. In 1950 she had seven operations on her back. Her 1951 *Self Portrait with Portrait of Dr. Juan Farill* shows her sitting in her wheelchair in front of her portrait of the doctor whom she credited with saving her life. The doctor gazes a little up and away, saintly and pale, on an easel not entirely unlike an altar. On Frida's palette lies her heart, like a pile of red paint shot through with blue.* She holds a bunch of paint brushes, sharp as darts or surgical implements, and dripping red. Here the heart is her martyrdom and her suffering as an invalid; also her gratitude to the doctor who has given her new life, and also, as paint and the tool of her self-expression, her salvation. At the same time it is wounded by the darts of the brushes, both medically and psychologically. And the whole lot—her suffering, her self, her art, her loving gratitude—is offered up to the saintly doctor. To point out the nunlike outfit of long black skirt and loose white *huipil* might perhaps be reading too much

---

*The heart as paint is an inversion of the written-on heart—see page 225.

into it, but it does look like a continuation of a tradition. On the one hand it recalls the passionate nuns; on the other it is a straightforward secular *retablo,* or ex voto. I have not been allowed to reproduce this picture or *Memory* here; you can find them in *Frida Kahlo: The Paintings* by Hayden Herrera.

Modern Mexican artists have been using bits of the body, and the damaged body, for some time, and must surely have influenced artists such as Damien Hirst and Marc Quinn. The performance artist Guillermo Gomez-Pena drank blood from a heart on stage for his piece *1991*; Ana Mendieta said of her 1970s work: "I started immediately using blood. I think it's a very powerful magical thing." *Los Caracoles Mas Bellos* by Silvia Gomes is six hearts linked by wires, recalling Frida Kahlo's *The Two Fridas*; it was made four years before Hirst sliced his cow in twelve. The early 1990s were good years for heart art: in 1991 Hirst produced "The Lovers": presented in pink, complete with a heart-shaped box of chocolates, a rose and painted nails; inside are four cabinets full of pickled body parts in jars, each cabinet accompanied by a short text on an attitude to love and death: Compromising, Committed, Detached and Spontaneous. They look like modern versions of curiosity cabinets, the chrestomathies in which eighteenth-century collectors would keep their strange little *objets.* At the same time they recall old-fashioned sweetshop jars in rows: sherbet lemons, mint humbugs, hearts, brains. And they are unmistakably medicine cabinets. The writing offers a modern moral pick 'n' mix. Take what you want, mean what you like. It's a shrine to freedom of choice and a demonstration of lost direction. It's both funny and chilling.

That same year Marc Quinn cast his own head in six pints of his own frozen blood (*Self,* 1991)—certainly more than Tony Hancock's armful. By making the head the blood-holder—a role traditionally played by the heart—he echoes the original notion which so bothered the ancients: where does life live? In the heart or in the head? Freezing the life force only makes the point stronger.

Alain Miller's *Eye Love Eye* (1997) is an oil painting in which the heart is neatly and weirdly transformed into a face, brown eyes gazing fondly from anatomically realistic ventricles, fat and vessels forming curls of hair and flesh. It is Arcimboldi made not in fruit and vegetables but in meat—living human meat. The heart here is a face, but it also echoes the unsleeping biblical eye seen in the seventeenth-century Emblems. This face has the same disconcerting expression.

Bill Viola's *Science of the Heart* shows a beautiful pristine double bed, and above it on the wall—where Frida Kahlo's mother had a votive Sacred Heart—is projected a simple film: a human heart, seen though the hole a surgeon cuts, beating, on a loop tape. Watching it, mesmerized by its swaying, rolling movements, by the miracle that lets us look at what could never be seen, you realize that it is gradually speeding up. Encouraged by the soundtrack of its beating, and by your growing fear for it, your own heart speeds up alongside. It is quite frightening: will it slow down in time? Will it be all right? Will *you* be all right? You want it to stop—but of course it must not stop, it will die. And then—way beyond what seems bearable—it starts to beat a little slower. And a little slower. You calm down with it. Thank God. And oh. No. It's getting too slow. Sluggish. Halting. Oh no. Fear kicks in again. A heart-stopping, breath-holding fear. Every angle of the heart's ever-slowing roll is visible; it's beautiful. But it's dangerous. It's going to stall. It's going to die. It is unbearable.

And it slowly picks up again. And the circuit repeats. And the bed, the clean untouched home of human love and physical passion, home of childbirth and sleep and dreams, potential deathbed, just sits there in front of this never-ending drama of the human heart.

THE HEART AS A HOUSE

Within the heart are unfathomable depths. There are reception rooms and bedchambers in it, doors and porches, and many offices and passages. In it is the workshop of righteousness and wickedness ... The heart is Christ's palace: there Christ the King comes to take his rest, with the angels and spirits of the saints, and he dwells there, walking within it and placing his kingdom there. The heart is but a small vessel, and yet dragons and lions are there, and there are poisonous creatures and all the treasures of wickedness; rough uneven paths are there, and gaping chasms. And there likewise is God, there are the angels, there life and the Kingdom, there light and the apostles, the heavenly cities and the treasures of graces: all things are there.

This is St. Makarios's elegant and graphic (almost in the cartoon sense) explanation of what the human heart could be to an educated fifth-century Christian. Of all the visual images which have represented the heart over the centuries, none is more charming than the idea of the heart being a building, a house—with, of course, chambers.

Plato described the heart as having separate chambers, like the male and female apartments in a house, but the image has other roots. *Educare* means both to raise up, as in build an edifice, and to educate. Educating a person—remember, the heart is where you keep knowledge—is akin to raising a building. Kephera, the Egyptian god of understanding and imagination, lived in the heart. The ancient Egyptian idea of the house of hearts, the safe place after death, influenced the Bible and thus the modern world. Equally the Egyptians expected to be united with God in the heart after death. It is no great leap to see the place where someone lives as house. St. Paul wrote: "Let the word of Christ dwell in you abundantly." The two sides of the heart echo the two stone tablets on which Moses received the Ten Commandments; here the heart has become a building material.

Hanuman revealing Rama and Sita in his heart (Indian).
© *Wellcome Library, London*

The dichotomous heart has also always been a hollow, fillable thing: it is sometimes seen as a chest or a jar, with the aorta as a narrow spout. The soul lives in the heart as the genie—a spirit—lives in the bottle. According to the Upanishads, the Hindu gods Siva, Hari and Indra reside in the heart when the heart is free from desire. In Islam, as al-Ghazzali tells us, "the heart has a window which opens on the unseen world of spirits. In the state of sleep . . . this window is opened and man receives impressions from the unseen world." (In Hinduism, when we sleep, we go into our hearts and bask in golden light—the heartbeat, which is fractal, does behave differently while we sleep, though it's not known how or why.) This window is another version of what in the heart's bloodier incarnation is the wound, through which love and wisdom go in and out. God said to Muhammad: "I am not contained in anything above or below, I am not contained in earth or sky, or even in highest heaven. Know this for a surety, O Beloved. Yet I am contained in the believer's heart." But God cannot live in the human heart unless that human lets him, and again and again we are told the story of how God enters and how good a host an individual is. This is al-Ghazzali again: "Human perfection resides in this, that the love of god should conquer a man's heart and possess it wholly." And this is an Orthodox prayer by St. John Chrysostom:

> I am not worthy, Master and Lord
> That you should come under the roof of my soul;
> But since, as you love mankind, you wish to dwell in me,
> With courage I draw near.
> You give the command:
> I will open the gates which you alone created.

NONENARBEIT

Eleven hundred years later these descriptions came to life in the Emblem tradition; but before that the image of the heart as a house for Jesus to live in seized the imagination of a late fifteenth-century German nun. Her name does not survive, but her work does.*

The Heart on the Cross, probably drawn for her own devotional purposes, shows a nun and the child Christ sitting happily inside a huge heart. Semivisible behind it, smiling down on the scene, is Christ on the cross. The nun has evidently climbed a ladder, each rung of which is labeled with the name of a virtue, in order to reach this happy union with God inside his heart. Her contemplation and imitation of Christ has paid off.

The cross is set like a tree in a garden; beautiful red poppies have sprung up where the drops of Christ's blood have fallen. It recalls the Song of Songs: "I will go up into the palm tree, and will take hold of the fruit thereof," which

---

*Jeffrey F. Hamburger has published an enchanting study, *Nuns as Artists*, without which I doubt I would have come across her.

The Heart on the Cross, by the anonymous nun. © *Staatsbibliothek zu Berlin— Preubischer Kulturbesitz, Handschriftenabteilung 417*

itself recalls the story of Bata. The picture demonstrates with elegant simplicity that as Christ came down to earth and suffered, before going back up to heaven, so we must make the effort to ascend and be with him there. Jeffrey Hamburger identifies an object dangling from the top rung as a seal: "Set me as a seal upon thy heart, as a seal upon thine arm, for love is strong as death." And here is the nun, sealed within his heart, in the cleft in his rock.

Banners spread out around the happy couple: "O heart, draw me to you, into you, and after you," they say, and "You are completely beautiful, my beloved," leading the educated on to the rest of the verse, which is not quoted in the picture but with which the nun would have been familiar: "The King hath brought me into his storerooms; we will be glad and rejoice in thee." Christ's heart is often referred to as his storehouse, full of his wealth, which is love. Our nun sits under a further banner: "That is my resting place, within which I will rest eternally without end." The heart, according to Hamburger, is "the bedchamber of the soul . . . mystical union [is] a foretaste of heavenly rest and repose." (Nietzsche put it: "The kingdom of heaven is a condition of the heart.") This is not an image of swooning sexual revelation; it is rather cuddly. The woman in Christ's heart looks very at home there, basking in the afterglow. The Christ child looks as if he's offering her a cup of tea (in fact it is a pyx, used to hold the host—tea of a kind).

Another drawing by this same nun makes the image even more explicit: the heart is portrayed as a house; steps lead up to a door in the side and the aorta sticks up like a chimney. Visible through a big picture window is the soul of the nun, sitting on Christ's knee, embraced by both him and God the Father, with the Holy Spirit alighting beside her. Sitting on the roof is the lamb;

The Heart as a House, by the anonymous nun. © *Staatsbibliothek zu Berlin—Preubischer Kulturbesitz, Handschriftenabteilung 417*

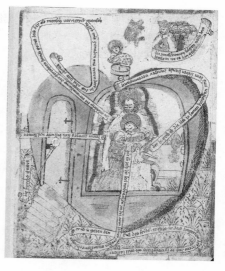

floating above is the biblical host of 144,000 virgins, led by St. Walburga. All around is a flowery meadow. Nothing could be sweeter. For a moment it looks almost like a gnome's house in a children's story. But look closer: a little dog, a Christian Cerberus, is half-visible by the steps, tethered to the closed door: he is the Fear of God. Not everybody can enter this little house. This time, the house is the nun's own heart, and she is completely at home. She has even dispensed with her habit—her end is achieved—and let her hair down. And this home is now sealed off—as she is sealed in the nunnery—and full of God. In one scroll of writing Christ is offering her the kiss of peace and the little finger of fidelity; the other scrolls speak of the transubstantiation of the soul from sinner to the noble image of Christ. The nun is sitting on the lap of God as Christ does, right in the middle of the Trinity; having entered Christ's heart, she has now taken Christ into her own bosom; she is the woman sitting with these male figures, imitating Mary (or possibly ousting her). The nun in real life must turn the picture round in her hands to read the scrolls which run around the edge. The Latin word *recordor,* from *cor* again, means to reflect yourself and recollect yourself: there is plenty of opportunity for that here.

These images are strongly reminiscent of St. Augustine, who in his *Confessions* referred to his heart as his innermost citadel, and offered this very clear and inviting vision of how man and God could unite:

> What place is there in me where my God can enter into me? . . . Lord my God is there any room in me which can contain you? . . . See the ears of my heart are before you, Lord. Open them and say to my soul, I am your salvation . . . The house of my soul is too small for you to come to it. May it be enlarged by you. It is in ruins: restore it. In your eyes it has offensive features, I admit it, I know it; but who will clean it up?

Augustine also referred to having used his heart as the temple of an idol, a false god: so it can be home to more than one's own soul and to God. For nuns and monks the heart could also be a convent or monastery. Texts called the *Herzklosterallegorien* (Heart Cloister Allegories) make this image clear: "A peaceful heart is a spiritual monastery in which God himself is the abbot," said one. "Resignation is the church, devotion the choir, meditation the cloister, remembrance of death the graveyard . . . chastity the dormitory." *De Claustro Animo,* by John of Soissons, went through each architectural feature in spiritual terms, starting in the wine cellar (Song of Songs again: "the Lord took me into his wine-cellar"). As the ancient Greeks used architectural mnemonics for learning rhetoric and law, a theater of memory, so the nuns and monks could remember their duties by looking around them. Learning by heart, in a way.

George Herbert's poems *The Church,* 500 years later, perform the same task. The collection opens with "The Altar," which even makes the shape of its subject matter:

> A broken altar, Lord, thy servant rears,
> Made of a heart, and cemented with tears:
> Whose parts are as thy hand did frame
> No workman's tool hath touch'd the same
> A HEART alone
> Is such a stone,
> As nothing but
> Thy pow'r doth cut
> Wherefore each part
> Of my hard heart,
> Meets in this frame
> To praise thy name
> That if I chance to hold my peace
> These stones to praise thee may not cease
> Oh let thy blessed SACRIFICE be mine,
> And sanctify this ALTAR to be thine.

(He refers here to Psalms 51:17; Deut. 27:2–6; Cor. 3:2–3; Ezek. 37:25–27; Luke 19–40 and no doubt many more.) A clearer image could hardly be made: the heart—the broken heart—is the place where communion between God and man takes place, and the poem itself is in the shape of the altar—the physical locus of Holy Communion during Mass. He continues with "The Church-floore," in which the building became one big sentence in sign language. Once again the heart is a microcosm: this time of the community in which the nuns lived, rather than of the world or the universe.

Another *Nonenarbeit* drawing shows our nun at a Eucharistic picnic/banquet, with Jesus presenting her to God the Father, and the Holy Spirit—a white dove—offering her the chalice on the picnic spread/altar. God is calling her beloved and inviting her to eat and get drunk with his love. Again, it all takes place inside a big heart. These pictures recall the *hortus inclusus* of the Song of Songs: paradisiacal, closed off, halfway to heaven. It ultimately represents the mystical union to which nuns in particular were so devoted and of which the Eucharist was so important a part. The taking of God into our own body is bound to mean something different to women than it would to a heterosexual man. Perhaps a woman's heart's desire is just to be in a private garden with her beloved, eating and drinking and achieving mystic union, like Adam and Eve, or Omar Khayyam: "A glass of wine and thou, beside me in the wilderness, the wilderness is paradise enow."

The heart of Jesus offered a way in which Christians—particularly females, it has to be said—could achieve this mystical union. The visions of the thirteenth-century Cistercian St. Mechtilde of Hackeborn were compiled by fellow nuns (including St. Gertrude) in the *Liber specialis gratiae.* In one, she sees Jesus with his heart open like a door. Inside is a circular room paved with gold, where she, Christ and Mary converse. He gives her a ring set with seven stones, each representing a stage of his love for mankind, the last of which is the opening of his heart on the cross. It seems she is marrying him within the chamber of his own heart. He describes the cross itself as the *thalamus,* the bridal bedchamber where he consummated his love for mankind:

> I entered the chamber of the cross; and just as the grooms gave their garments to the players, so I gave my clothing to soldiers, and my body to the crucifiers. Then I extended my arms with the hardest nails in your sweet embraces, singing to you in the chamber of love . . . I opened my heart to you so that you could enter as I, dying with you on the cross, suffered the sleep of love.

Here Christ, with his openness, the phallic nails and the orgasmic song, is like a woman welcoming a male lover.

The Lord showed her the most beautiful home, extremely lofty and wide, in which she saw another little house made from cedar wood, its interior covered over entirely with a layer of magnificent silver, in whose centre resided the Lord. She easily recognised this home as the heart of God . . . truly the innermost little dwelling represented that soul which, just as cedar trees are beyond putrefaction, is immortal and eternal. The door of this little house was placed towards the east and had a golden bolt, from which hung a golden chain, extending to the heart of God, so that when the door was opened, the chain could be seen to move the heart of God. The door, she understood, designated the desire of the soul; the bolt, its will; the chain, the true desire of God, which always comes before the desire and will of the soul and stimulates and draws it to God.

The descriptions of these little houses are reminiscent of the instructions God gave for the manufacture of the Ark of the Covenant, wherein God's law would be kept (as well as in the hearts of believers).

As well as living in the heart, St. Mechtilde and Christ exchange gifts of the heart: "If it please thee, I would make a delectable and seemly present to you of my heart," she says, and Christ answers: "Thou may never give me a dearer or more delectable present than to make a little house of thy heart, in which I might delight and dwell. This house shall have but a window through which you may speak to men and send forth my gifts." She had, she said, "*nimia devotio circa divinum Cor Jesu Christi*"—excessive devotion to the divine heart of Jesus Christ.

The heart also appeared as various household accoutrements. One image on which nuns meditated was that of the Christ child asleep in the cradle of their heart. The mystical sexuality of entering Christ's body—his heart—and him entering theirs (in the form of the Eucharist) and uniting with him is more than a love affair; it is a marriage with a baby, conceived in the heart (Augustine and Martin Luther also felt pregnant in the heart). Sometimes nuns kept Christ-baby dolls which they would care for and put to bed in exquisite gold cradles to demonstrate their undying love for him. The heart is easily identified with the womb (which in medieval allegory was itself seen as a chamber in a house); particularly Mary's womb, in which Christ, who was after all love personified, was conceived. Most women who have been pregnant know something of how love grows in the heart as the child grows in the womb. (Phantom pregnancies were not unknown among nuns for whom the metaphor proved more than just spiritual. The film *Agnes of God* deals with such a story.) In effect, these images re-create the family for women whose birth families are lost to them and who will never have earthly emotional and sexual fulfillment. In these pictures and visions, the nun is a mother with a husband and a baby, a kindly father-in-law and a nice little house, cut off from the difficulties of the world. There could almost be roses around the door. And the whole scene takes place inside her own heart.

THESE NUNS' HEARTS are pretty pure: what of the average sinner? A contemporary of the drawing nun, echoing St. Augustine, wrote in a sermon:

> You should prepare the house, so that when the Lord comes he finds it beautiful and well-prepared . . . That our heart is our Lord's house he says himself: "My father has given me this house as my proper inheritance."* This house we should prepare. In faith, we should drive out sin. And then we should decorate it with virtuous works, and our hearts will really bloom with virtuous thoughts.

In Mexico in 1574 we come across Fray Bernardino de Sahagún telling the surviving Aztecs to ask Christ: "How am I to adorn for you my soul, within which you wish to enter and lodge? For I know that first of all I need to drive out all my sins . . . Like one who maintains a household, I am to sweep well, I am to clean well."

George Herbert, a century later, wrote:

> A servant with this clause
> makes drudgery divine:
> Who sweeps a room as for thy laws,
> makes that and th'action fine.

Pádraic Pearse, writing in the early twentieth century, also used the image:

> What if the dream came true? And if millions unborn shall dwell
> In the house that I shaped in my heart, the noble house of my thought?

---

*Psalms 2:8 and 15:5.

And in "Christ's Coming":

> I have made my heart clean tonight
> As a woman might clean her house
> Ere her lover come to visit her:
> O Lover, pass not by!
> I have opened the door of my heart
> Like a man that would make a feast
> For his son's coming home from afar:
> Lovely Thy coming, O Son!

In the seventeenth century the image took off in the second type of Heart Emblem series. The first showed the heart being tried and tested (see page 130); here we see Jesus preparing the human heart to make it fit to receive him—and eternal life. First he purges it, then he illuminates it, then he unites with it by taking up residence; the charm and elegance with which he does so has the modern reader ricocheting between laughter and tears.

In the 1630s Henry Hawkins, a recusant Jesuit, produced a series in English called *The Devout Hart,* a translation from the Latin of F. St. Luzvic, and a book so delightful that I can only recommend the 1975 edition from the Scholar Press. The book was published in Rouen: it would have been written in secret and smuggled back to England for the comfort of oppressed British Catholics. Only one copy of this book with its plates has survived. The story tells of the young Jesus—Iesule, as he is sometimes called—and all he does for the heart that loves him. He saves it when "the world, the flesh and the divel" come assailing it; he knocks, "most amourous," at its door; he searches out the monsters lurking in its dark corners; he sweeps out the dust of sins; and he becomes "a living fountaine within the hart," with blood and holy water pouring from all his wounds, a divine *mannikin pis.** As a result the heart becomes a flourishing garden set about with roses. Jesus sings in the Quire of the hart and plays on the harp while angels sing (see page 259); finally he crowns his "dear hart with Palmes and Laurels," celebrates his heavenly nuptials therein

---

*The Christian heart was often a fountain—so-called by Plato because of the expulsion of blood; it developed into the fount of knowledge. In Islam the image takes a different form with the heart as a well, fed by five streams—the five senses—which bring in a lot of muck that needs cleaning out.

Jesus sweeping demons from the heart, from Hawkins's *The Devout Hart.* © *The British Library 1578/15*

and uses the heart as a mirror, to see a perfect reflection of himself.

Throughout, Iesule is small enough to treat the heart as a wendy house, or a big and much-loved pet; the accompanying text, however, is wild and poetic. "When IESVS enters into the hart, and therein pours his light, Good God? What foule, what horrible prodigies of vices the mind discovers there which the eye had never yet detected? I say when IESVS puts forth his rays, what bestial manners? What perfidiousness? What blots of an ungrateful mind?"

Darkness of heart has lasted as an image of internal fear and shame: from Hawthorne's *The Scarlet Letter* ("What other dungeon is so dark as one's own heart?") to the scene in William Golding's *Lord of the Flies* where Ralph mourns Piggy and weeps "for the darkness of man's heart," to Conrad's terrible *Heart of Darkness.* In *The Devout Hart* the darkness fades, "the clouds being vanished quite and slunke away," and the horror becomes apparent: the "swarme of lewd concupiscences which even here pester the miserable heart . . . O how I tremble to see how many . . . busy buzzing gnats, peevish wasps, ill-favoured butterflies! What a vast throng of worms there is, and what a stench from thence exhales to heavenwards!" But soon enough, with enough love and devotion and heavenly house-cleaning, the stench will be replaced by "the most sweet odour of the white and ruddye rose, which IESVS is," which "recreates and refreshes man and Angels," as Jesus, like Solomon, builds a throne for himself in the heart of his lover, and "there is nothing here that breathes not admirable sweetness to the smelling."

In fact Iesule treats this heart in much the same way as the mystic nuns treated his. This is Jesus as the man from the council come to get rid of the pests, a charming domestic view of the immortal battle between Good and Evil within man's soul. (When Patience and Wrath met in this battle, as

An angel chases demons from the heart in *The Heart of Man.*

recorded in Prudentius's *Psychomachia,* Patience won without even drawing her sword, because Wrath exhausted herself in a frenzied attack then, mad with frustration, seized a spear and struck herself through the heart with it. Which is pretty much like life, I find.) Hawkins went wholesale on domesticity and continued the theme with the sacred garden in his *Parthenia Sacra* (1633).

The emblematic approach is not dead. A theosophist text published in Madras in 1912 speaks of the "Five Symbols on the Razor-Edged Path to the Three Great Initiations." The first is the Flaming Sword, which pierces "every dark and hidden corner of his aspiring heart—till every sin has been pierced and slain . . . and clears the way for the blooming of the heavenly flowers of Love, Purity, Truth, Devotion, Gentleness and Service." (This text also offers a good example of the many duties Christ's heart had to fulfill: it pours forth an eternal river of glowing light and an eternal fount of pure joy; in it blossoms a flower of the heaven world called tender sympathy, whose root is love, which has its source in "the flaming Heart of Love, from whence the Master's heart caught fire . . . Another shining jewel is divinest patience, the gentle dove of patience nestling close down beside the giant courage . . . what sweet patience, this waiting for hard hearts to open . . . neither the Master, nor Buddha, nor Krishna, may force the soul's locked door.")

A booklet called *The Heart of Man,* published in South Africa in forty African languages in the early 1960s, gives ten tableaux of the various states of the heart of man. One shows the sinner's heart, full of animals representing weaknesses (the tortoise of laziness, the peacock of pride and so on), with a triumphant devil in residence and the Holy Spirit looking on sadly from outside; another shows the heart in search of salvation (an angel clutching a skull fights off the frog of avidity and the billy goat of carnal covetousness); there is also the repentant heart (full of fluttering flames of holy love, while nasty an-

The Heart Sutra in the shape of a pagoda: Chinese, ninth century. © *The British Library Or. 8210/S. 4289*

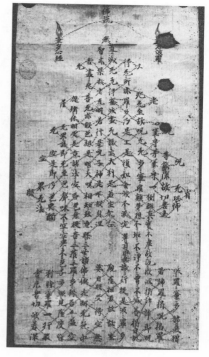

imals leave with their tails between their legs); and finally the heart as the Temple of God, festooned with grapes. Each heart has also in place of the aorta its owner's face expressing troubled sinfulness or beatific salvation. The use of the heart as an image, and as the part of the human being to which imagery speaks, has hardly changed in 300 years.

THE HOUSE IN THE EAST

The heart is not only a Christian house. The brevity of the Buddhist Heart Sutra (see this page) meant that it could be illustrated in ways which longer texts could not, and in China, Korea and Japan it was written out in the form of a pagoda, like concrete poetry or George Herbert's altar. Commissioning and copying texts, and placing them in, for example, pagodas and stupas, spreading the word, were considered acts of great merit, so perhaps this is a metaphysical and devotional pun, comparable to the nun's heart houses and the cordiform maps of the seventeenth century (see page 236). In all three examples—the pagoda, the house and the world—the heart is being used as microcosm represented as the macrocosm: both itself and the bigger place in which we—or God, or both—live.

In Hinduism, too, the heart was seen as God's house. The Chandogya Upanishad describes it thus:

> Within the city of Brahman, which is the body, there is the heart, and within the heart there is a little house. This house has the shape of a lotus and within it dwells that which is to be sought after, inquired about and realised.
>
> What, then, is that which dwells within this little house, this lotus of the heart? What is it that must be sought after, inquired about and realised?

Even so large as the universe outside is the universe within the lotus of the heart. Within it are heaven and earth, the sun, the moon, and the lightning and all the stars. Whatever is in the macrocosm is in this microcosm also.

All things that exist, all beings and desires, are in the city of Brahman; what, then, becomes of them when old age approaches and the body dissolves in death?

Though old age comes to the body, the lotus of the heart does not grow old. It does not die with the death of the body. The lotus of the heart, where Brahman resides in all his glory—that, and not the body, is the true city of Brahman.

In the Mundaka Upanishad we read: "Within the lotus of the heart he dwells, where the nerves meet like the spikes of a wheel. Meditate upon him as OM, and you may easily cross the ocean of darkness."

The image is of the body as a noisy city, the heart as a shrine in the center of that city within which God dwells. Peace and self-knowledge can be attained, and unity with the *atman* (the reality, as opposed to the apparent; the real self, God within the creature, the soul in the individual) is the start of traditional Hindu ritualistic worship.

Sometimes the heart is the city, and the city is the heart. Jerusalem—*al-Quds*—is the heart of Islam. In October 2000, as the Middle East peace process began to fall apart, Mustafa al-Bakri addressed Israel in *Al Osbo'u,* an Egyptian weekly: "Jerusalem is our life; it is the future for which we have been waiting for long decades, the soul without which a body would decay. Have you known anyone to surrender his soul?" The problem is the Israelis see it the same way.

THE HEART AS A LOCKED BOX

Of course, hearts have keys: all the better to lock them away from the world, to resist the appeals of God or a lover; and all the better, in the end, to surrender. Elton John offered up his key in "Don't Go Breaking My Heart": presumably if you give someone the key they don't need to break in. John Donne invited God to "Batter my Heart" (see page 316), spawning hundreds of pop songs about love knocking and thumping on the doors of hearts. The key and the keyhole are also charmingly sexual images of gaining access, particularly to love. A version appears in an Angolan folktale, "The Widow's Children," in which the key to someone's house is concealed inside his heart.

You can lock your heart up against marauders, or you can lock qualities inside it: "O most loving IESV," Hawkins wrote, "imbue my hart with the colors of Heaven, paint not shadows, but genuine and native images, snowy innocence, greenes of hope, the purest gold of charity, that so the closet of my hart may come to be a certain Cabinet or Reliquary of al perfections." In practical terms, the physical/spiritual heart is a most logical shape to hold and protect bits of dead loved ones: it's enclosable, lockable, full of love and religious virtue. Or one can lock up one's living self: an Alsatian nun, Clara von Ostren, wrote:

> I enclose myself every day in three locks: the first lock is the pure clear and maidenly heart of the noble Virgin Mary, against all temptations of the evil spirit; the second lock is the good heart of our beloved Lord Jesus Christ, against all temptations of the body; the third lock is the Holy Sepulchre, in which I hide myself with our Lord from the world.

Herbert again (in "Confession") wrote:

> . . . within my heart I made
> closets; and in them many a chest;
> And like a master in my trade,
> in those chests, boxes; in each box, a till:
> Yet grief knows all, and enters when he will.

This is "The Heart's Little Keys" (from Middle High German):

> You are mine, I am yours;
> Of that you should be certain.
> You are locked
> In my heart
> The little key is lost
> You must forever remain within.

It is a secular poem, but sacred and secular love shared a good deal of territory by the fifteenth century, and attempting to separate the two is an exercise

Donatello's *Miracle of the Miser's Heart.* © *Scala*

which parts of humanity have been attempting for thousands of years with remarkably little success.

One of the four miracles of St. Anthony of Padua was the story of the
miser's heart. A bronze tablet by Donatello, on the high altar in San Antonio,
Padua, tells the tale. A miser's corpse lies on a dissection table, split from his
guggle to his zatch, surrounded by a crowd of onlookers gazing in wonder—
dissections and anatomical knowledge were still in their early days—at the interior of man. But in the chest cavity, where the miser's heart should be, there
is nothing. St. Anthony, overlooking the proceedings, knows his Bible: "For
where your treasure is, there will your heart be also." In decent Christians,
their treasure should be their love; for the miser, it's his money. Way off to the
left we see a strongbox and, dangling by the trachea, the miser's heart being
lifted out of it.

Human dissection was legalized in Padua eighteen years before this tablet
was made in 1429, so it is possible Donatello witnessed one at a medical
school. Ghiberti wrote to him from Florence around the time the relief was
made, recommending "*avere veduto notomia*"—having seen anatomy. The
heart of the miser was the last of Donatello's bronze series of the Four Miracles to be cast. He didn't get it quite correct anatomically: the opening in the
miser's body is in the wrong place, and the presence of the trachea goes back
to Aristotle's notion that it led into the heart, and would therefore be the logical way for external things (money, for example) to enter it. (St. Anthony, by
the way, is the patron saint of finding lost things: "Holy Tony, look around,
something's lost and must be found.")

Daniel Cramer's Heart Emblems 32 and 16 hark back to St Anthony: in one, God releases the heart from being chained to a treasure chest: "if riches increase, set not your heart upon them"; in 32, a miser finds his heart in a chest of coins. This is another image shared with Islam: as al-Ghazzali wrote, "the treasuries of God are the hearts of the Prophets." A good Muslim should examine his heart every day to see if his spiritual capital has grown or declined, in case his heart has sneakily presented its own selfish desires as the will of God. There is an echo here of the ancient Egyptian heart which could speak against you.

In an Italian attic I recently came across *Il Cuore e il Portafoglio* (The Heart and the Wallet), a leaflet published in 1931 which explains that these two are constantly at odds—except when they both recommend that the dutiful citizens of Italy buy National Bonds at 5.78 percent. It is illustrated with a drawing of a besuited man being pulled in half by on the one hand a wallet with long muscly arms and on the other a winged heart. The happy unification at the end of the tale is symbolized by a fat, hollow heart overflowing with coins. Thus fascism warped the Bible to its own ends: the treasure in your heart was never meant to be your cash. As the Johnny Guitar Watson song goes: "Love of money is the root of all evil/ Think you'd better read first Timothy six."

THE HEART AS A MIRROR

Mankind is made in God's image, so God likes to see himself when he looks at us: we are mirrors to reflect him. We can see ourselves looking like him, and he can see himself in us. The mirror must be spotless—but of course in the well-kept house that is the devout heart, it will be.

Hawkins's Iesule uses the heart as a mirror, to see a perfect reflection of himself. The cleaning and the mirror are frequent biblical images. In the Hindu Brhadaranyaka Upanishad we learn that the cleaned human heart becomes "a polished mirror" in which God can see himself; "when all the desires he carries in his heart have been cast away, then the mortal becomes immortal and from that time onward he delights in Brahman." Above all in Sufism clean hearts reflect God: "In meditation they become mirrors," as Rumi put it.

The purpose of Allah's 124,000 prophets on earth—one of whom was Jesus—is to teach men how to purify their hearts in the crucible of abstinence. "The aim of moral discipline," wrote al-Ghazzali, "is to purify the heart from the rust of passion and resentment, till, like a clear mirror, it reflects the light of God." Hafiz places the image in a different context:

> Not one is filled with madness like to mine
> In all the taverns—my soiled robe lies here,
> There my neglected book, both pledged for wine.
> With dust my heart is thick, that should be clear,
> A glass to mirror forth the Great King's face . . .

In "The Broken Heart" John Donne uses the image steeped in erotic love:

> . . . what did become
> Of my heart when I first saw thee?
> I brought a heart into the roome,
> But from the roome, I carried none with mee:
> If it had gone to thee, I know
> Mine would have taught thine heart to show
> More pitty unto mee: but Love, alas,
> At one first blow did shiver it as glasse.
>
> Yet nothing can to nothing fall,
> Nor any place be empty quite,
> Therefore I thinke my breast hath all
> Those peeces still, though they be not unite;
> And now as broken glasses show
> A hundred lesser faces, so
> My ragges of heart can like, wish and adore,
> But after one such love, can love no more.

In Hungary, meanwhile, enthusiastically decorated gingerbread hearts, with a mirror set in the middle, are symbols of true love: lovers would swear devotion in the mirror. Similar ones are still found in Croatia, where they are called *licitarsko srce,* and given on Mother's Day.

3

THE HEART AS A BOOK

In the book of Exodus when God gave the law to Moses, "two tables of testimonie, tables of stone, written with the finger of God," he told him that the words of the law were to be kept in the hearts of men. The two tables of stone lent themselves easily to the two sides of the heart, and from this arose a strong and lasting image: the written-on heart, from which, along with the ancient beliefs that memory and knowledge lived in the heart, evolved the complex and charming idea of the heart as a book.

The law written in the heart appears over and over in the Old Testament: "I will put my law in their inward parts, and write it in their hearts"; "My son . . . let your heart keep my commandments . . . write them on the tablets of your heart." What is written in the heart cannot be erased. It is as indelible as if it were written in stone. (Even the philosopher Thomas Hobbes, to whom metaphor was anathema, believed that before the Ten Commandments natural reason was written in men's hearts.)

This fit in nicely with the idea conceived by the classical Greek poets that the self—memory, knowledge, destiny—was written on a text or scroll concealed within the body. The Egyptian *ib* could be tied up with strings like a papyrus scroll, so that its secrets didn't spill out. Plato spoke of writing in the soul and of "the marks branded on the soul by every evil deed." This reappears in the Old Testament: sin is written "with a pen of iron, and with the point of a diamond; it is graven upon the table of their heart, and upon the hornes of your altars." The ancient Egyptian heart spoke as a spiritual adviser. All this contributed to the biblical and Islamic idea of human hearts revealing, after death, the record of their owners' sins and virtues.*

---

*In Rome reading and writing metaphors were common for thought, as a swift tour of the vocabulary of mental activity shows: "evolve" comes from the Latin to unroll, "explicate"

Amor shown writing on the heart, from Harvey's *Schola Cordis*. © *The British Library 11623.a.45*

So when Jesus came along, as the word made flesh, the image of a precise piece of flesh with the word on it was revived. (In the Gospel parable of the seeds and tares, the word of God is the seed which grows in the heart and brings forth good fruit. Thus are the metaphors mixed.)

In the opinion of St. Paul, who knew a good image when he saw one, the heart held both ancient law and the revelation of Christ. It was spiritual, and fleshly too, as befitted an organ so closely connected with an incarnate god. At the same time the individual conscience of man lay in his heart. "You yourselves are our letter of recommendation, written on your hearts, to be known and read by all men . . . written not with ink but with the Spirit of the living God, not on tablets of stone but on the tablets of the human heart," he wrote to the Corinthians, introducing the notion of the letter and the spirit of the law: a personal moral responsibility, based in the heart. By rescuing the physicality of the heart, St. Paul provided Christianity with a metaphor that would run and run. The heart as a book was an elegant and central part of this.

The idea that the deeds of the living were recorded in writing by God and his scribes, to be opened after death for ultimate judgment, occurs in ancient Egypt, in the Tablets of Zeus, in the Bible (in Daniel, Revelation and the Psalms) and in the Qur'an. The Book of the Dead, the Book of Life, the writing in the heart of the Old Testament and the opened books of judgment all paved the way for the allegory of the book of the heart. The allegory offered many useful details. The wax of the heart must be smoothed; the papyrus of the heart washed clean (as in baptism and the Egyptian washing of the heart)

---

from to unfold, "complicated" from wrapped up. "Implicit" and "explicit" also come from *plicare*, to fold. "Character" is from the Greek *kharakter*—impression, as in impression made on a wax tablet in writing.

of previous beliefs and previous sins, so that Christian law could be entered (remember Marguerite-Marie Alacoque cleaning her blank canvas). The technical terms of writing, reading, inscribing, correcting, recording and so on gradually became commonplace in prayer and contemplation. John Chrysostom, John of Egypt, Basil of Caesarea and the Desert Fathers of the fourth and fifth centuries found the heart as a book exceptionally useful both as an image for converting others and for the daily duty of moral self-examination. St. Ambrose of Milan emphasized the individuality of the book of heart, gave it a neat and usable name—"*liber cordis*"—and passed it on to St. Augustine, who wrote from the heart, about his heart's memories and morality. "*Coram te cor meum et recordatio mea,*" he wrote, addressing God: "my heart and my memory are open before you," using three words out of seven which are based on *cor,* the Latin for heart. Augustine had his magnificent conversion—change of heart—while reading. His *Confessions* could be given to God on Judgment Day—they are, in this sense, his heart.

"If you have lived righteously," St. Ambrose wrote, the word of God would remain written in your heart. "See that you do . . . not erase it and write with the ink of your evil deeds." For St. Paul, God wrote the heart; for St. Ambrose, we get to write it too; for St. Augustine, God's writing could be renewed by grace. It has become a kind of developing narrative, an autobiography.

BOOKS OF THE HEART AND HEART-SHAPED BOOKS

Mostly the book of the heart was an idea which anyone educated enough could use to marshal their thoughts and feelings. By the fifth century A.D. the book of the heart had become physical. John Climacus saw monks carrying little texts in which they would record their good and evil thoughts and deeds. This, as Eric Jager points out in his excellent *Book of the Heart,* introduces the idea that writing "is a valuable means of self discovery." Thomas Keneally, author of *Schindler's Ark,* said something very similar: that it's foolish to want writers to write about what they know, because until they've written it, they don't know it. God, angered by his people's idolatry of the Golden Calf, broke the first set of tablets that he had given Moses and had Moses write out the law himself on a new set. We know better what we have written down.

When God sent his new book down to Muhammad in the seventh century A.D., it fit nicely with existing heart/book imagery: "There are guardians over you, honoured recorders, who know all that you do . . . it is a book written comprehensively . . . his book of record . . . Allah knows best what they keep hidden in their hearts."

By medieval times books had become the two-sided objects opening down the middle with which we are familiar now. The correlation was too good to miss: two-sided biblical tablets, two-sided heart, two-sided book. Medieval artists took this combination of imagery a step further and came up with a pictorial image of the book of the heart: the two-sided book and the two-sided human heart combining like an openable diptych. It could be represented in painting or illumination; and it could be actually made, in which case it would actually hold words, as the heart is meant to. Like the hearts within hearts and boxes within boxes of medieval saintly visions, you could have heart books within heart books within heart books, embodying all those qualities of secrecy and union. A fifteenth-century codex from St. Augustine's *Confessions* shows him in a miniature, enclosed in the opening letter of the book: he is sitting holding a pen and a heart and pondering over an open book—perhaps the *Confessions*—on his desk (see page 219). The heart as a book was replete with allusions: clean vellum was piety, the lock was secrecy. Its accuracy was a reflection of your care and attention; reading it was a duty to God. In the thirteenth century Richard de Ste. Victoire put it like this:

> Truly our hearts, which we say are figured by parchment, and in which this writing of the spirit is inscribed, are prepared by bitter penitence in the same way as material skin. They are stretched by regular abstinence, they are scraped by removing all carnality, and they are formed into quires by unflagging constancy.

Other versions offer the parchment of pure conscience: the knife of the Fear of God scrapes "all the roughness of sin and vice" from it; the pumice of Heavenly Desire makes it smooth; fine particles of the chalk of Holy Thoughts whiten it. The devil is a wicked scribe who will try to rub out the good that you write and insert the deadly sins instead, sabotaging the desk of tranquility-of-heart, the ink of humility, and the double nib of the love of God and thy neighbor. Once properly written, the book of the heart must be locked up to keep it secret and safe. The idea came to the fore during the twelfth century, when books, silent reading and the individual were all invented.

St. Augustine enclosed in the opening letter of his *Confessions.*
The British Library, Harley 3087

And what was written in this imaginary book? On one page, the laws pertaining to the love of God; across from that, the laws pertaining to the love of thy neighbor. On one side, the page of sinners, your sins and how you love them; on the other, the page of penitence, your sins and how you regret them. There is scope for moral ambivalence, for present and past, for temptation and redemption. You could also list your good deeds. You should concentrate on your own book and not poke about in other people's. By writing and reading this book, man comes to know himself. As the Delphic Oracle said: *gnothe te*

"Belle, Bonne, Sage, Plaisante . . . ," the heart-shaped love song by
Baude Cordier, c. 1400. © *Musée Condé/ Bridgeman Art Library*

afton; nosce te ipsum, know thyself. By turning the pages, a person has a chance
to change. Weeping over your sins helped to erase the wickedness of the world;
the tears washed sins away from the heart.* It was an internal prayer book, an
object of contemplation carried within the body; it was free, it required concentration, it was humble. After the Fourth Lateran Council declared that all
Christians should confess at least once a year, it became a kind of moral diary
of self-knowledge, available to Everyman.

---

*Dolere—to weep; *delere*—to erase; is this a kind of self-baptism?

Another version of the book of the heart recorded romantic love stories. Twelfth-century troubadours sang of wounds, scars, pictures and marks left on the heart; later this became writing. Cupid's arrow could be a pen (as God's was when the Holy Spirit wrote Jesus in Mary's womb); *calamus* in Latin can mean both pen and arrow, and there is an obvious connection between an arrow and a quill. It could be a phallus too, and a heart could be a womb or genitals (see page 126). Cupid, after all, pierced Ovid's heart with an arrow with his name written on it, as inspiration for his love poetry. The fletched arrow becomes the feathered quill, the writing becomes the wound, the piercing changes the heart. According to the troubadour Sordello, the arrow in his heart was what made him sing. Just as God's law could affect your behavior, so could the image of the lover:

> Love engraved
> Your features in an image
> Cut deeply into my heart
> And so I've handed myself over
> To do whatever pleases you
> Finely and firmly through all my life.

This is a nice and very early example of religious imagery being used for specifically erotic ends, rather than a sexual love for God. This marks the beginning of the worship of idealized romantic love now so taken for granted.

Text itself first took on the shape of the heart around 1400, in *The Chantilly Codex*: a love song, both lyrics and music, was beautifully and decoratively written out in the form of a scallop-topped, pointy-bottomed heart. Thus the shape becomes part of the declaration made in the song:

> Beautiful, good, wise, and elegant lady
> On this very day when the year begins anew
> I make you the gift of a new song in my heart
> Which presents itself to you.

So the poet has a song in his own heart; he puts the song on paper in the shape of a heart; and he gives the whole thing to the beloved: an elegant conceit.

It was only a matter of time before heart-shaped books appeared. Some survive, containing prayer, poetry and recipes: versions of religion, love and domesticity. Around 1485 a Dutch painter known only as the Master of St. Gudule produced two very similar paintings of gentlemen with heart-shaped books: one is reading; one, depicted with a pen and inkwell, seems to have been writing too. Both paintings have churches in the background. They could simply be straightforward portraits, showing cordiform prayer books such as the Book of Hours which is now in the Bibliothèque Nationale in Paris. Or they could refer to the metaphorical book of the heart: the man's own internal spiritual record. Thomas à Kempis had just written: "Write my words upon your heart and earnestly reflect upon them"; "heart prayer" was becoming widely known and accepted. Perhaps an evocation of St. Augustine was intended, with the pen and the heart and the book. The heart book is clearly associated with the man's prayer; at the same time it is the man himself. The spine is down the middle, so the book opens out to make one heart; the writing is visible but illegible. He is open but mysterious.

The *Hjertebogen* (the Heart Book) is another example of the book itself. It was made by Albert Muus, the royal chef of Denmark, between 1553 and 1555, bound in leather and decorated with gilt. It contains an anthology, which includes the earliest collection of Danish ballads. Like the books in the paintings, open flat it forms the shape of a scallop-topped heart. Anna, Electress of Saxony and a Danish princess, had a heart-shaped book of prayers and household remedies bound together in 1590; she may have gotten the idea from the *Hjertebogen*. The late fifteenth-century *Chansonnier* made for Jean de Montchenu, a noble cleric, has a complete heart on either side of the spine. Open, it makes the shape of two hearts, united at the spine (an image of romantic love, perhaps—individual yet connected, open to each other even when closed to others). The songs are love songs, full of references to both hearts and writing. The delicacy of the musical notes on the stave, the allegorical animals in the margins and the perfect miniatures—including one of the god of love shooting a victim in the heart—all enclosed in a red leather heart make it quite beautiful, both conceptually and actually: a heart full of music and beauty. The wonderfully named sixteenth-century poet Tempesta Blondi had a heart-shaped volume of lute tunes in which he wrote, over a period of years, love poems and some personal records. The ever-adaptable heart makes perfect sense as a shape to carry all these different kinds of writings.

Lucas Cranach painted a heart-shaped altarpiece, folded on hinges down the middle: on the outside one side of the heart shows Adam and Eve at the

Portrait of a Young Man, by the Master of the View of St. Gudula,
late fifteenth century. © *The National Gallery, London*

Fall; on the other is the Annunciation—the failure of marriage and the purest
of marriages. Closed, it presses the example of Mary, as pictured in the Annunciation, upon humanity just as humanity is about to fall. Inside the heart,
when it is opened, we see portrayed the Passion of Christ on the cross. The
shape of the altarpiece is transformed, as the hearts of those who look at it are
meant to be transformed.

The Extraction of the Heart of St. Ignatius, by Botticelli, fifteenth century. Christ's name was written on the heart, "all of letters of golde." © *Scala*

WRITING ON THE HEART

The next step is actual writing on an actual human heart. It happened in literature: Dante's *La Vita Nuova,* which can be seen as a book of the heart, ends with his lady's name being written in his heart by his thoughts and his sighs. Fiametta, in Boccaccio's *Amorosa Visione,* takes the phallic pen herself, opens up her lover's breast and writes her name in gold upon his heart—something of a gender revolution. But for the real thing we must turn to the saints.

St. Eulalia saw the scars of her martyrdom as "Thy name . . . written on me"; St. Cassian, a fourth-century teacher, was stabbed to death by his pupils, using the sharp-nibbed styluses with which they had written on wax tablets and cracking jokes about how he had taught them to write. By the fourteenth century tales abounded of the hearts of early Christian martyrs marked with the sign of the cross or the name of Christ: it was seen to evoke the wound, to imitate the Passion, to mark the heart as God's property, to demonstrate that God was truly impressed on this heart, to create a quality relic and tool for conversion and to challenge the romantic and carnal heart tropes of troubadour love songs and poetry.

St. Ignatius of Antioch was an early martyr. Throughout his "dyvers grete turmentis" he called on Christ's name: "I hafe that name wretten in my herte, and therfor I may not sese fro calling ther-uppon." Sure enough, when he died they "tuke hys harte oute of his body & cut it sonder be the myddeste" and there was Christ's name, "all of letters of golde." He was recalling a passage from Jeremiah: "Because the word of the Lord was made a reproach unto me . . . his word was in mine heart, as a burning fire in my bones." Likewise Psalm 119: "Thy word I have hid in mine heart; that I might not sin against thee." In another version his heart was chopped into bits to make more relics, and each one bore the name of Christ in gold—like a manuscript reproduced in order to reach more people; a kind of divine photocopying.

Santa Maria Maddalena de' Pazzi (St. Mary Magdalen of the Madmen) was visited in the early 1600s by St. Augustine, who wrote on her heart "*verbum caro factum est*"—the word is made flesh. He wrote it twice, once in blood, once in gold. Where St. Teresa's heart was pierced by an angel's dart, St. Maria Maddalena's is inscribed by Augustine's feathered quill; the sexual overtones are quite apparent, and were made explicit by Bernini and Sagrestani, Renaissance artists who reveled in divine orgasms.

Ted Hughes used this imagery of flesh and judgment, writing and wounding, pen and arrow, in *Birthday Letters,* his poems about his marriage to Sylvia Plath. In "The Cast" Hughes describes Plath's words and accusations against her father as arrows piercing him as he endures a stake not through the heart but upright, and him tied to it. I would quote this for you but Hughes decreed that the poem should only ever appear in the context of the collection, so I can't show you directly how exquisitely, and painfully, he uses the image (it's on page 179 of the paperback edition).

It is painful for the heart to be written on, engraved, branded; and painful to be opened up and read. This is another form of the creative wound through which love and communication (literally, in the case of Ovid's poetry) pass. Piercing the heart with the arrow picks up another role: if the arrow is a pen, and the heart is full of blood, then blood can be ink and the heart an inkwell. Sure enough, from the seventeenth century heart-shaped inkwells abounded. (For Frida Kahlo, remember, the heart was a pile of paint.)

Henry Suso took both the male and the female role in his heart-writing experience: piercing and being pierced, his body the page and his heart's blood the ink. Here it is, a supreme example of physical and emotional, erotic and religious fervor, in his own words (in the third person):

The Ecstasy of St. Teresa, as the angel prepares to pierce her heart, by Bernini, seventeenth century. © *Santa Maria della Vittoria / Bridgeman Art Library*

He cried out: "Oh sweet lord! If only I could devise some love token that would be an everlasting badge of love between thee and me, an authentic document that I am all thine and thou art the only beloved of my heart, written in letters which my fickleness can never erase." In his burst of fervour, he pushed back his scapular, bared his bosom, took a sharp stylus, and called on

God to help him, saying: "Almighty God, give me strength this day to carry out my desire, for thou must be chiselled onto the core [the heart] of my heart." Then stabbing the stylus backward and forward, in and out of his flesh, he engraved the name of Jesus (IHS) over his heart. Blood gushed out of the jagged wounds and saturated his clothing. The bliss he experienced in having a visible pledge of oneness with his truelove made the very pain seem like a sweet delight.

One of his female followers embroidered the IHS in scarlet on pieces of cloth, and had him hold them to his devotional scar, and passed them around: another medieval photocopying system. Suso's early heart tattoo has all the attributes of the modern tattooed love heart: the name of the beloved written on a banner, the blood, the arrow/quill. It also prefigures teenage girls picking out the name of their boyfriend on their arm with compass-point and pencil lead: physical self-abuse, devotion, a longing for eternal oneness.

The tattooed love heart is an all-encompassing emblem. It's Catholic, devoted to Mary, with its blades of sorrow and its roses, its banners like a Mexican *retablo,* its spear of Longinus letting out a fountain of love. It's Protestant, with its graphic shape and cartoon quality. It's ancient, with naughty Cupid's random arrow and undertones of death and sacrifice. It's Old Testament, with its echo of Deuteronomy: "And thou shalt love the Lord the God with all thine heart and with all thine soule and with all thine might. And these words which I command thee this day shall be in thine heart." It's Augustinian, with its arrowed quill inscribing the name of the beloved. It's sexual, with its long hard piercing of a soft red recipient. It is in fact a crossroads of religious and romantic love, which is why you can have either MOTHER or LULA MAE written in the banner without it being improper: for once the Madonna and the whore belong in the same place. It is the heart doing what it does best: being both.

St. Marguerite-Marie Alacoque, an-

A HEART TATTOO

From the *Guardian,* November 10, 1999: "A man from Bristol has had the name of the heart surgeon who saved his life tattooed on his arm." The life-saver is in practice the life-giver, i.e., God, and worthy therefore of being united forever with the saved, in writing on the saved body. I don't know whether the tattoo was heart-shaped. I hope so.

other devotee of sadomasochistic sanctity, had written on her heart, among other things, the word JESUS. Mary Tudor we all know about: Calais, they say—or "callous," if you prefer the *1066 And All That* version. As Robert Browning wrote:

> Italy, my Italy!
> Queen Mary's saying serves for me
> (When fortune's malice
> Lost her Calais):
> "Open my heart and you will see
> Graved inside of it, 'Italy.'"

In the twentieth century the heart-surgery pioneer Christiaan Barnard said that written on his was: "Owen Harding Wangensteen—father, teacher, friend."

The seventeenth-century emblematists loved the image of the heart as a book. Christopher Harvey introduced his *School of the Heart*: "Bend thine eye inward, consider where thine heart doth lie . . . looke what thou hast writ thyself in thine own booke, thy conscience: ere set thou thyself to school." John Donne wrote of the individual's "manual, his bosom, his pocket book, his Vade Mecum, the Abridgement of all Nature and all Law, his own heart and conscience." This is recalled again in Harvey's emblem *The Table of the Heart*, where Amor is seen writing on the heart with a quill (see page 216).

George Herbert unites the broken and the written-on heart in this poem:

> IESU is in my heart, his sacred name
> Is deeply carved there: but th'other week
> A great affliction broke the little frame,
> Ev'n all to pieces, which I went to seek:
> And first I found the corner, which was *I*,
> After, where *ES*, and next where *U* was graved.
> When I had got these parcels, instantly
> I sat me down to spell them, and
> That to my broken heart he was *I ease you*,
> And to my whole is *IESU*.

And, recalling the heart as a house as well:

The Passion

Since blood is fittest, Lord, to write
Thy sorrows in, and bloody fight;
My heart hath store, write there, where in
One box doth lie both ink and sin
That when sin spies so many foes
Thy whips, thy nails, thy wounds, thy woes,
All come to lodge there, sin may say,
No room for me, and fly away.
Sin being gone, oh fill the place,
And keep possession with thy grace;
Lest sin take courage and return,
And all the writings blot or burn.

It was not an exclusively Christian image. In this poem Rumi uses a handful of imagery familiar in the West from the Bible: the heart as a tablet for writing, as a fountain or spring, as a box or container, and as the source of a person's deeper truths.

There are two kinds of intelligence; one acquired
As a child in school memorises facts and concepts
From books and from what the teacher says,
Collecting information from the traditional sciences
As well as from the new sciences
With such intelligence you rise in the world.
You get ranked ahead or behind others
In regard to your competence in retaining
Information. You stroll with this intelligence
In and out of fields of knowledge, getting always more
Marks on your preserving tablets.
There is another kind of tablet, one
Already completed and preserved inside you.
A spring overflowing its springbox. A freshness
In the centre of the chest. This other intelligence
Does not turn yellow or stagnate. It's fluid,
And it doesn't move from outside to inside
Through the conduits of plumbing-learning.

> This second knowing is a fountainhead
> From within you, moving out.

This last couplet echoes the Gospel teaching that man is defiled not by what goes into him (food and so on) but by what comes out: bad words, evil thoughts.

The book of the heart could contain law, diary, prayer, poems, love stories, music, memories, autobiography, thoughts, moral records and accounts, secrets, desires, the ledger of our conscience (*Bridget Jones's Diary* is a classic book of the heart). It can be known only by ourselves and by God or the lover. For Thomas Watson, the seventeenth-century divine, writing the year that Charles I was executed, God read our hearts as if he were dissecting them:

> Brethren, did our hearts stand where our faces do, this would be a day of blushing, we would be ashamed to look one upon another; remember God hath a key for the heart . . . We have here a Map of God's Knowledge . . . all things are naked. Some expositors render it *Excoriate* . . . it is a metaphor for taking off the skin of any beast, which doth then appear naked. Thus our hearts are said to be naked; they lye open to the eye of God . . . they are naked and open . . . the word alludes to the cutting up of Sacrifices under the Law . . . or may allude to an Anatomie, where there is a dissection and cutting up of every part . . . Such an anatomy doth God make in the soul; an Heart-Anatomy: He doth cut up the inward parts and makes a difference; This is Flesh, that is Spirit; this is Faith, that is Fancie; this is Grace, that seems to be so . . .

It is impossible, reading this, not to think of Donne's "naked thinking heart": the word and the flesh laid open for sacrifice and self-knowledge.

Is it any wonder that, as Cupid recolonized the heart, and as medieval romance and Renaissance epic moved into the novel, the read and written-on heart became and remained a much-used symbol?

A WORD ON MAPS

Medieval maps were not geographical so much as of a specific cultural and religious world; maps were a way of seeing things at a certain time in history.

A WORD ON WORDS

The English word "heart" comes from the Latin *cor* and the Greek *kardia*, which are the same as the Sanskrit *hrid*. The letters "h" and "k" are related, according to Grimm's Law. Dr. Boyadjian quotes a researcher called Pictet who reports that *krid/kurd* in Sanskrit means to leap, and leads through *krid* to *hrid*, to *kardia*, to heart: so the heart is the thing that leaps (as indeed is the hart, the same hart which pants for cooling streams, so pants my soul, oh Lord, for thee). It is a very nice and extremely probable idea that the heart is named for its movement: the beating, the transforming, the uniting—the heart is in many ways active. I would like to believe that the Italian *lepre*, meaning hare, is somehow connected with English leaper, as in leprechaun, a little creature that leaps out at you. But this is wishful thinking, not etymology.

The Arabic word *qalb* is itself a root from which, as is the way with Arabic, other words—sometimes obvious, sometimes surprising, often poetic —develop. From the root of the beating heart, *qalb*, branches *qalab*, to overthrow; *maqlab*, a dirty trick or a rubbish dump; *maqloub*, upside down; *mutaquallib*, changeable; *inquilab*, a coup. Changing and moving is a fundamental part of the heart's identity: the pulse changes; the heartbeat (*debdeb, lubdub*) suggests something flopping over in a constant pulsating movement. It also works beautifully as an emotional and spiritual image: the heart has to be in the right place, and upright, but it is constantly flexing and changing and desiring, pushed and pulled by the emotions that inhabit it, constantly temptable, redeemable, transformable and transforming.

This is central to how we use the image of the heart: each use incorporates the possibility of its own opposite. Warm-hearted, cold-hearted; soft-hearted, hard-hearted; big-hearted, heartless; heart in the right place, heart in mouth or boots; stout-hearted, chicken-hearted; lighthearted, heavy-hearted. "At the heart of all things is the germ of their overthrow," as Ahdaf Soueif put it; Hafiz wrote:

O Hafiz, why complain of the grief of absence?
Union lies hidden in absence
As the light of dawn
lies hidden in the darkness of the night.

Lands and races far away were neither relevant nor accessible: the voyage was within, and the map was an object for guidance on a spiritual plane.

When the Europeans of the age of discovery began to consider geography, mapmakers discovered the limitations of their knowledge, and they used a cocktail of imagination (here be monsters), likelihood and mathematics to deal with the problem. Trying to fit ever-expanding knowledge, gridlines of latitude and longitude, and the surface of a complete sphere on to a plane was a practical and intellectual challenge which provoked some wonderful solutions. The world could be mapped on a modified cone projection: take a cone, snip its tip off, slice down one side and lay out flat. Or as a disc, or two discs, or a long eye shape, a wide extended oval or six segments—gores—as if to be cut out and pasted on to a globe. The names are magical: azimuthal or zenithal, equidistant, stereographic, orthographic, gnomonic, homoetheric, first and second Ptolemaic, trapezoidal and based on the projection of Marinus of Tyre. Or cordiform: heart-shaped.

First came the pseudocordiform projection. If the grid of the modified cone is extended and the corners rounded off, it becomes a wide, splayed heart shape. This wide projection was used as early as 1507 and as late as 1564, when Abraham Ortelius used the extra space it allowed to include puffing wind heads, cannibals dismembering each other (in Brazil), a caravan of camels galloping across Tartary and a flying turtle off Greenland. This wide heart shape was also used in the famous Fool's Cap Map of 1590 (there was an earlier one in Paris in 1575 as well), where the map is the face of a belled and tasseled fool, and the useful bits of information inscribed include: *caput Helleboro dictum*—"I purify my head with Hellebore" (which was said to cure madness); *stultorum infinitus est numerus*—"The number of stupid people is infinite"; and "Who doesn't have ears next to each other?" On the fool's little cymbals is written "vanity of vanities, all is vanity," referring presumably to the voice as a clashing cymbal, in Corinthians. This fool is a Christian allegory; the heart shape merely gives it another level. On a badge is written: "*Stultus factus est omnis homo*" (Every man is made stupid) and, just to make it crystal clear, "*Nosce te ipsum*" (Know thyself). This map is mentioned in Burton's *Anatomy of Melancholy*, when he observes that "all the world is mad."

The first recognizably heart-shaped map, plump and compact with a pointed tip, was a beautiful double-sheet woodcut designed by Oronce Fine in

Peter Apian's cordiform map of 1530. © *The British Library, c.7.c.16*

Paris in 1519 for Francis I, though not printed until 1534. The heart shape took off: in 1530 Peter Apian made one which is very similar to Fine's and probably based on it. It has two little portraits at the top: one of Ptolemy, on whose ancient maps it is based, holding an empty heart shape containing an oval world map; the other of the explorer Amerigo Vespucci, holding a corresponding heart shape with an empty oval. The message is clear: this map combines the ancient geography of the Old World with the modern exploration of the New World.

As Fine and/or Apian extended the gridlines of Ptolemy's map in order to include the new discoveries, the heart shape probably emerged of its own accord. At the same time, the use of the internal, hidden, fundamental heart as a template for the wide, open, new, discoverable world was a conceit which must have appealed to a Renaissance mind. It is just another form of microcosm and macrocosm; of relating the individual to the universal and the inner to the outer. A world the same shape as our own heart is at once familiar and mysterious. A world made of a heart is at once metaphysical and sensible. God created the word, the word was God, the word became the world, and what could be nicer than the world being, for example, God's heart? It fits nicely with the cleft in the rock, in which Jesus' body with its wound is a part of the landscape. We've had the heart as a house and a storehouse; we will see it as an enclosed garden wherein the faithful gather for sublime union with God; we've seen it written on; we will see it plowed and sown, fertile and sprouting fruit—the heart as a whole world is a logical extension of all that imagery. Hearts still quake; in the seventeenth century they had heartquakes as the earth has earthquakes.

In addition, the connection between the inward journey of self-knowledge and devotion and the actual journey, of pilgrimage or voluntary exile, had existed since classical times, with Scandinavian and Arab (Sindbad) versions, and Christianized texts such as St. Brendan's *Navigatio* (a fifth-century tale written in the ninth century) and the Arthurian quest for the Holy Grail. When it became apparent, in the age of discovery, that heaven was not on earth, not second on the right past Jerusalem, another location was needed. Some placed heaven in the sky; some (the more educated) decided that "within"—in the heart—was a safer and more interesting bet.

When in the seventeenth century Thomas Watson referred to the heart as a map for God to know us by, it was not an original image. The heart-shaped maps of the previous century incorporated the mysticism of the medieval religious maps alongside Ptolemy's geography and the knowledge of the explorers. Hendrik Niclaes, leader of the religious community called the Family of Love, produced a kind of cordiform map that had no connection whatsoever with physical geography, yet is a map of a world as he saw it. The print, from his *Huis de Liefde* (1576), shows a Progress of the Soul taking place entirely inside a heart. A righteous skeleton, armed only with the shield of Hope and accompanied by the warrior Intelligence (armed with the sword of the

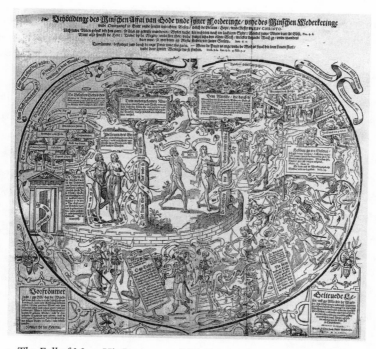

The Fall of Man, His Progress and His Return, from *Huis de Liefde,* by Hendrick Niclaes, 1576.

Spirit—*Geest*), starts from the tree of knowledge, where Adam and Eve are in the process of falling, battles through a forest of vices, and passes through the "strait gate"—a stylish portico with Doric columns—in the wall which separates it from the forest of virtues. He ends up under the tree of God, where a new and reformed man and woman stand lovingly entwined. This heart is divided into two sections, two chambers, with a wall between them: one is heaven (forest of virtues), one is earth (forest of vices). Arguments about how many chambers the heart had were still continuing at this time, and two was not an unorthodox estimate. A biblical quote accompanies the image: "Because strait is the gate, and narrow is the way, which leadeth unto life, and few there be that find it." (Matthew 7:14—the strait and narrow of familiar phrase was originally the narrow—as in Straits of Gibraltar—not the straight.) It seems strange yet somehow inevitable that the valves between the chambers of the heart should have become a metaphor for the difficulty of achieving a place in heaven. And it's true, too, though Niclaes can have known nothing of it, that stenosis—narrowing—of the valves can preclude the possibility of continued, let alone eternal, life (at least on earth). That said, given the date, it's more likely that Niclaes would have taken Galen's septal pores as the model for his strait gate from chamber to chamber of the heart: gates so strait that, as it turned out, they didn't exist at all. There is another possibility here too: in medieval times Christ's heart's wound was known as the gate of heaven, "the well of eternal lyffe." So this can be seen as the wound, playing its role actually inside the heart.

And then there were the double cordiform projections in which the world was presented as two hearts, lying as it were on their sides and joined at the tip like Siamese twins. This form was made by Fine in 1531, surrounded by mermaids and cherubs, and by Gerald Mercator in 1538, an important map which showed North America as separate from Asia, setting off an argument that ran for 200 years.

4

ROSES, TREES AND FRUIT

The rose and the heart have a special relationship, a common history through religion into romance. The rose is as sweet as Christ's heart; its thorns as sharp and bitter as his heart's wound. Like his heart, it holds the exquisite sorrow, the agony and ecstasy at once. It is blood-red and transient; it evokes great love and great suffering. It is a Christian image and an image from courtly love, both religious and worldly. It gives sex to sacred verse and spirituality to love poetry. It is wonderfully beautiful; it carries the odor of sanctity (even after death, if you dry it); it lives and then it dies; it is reborn over and over.

THE ROSE GARDEN

A rosary, a string of beads representing a circuit of prayers, or the ninety-nine names of Allah, is named for a rose garden. Mary—the Rose without Thorns, the rosebush from whose virgin stock Christ grows—plucked roses from the mouths of praying saints and made chaplets of them; saints made chaplets of prayers and crowned Mary with them. Mary's Immaculate Heart is often portrayed with a chaplet of roses entwining it as the chaplet of thorns entwines that of her son: I have a plastic plate showing the pair of them like proud siblings in a double-frame of graduation photographs, displaying his 'n' hers visible hearts, mix 'n' match roses and thorns. My local religious tat stall also has a plastic statue labeled "Maria Rosa Mistica": instead of the heart that usually gleams from the front of her robe, this Mary displays a single rose, a mystical corsage.

On Christmas Day 1280 a nun called Christina von Hane

> had a spiritual vision in which the most beloved little child Jesus was playing . . . and all about him the most beautiful roses. They were not earthly

Madonna and Child with Four Saints, by Piero della Francesca, fifteenth century: note her rose. © *Clark Art Institute / Scala*

roses, they were heavenly . . . There she saw the tender most beautiful child standing in front of the altar in a cradle, and it was blanketed with a cover of roses, and on each and every rose petal was written: "Pater Noster."

In 1667 a rosary was described as "a Chaplet of good Works to present to God at night." An early fifteenth-century sermon used the image thus: "Collect in the little basket of your heart the rose petals that the rosebush of Christ let fall in the fear of his suffering as he knelt on the Mount of Olives and as he carried up the cross." This delicate transubstantiation of

Cramer's emblem *Qui Sitit, Bibet* (Who Thirsts, Let Him Drink): God gives the drink, which pours straight out through the heart to feed the rose. © *The British Library 95.a.22*

roses for blood gives a less ferocious and bloody version of the Passion.

St. Mechtilde had a vision: she was with Christ in a beautiful garden. "Look into my heart," he said, and his heart appeared to her as a great rose with five petals, almost covering his torso. (Another drawing by the St. Walburga nun shows Christ's agony in the garden, taking place in the center of a red rose.) The rose, as a red thing you can go into, gaze into, contemplate, matches the wound and the heart. A rose even has a heart.

It was the chosen badge of Henry Suso: white roses for purity and red roses for patience in suffering. The Rosy Cross, stained with Christ's blood, lent its name to the brand of hermetic Christianity called Rosicrucianism. Many of their texts are called rosaria, rose gardens. German innkeepers hung roses in their taverns to indicate that what was said there should never be repeated: sub rosa—beneath the rose; in secret. Like the heart, the rose concocts miracles; like the heart, the rose keeps secrets.

The Heart Emblem series of Daniel Cramer is a Rosicrucian rosary. Henry Hawkins, the Jesuit emblematist, made a rose-garlanded sacred garden out of the heart in *The Devout Hart*, in which each flower was compared to a heart pure and delightful enough for God:

> Here the Lilly . . . in forme of a silver cup, shewes forth her golden threads of saffron in her open bosom; a noble Hierogrifike of a snowy mind, a candid purity, and a cleane hart . . . Here now besides the pourpourizing rose, the flower of martyrs dyed with sanguine tincture of their bloud, represents that incredible love which put thee (O love piously cruel!) and nayled thee on the Crosse.

THE ROSE AND SEXUALITY

The red rose, like the heart, joins love and sexuality. Lovers have argued for centuries against maidenly rejection by pointing out that unless she gather her rosebuds while she may, petals will wither, and then what? As Fletcher put it, "Ladies, if not plucked, we die."

> Darling, each morning a blooded rose
> Takes the sunlight in and shows
> Her soft, moist and secret part.
> See now, before you go to bed,
> Her skirts replaced, her deeper red –
> A colour much like yours, dear heart . . .
> Then scatter, darling, your caresses
> While you may, and wear green dresses;
> Gather roses, gather me –
> Tomorrow, aching for your charms,
> Death shall take you in his arms
> And shatter your virginity
>
> PIERRE DE RONSARD, TR. ROBERT MEZEY

The rose in William Blake's poem is love, the passive female heart and vagina—the wound—again:

> O Rose, thou art sick!
> The invisible worm
> That flies in the night,
> In the howling storm,
> Has found out thy bed
> Of crimson joy:
> And his dark secret love
> Does thy life destroy.

There is a parasitic nematode known as the heartworm which infests the hearts of some carnivores. Usually, what eats the heart is envy or sexual jealousy: eat your heart out.

From "Red" by Ted Hughes
Red was your colour.
If not red, then white. But red
Was what you wrapped around you.
Blood-red. Was it blood?
Was it red-ochre, for warming the dead?
Haematite to make immortal
When you had your way finally
Our room was red. A judgement chamber.
Shut casket for gems. The carpet of blood
Patterned with darkenings, congealments.
The curtains—ruby corduroy blood,
Sheer blood-falls from ceiling to floor.
The cushions the same. The same
Raw carmine along the window-seat.
A throbbing cell. Aztec altar—temple.

Only the bookshelves escaped into whiteness.

And outside the window
Poppies thin and wrinkle-frail
As the skin on blood,
Salvias, that your father named you after,
Like blood lobbing from a gash,
And roses, the heart's last gouts,
Catastrophic, arterial, doomed.

Your velvet long full skirt, a swathe of blood,
A lavish burgundy.
Your lips a dipped deep crimson.
You revelled in red.
I felt it raw—like the crisp gauze edges
Of a stiffening wound. I could touch
The open vein in it, the crusted gleam.

Everything you painted you painted white
Then splashed it with roses, defeated it,
Leaned over it, dripping roses,

Weeping roses, and more roses.
Then sometimes, among them, a little bluebird . . .

Dorothy Parker wrote, in 1937:

Why has no one ever sent me yet,
One perfect Limousine, do you suppose?
Ah no, it's always just my luck to get
One Perfect Rose.

The perfect rose is a simple point of sympathetic magic: the man sends a heart/vagina symbol, full of sweetness and the hope of rebirth, hoping that the woman will in exchange give him her heart, vagina, youthful beauty and possibly babies. A limousine is a phallic thing: it makes a different point altogether.

John Donne, in one of his direct chats with his heart, warns it of its similarities with a blossom which can only be a rose.

The Blossome
Little think'st thou, poore flower,
Whom I have watch'd sixe or seaven dayes,
And seene thy birth, and seene what every houre
Gave to thy growth, thee to this height to raise,
And now dost laugh and triumph on this bough,
Little think'st thou
That it will freeze anon, and that I shall
To morrow finde thee falne, or not at all.

Little think'st thou poore heart
That labour'st yet to nestle thee,
And think'st by hovering here to get a part
In a forbidden or forbidding tree,
And hop'st her stiffenesse by long siege to bow:
Little think'st thou,
That thou to morrow, ere that Sunne doth wake,
Must with this Sunne, and mee a journey take.

But thou which lov'st to bee
Subtile to plague thy selfe, wilt say,
Alas, if you must goe, what's that to mee?
Here lyes my businesse, and here I will stay:
You goe to friends, whose love and meanes present
Various content
To your eyes, eares, and tongue, and every part.
If then your body goe, what need you a heart?

Well then, stay here; but know,
When thou hast stayd and done thy most;
A naked thinking heart, that makes no show,
Is to a woman, but a kinde of Ghost;
How shall shee know my heart; or having none,
Know thee for one?
Practise may make her know some other part,
But take my word, she doth not know a Heart.

Meet mee at London, then,
Twenty dayes hence, and thou shalt see
Mee fresher, and more fat, by being with men,
Then if I had staid still with her and thee.
For Gods sake, if you can, be you so too:
I would give you
There, to another friend, whom wee shall finde
As glad to have my body, as my minde.

THE NIGHTINGALE AND THE ROSE

In Persian poetry the rose was the beloved, the nightingale the lover, their relationship complex. The nightingale pours out his heart—his song, his love, his life—to the rose; the rose answers back.

A nightingale said to a new-blown rose at dawn
"No need for airs.
Many in this garden have bloomed like you."
The rose smiled and replied:
"I do not fear the truth.

But no lover speaks rudely to his beloved."
If you wish to drink from that jewel-encrusted cup
You must first thread your eyelashes
With many a pearl.

At dawn the nightingale said to the breeze,
"You see where love of the rose has brought me.
That charm and gentleness
brought a turmoil into my heart,
and the glory of the garden
Impaled me on a thorn."

Once again the steadfast nightingale
Sings from the stately cypress
Pleading for the safety of the rose
From the spell of the evil eye.
O rose, be grateful
That you have flowered as an emperor of beauty
Do not parade your pride by disdaining the lovelorn nightingales.
I do not complain at your absence,
For without absence one cannot savour presence.
Others may indulge in festivity and rejoicing;
For me, suffering in the absence of the Beloved
Is my sole source of delight.
The zealot set his hopes
On houris and palaces in the life to come;
My palace is the tavern, my houri the friend.
Drink wine to the sound of the harp,
and if anyone say "drink not"
reply "God is merciful."
O Hafiz, why complain of the grief of absence?
Union lies hidden in absence[*]
As the light of dawn
lies hidden in the darkness of the night.

---

*The hackneyed English version of this, "absence makes the heart grow fonder," is from Francis Davison's "Poetical Rhapsody" (1602).

The nightingale received its song
from the bounty of the rose—
How otherwise would its beak encompass
Such beauties of thought and rhyme?
FROM *GHAZALS* BY HAFIZ

In Oscar Wilde's story, the nightingale gives up his heart's blood on the rose's thorn, singing his heart out the while, in order to dye the rose red, so that a poor lovesick student can give it to a fussy wench who in the end rejects it, and him, anyway. The nightingale dies on the rose's thorn, the rose ends up crushed under the wheel of a passing wagon, the student gives up on love and the girl goes off with a richer man.

The nightingale and the rose are not the only images Wilde borrowed from Islam. In "The Birthday of the Infanta" the little dwarf believes himself beloved by the Infanta: she gives him a rose, no less—as a token, he thinks. Then he sees his grotesque reflection in a mirror, imitating his movements, and his heart breaks in shame and he dies. Just as Allah looks in the mirror of man's pure heart to see himself, so a man looks into his own heart to see his own nature. The Infanta is piqued: in future, she says, let those who come to entertain her have no hearts.

THE LOTUS

As the rose is to Christianity, so the lotus is to Hinduism and Buddhism. The Lotus Sutra is the King of Sutras, twenty-eight chapters of the final, perfect and complete revelation of Buddha Sakyamuni. The lotus, in Hindu tales, is an emblem of Vishnu, a beautiful and benevolent thing, golden, red or white: it falls from heaven in a dream and a divine woman or heavenly youth emerges from it; a beautiful woman looks like a golden lotus floating on the Ganges, or has eyes like a blue lotus; a pregnant queen longs to fly in a magical chariot shaped like a lotus; a lotus makes lakes fragrant. In the story of Devasmita, a clever, faithful and determined wife who fights off would-be seducers with considerable élan, Shiva gives her and her husband a lotus each, which remain lustrous, red and unfaded so long as they are faithful to each other. "Each beheld in the hand of the other a red lotus, and it seemed as if they had got one another's hearts." The lotus of the heart (*hrdaya pundarika*) is the center of spiritual consciousness; it shines with inner light and is beyond sorrow; it fills those who see it with an extraordinary sense of peace and joy. It is, of course, for meditating upon.

THE TREE AND ITS FRUIT

When Anubis fed Bata's heart to him in a glass of water to bring him back to life, it looked like a fruit. At the Fall, Adam and Eve ate the fruit of knowledge and became aware of themselves—their weakness, their desires, their passions, each other. (Knowledge and emotions, remember, lived exclusively in the heart at that time.) As a direct result, Christians eat the body of Jesus, the "perfect man," to make up for it: to cleanse their hearts. Sins (acquired after eating that fruit) are confessed—given up through the mouth. The body of Christ, and his heart's blood, is taken in to redeem those sins. Eating the apple separated Christians from God; eating the body brings them back together. A link, rooted in ancient myth, has developed between God, the heart and fruit—particularly, despite the apple, grapes, peaches and pomegranates. The heart is both the tree and the fruit; so, again, it is the place where two things can be one.

The similarities between a tree, with roots and branches, and the cardiovascular system had been noted in ancient times. How could the heart not be a tree, with all those branches coming off it?—particularly before the anatomical reality was known and accepted that the branches joined up again in circulation, rather than just branched out. The ancient Greeks thought thus, though they couldn't decide which way up it grew. Aristotle rooted the tree in the

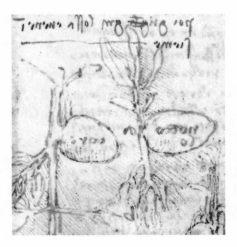

A sketch by Leonardo, from 1504–6: the left-hand figure is labeled "heart" and the right-hand one "seed." The note beneath says "The plant never arises from the branchings, for the plant first exists before the branches, and the heart exists before the veins. The heart is the seed which engenders the tree of the veins." This is the Aristotelian view; Galen held that the heart was more like a fruit on the tree—though of course fruits contain seeds. © *The Royal Collection 2001, Her Majesty Queen Elizabeth II*

Dionysus, the ship and the vine, on a sixth-century B.C. kylix by Exekias. © *Staatliche Antikensammlung und Glyptothek, Munich / Bridgeman Art Library*

heart; Galen, in the liver. He wrote: "From the heart springs out an artery as does the trunk of a tree from the earth [and] just like the trunk of a tree divides into branches." The image of a tree growing from the heart also owes something to the Gospel of St. Mark, in which is written, much to the confusion of devout Christian anatomists: "There is a seed in the heart which grows." (This might also have contributed to the "black grain," see page 23.) Leonardo picked up on this and the ancient Tree of Life, and drew some exquisite little anatomical hearts sprouting blood vessels which look more than anything like the broad beans in jam jars of primary-school nature lessons.

William Harvey owned his own trees of life, the roots and branches laid out for all to see: entire cardiovascular systems were painstakingly removed from corpses, elegantly spread out for maximum educational and reference value—on wooden boards—and varnished. They look like the skeletons of dead leaves in winter. Here anatomy reinforced imagery.

THE GRAPE AND THE VINE

"I am the true vine and my Father is the husbandman ... I am the vine, ye are the branches ..." John's allegory of Christ as the vine offers a full hand of further imagery: growth, fruitfulness, spreading, pruning, nurturing and more. Also, like any metaphor built to last, it harked back to previous imagery. Grapes were already associated with eternal life in classical times, through Dionysus, the Greek god of wine, who had died and rose again because his father saved his heart. Ovid tells how Dionysus, on board a pirate ship, caused a great vine to grow up out of the sea and swamp it: the image of the mast entwined by the grape-laden vine (while the godless pirates turned into dolphins and the faithful pilot was saved by the god) is a forerunner of the later Christian image of the vine cross.

Christ crucified on a vine, c. 1435, German.
© V&A Picture Library

The cross on which Jesus died was often referred to as the tree and represented as a vine. In this, Jesus himself becomes the fruit, but this image is endlessly flexible. A German plaster rondel of the mid-fifteenth century shows a vine cross bearing the heads of the apostles as fruit and, in another interesting sexual reference, the words *Pater umificat* (the father waters) and *Maria fecundat* (Mary makes fertile). Late-medieval German crucifixes can be seen with grapes sprouting from the cross. St. Bridget of Sweden was very taken with the vine imagery, and saw her order as a vineyard whose branches "will be brought to take root." With the charming literality of early imagery, if Jesus produces wine then he must be a bunch of grapes; specifically, if the blood is wine, the heart is the grapes. St. Augustine declared Christ to be "the cluster of grapes of the promised land, and the grapes placed under the press"; this refers to the grapes brought back on a staff from Canaan by Moses' spies. And also, when Isaiah prophesies that the avenging God will trample his enemies in the wine press—"I will tread them in mine anger, and trample them in my fury; and their blood shall be sprinkled upon my garments, and I will stain all my raiment"—the enemies become the sins of humanity, and as Christ became sin for us so Christ is trampled in his father's anger, and the blood that is sprinkled on God's garment is God's own blood, the eucharistic wine. So when "Mine eyes hath seen the glory of the coming of the Lord, He hath trampled out the vineyard where the grapes of wrath are stored," the grapes were his own son whom he gave to suffer for the redemption of Christians.

Christ in the wine press, standing in a bowl, blood pouring from his wounds and a press weighing heavily on his stooped back, was a common image in the religious art in medieval Europe, and it lasted long enough to be of use to George Herbert in "The Bunch of Grapes":

. . . much more him I must adore
Who of the laws sowre juice sweet wine did make,
Ev'n God himself, being pressed for my sake.

Allegory of the Sacrament, by Juan Correa. © *Denver Art Museum*

The imagery comes together in Juan Correa's *Allegory of the Sacrament* (1690, see this page): a vine grows out of Christ's heart, out of the wound in his side, up a tree and back down with ripe grapes which Christ is squeezing into a bowl to make the sacramental wine.

O du eddele sedderenbom (O you noble cedar tree)
As you hung, Lord
On the wide cross

Your mild divine heart
Was pierced by a sharp spear
Oh! If only my heart were a garden
Full of fine noble flowers
I would plant within it
A little chaplet for my love.
The flowers that I have in mind
Are called humility,
The others shall be called
Faith, hope and charity.
From my beloved's heart
There springs a runnel
I will channel that little river
Directly into my garden.
My beloved's arms
Stood wide outspread
I would like to rest in them
So I could forget all my sorrow.
. . . In my beloved's side
stands a golden shrine
Oh! If only I were enclosed in it
As I desire.
I ask sweet Jesus that
Through the power of your love
You place my wild heart
Upon the branch of the tree,
So that my heart may rest
Entirely in your wounds,
Entirely between your breasts
Just like a bundle of myrrh.
Lift me up, beloved lord
Now and for eternity
So that I may find your love
In the gourd of my heart.

THE TREE OF LIFE OF THE CABBALA

The Cabbala is a development from the Old Testament, a mystic tradition which Abraham learned from Melchizedek, and which has been passed down since. The cabbalistic Tree of Life is a picture of creation, a template of the nature of everything.

On this tree hang ten radiant emanences, the *sephirot*. The first three are beyond human comprehension; the fourth, created on the first day, was *Hesed*, loving kindness. On the second day *Din*, judgment, was created to temper loving kindness. On the third day *Rahamim*, mercy, and *Tepheret*, beauty, were created to temper judgment and balance the tension between judgment and loving kindness. The benign influence of *Tepheret* radiating over all the other *sephirot* is compared to the sun in the center of the heavens. As God created man in his own image, each *sephirah* is associated with a body part of the archetype. *Tepheret rahamim*, merciful beauty, the sun, belongs in and with the heart.

The twelfth-century *Book of Bahir* says:

> Holy Israel occupies the top of the tree and its heart: just as the heart is the splendid fruit of the body, so is Israel likewise the fruit of the splendid tree. So is Israel, likewise, at the top of this tree, and this top is its heart; and the treetop corresponds to the spinal cord of man, the most essential part of the body.

There is a correlation here to Bata's heart at the top of the tree and to St. Mechtilde, who wanted her heart left in the tree for good biblical reasons. The vine cross, by becoming the tree of death and regeneration, is another branch of the same root as the Tree of Life (which was, incidentally, adopted and adapted by St. Thomas Aquinas, who used it to revivify the intellectual life of the medieval Church).

Looking at a diagram of the Tree of Life, it is impossible not to notice similarities with the yoga chakras (see page 269), where the heart is the fourth of a series of hubs in the microcosm which is man. Once again the heart is the crossover point between earthly and divine.

POMEGRANATES, PEACHES AND PAPAYAS

Lounging on his mother's lap, the baby Christ dandles a pomegranate. It is a symbol of the Passion, his fate, in which as he dies his heart will be opened to mankind by Longinus's spear. A pomegranate is a similar shape to a heart—perhaps halfway between the physical heart and the adapted emblematic heart; certainly similar to the peachy heart which followed the pine-cone heart. Its spiky crown serves equally well as the shorn aorta, the crown of thorns, or the flames of the Sacred Heart. The color is right (yellowy red like a real heart with its layers of fat, ripening to the glorious crimson of the emblem). It is tough, like real heart muscle. Open it, and it has its pith-constructed chambers, full of scarlet drops—a clear transparent scarlet, like the blood mixed with water in Christian imagery, the blood that feeds and redeems and the water that cleanses, to ensure rebirth.

But this is not just a Christian and anatomical connection. When Zeus brought back Dionysus's heart from the Titans, it dripped blood, and where that blood fell pomegranate trees sprang up. When Hades took Persephone (daughter of Demeter and Zeus) down to his deathly kingdom, she ate pomegranate seeds, which condemned her to spend six months of each year on earth and six months in the Underworld, thus introducing the seasons (before this all fruit and flowers were constant, courtesy of Demeter) and promoting her to the ranks of the born again, alongside Osiris, Bata and Dionysus, to be joined later by Jesus. Demeter hated pomegranates as a result, and Hera, Zeus's wife, is portrayed with a pomegranate, possibly as a symbol of her victory over Demeter.

According to Philostratus, the Furies caused a pomegranate tree to grow on the grave of Eteocles, and when the fruit was plucked, blood flowed from it; the suicide Menoeceus also sprouted a pomegranate tree, and to dream of pomegranates, according to Artemidorus, presaged wounds.

At the same time the pomegranate, rounded and closed and full of seeds, is a fertility symbol, a womb. In this sense, Hera has a pomegranate appropriate to her role as goddess of marriage, and Hades made Persephone taste her own fertility, her sexuality, her own flesh, which is necessary to the continuation of the race and rebirth through having children. The apple Eve tasted—the fruit of the tree of knowledge—has frequently been identified as a pomegranate. (Nan, the mother of Attis, by the way, conceived him by putting a pomegranate in her bosom.) Frida Kahlo wrote of "the blood of the pome-

Madonna with the Pomegranate, Botticelli, c. 1482. © *Scala*

granate" in Diego Rivera's kiss. Diego Durán described Aztec human sacrifices: "With a knife dropped on to his chest, a man could be sliced open as easily as a pomegranate." The hearts of the sacrificed were known as *quauhnochtli tlazotlil*—the eagle's precious Barbary figs.

In an Indian fairy story called "The Pomegranate Raja" a wicked stepmother tries repeatedly to kill her stepchildren, but they keep coming back to life. She has the son made into a curry which she tries to feed to his father; she has their livers taken out for her to stand on while she bathes; then she buries the livers in the garden and from them grow first two beautiful flowers which she cannot pick, then two beautiful pomegranate trees, with beautiful fruit which grow out of her reach when she goes to pluck them. She cuts the trees down—their fruits fly up into the sky—only for the whole caboodle—trees and fruit—to grow again during the night. In the end the fruit jump into the hands of the Pomegranate Raja; late at night he hears voices inside them and carefully cuts them open to find his two children safe and sound. (Their dead mother, the Pomegranate Flower, comes back to life too, after a sojourn as a beautiful bird who weeps pearls and laughs rubies.)

I've wondered why, when the evil stepmother—Snow White's, for example—asks for proof of the innocent child's murder, she asks for the heart rather than something recognizable like the head. The answer is that any halfway effective magic can put dead and dismembered people back together again; but without the heart a person, however well reconstructed, cannot be himself again. Perhaps the reason why the Pomegranate Stepmother fails is because she asked for livers, not hearts. Heart-seeking stepmothers usually fail too, often because the compassionate executioner substitutes an animal heart for that of the person he was to kill.

The pomegranate, like the heart, holds knowledge: Gustave Courbet painted worm-eaten pomegranates when he was in prison after the collapse of the Paris Commune. Was he thinking of worm-eaten hearts or worm-eaten wisdom, of spoiled fertility, of spoiled chances of reemergence from the dark? Francis I of France, the king who kept the *Mona Lisa* by his bed, filled Fontainebleau with images of the pomegranate as a symbol of the state: the parts—seeds—were ruled by the whole—the king, demonstrating that even nature obeys the state.

From "Pomegranate" by D. H. Lawrence
Now in Tuscany,
Pomegranates to warm your hands at;
And crowns, kingly, generous, tilting crowns
Over the left eyebrow.
And, if you dare, the fissure!
Do you mean to tell me you will see no fissure?
Do you prefer to look on the plain side?
For all that, the setting suns are open.
The end cracks open with the beginning:

Rosy, tender, glittering within the fissure.
Do you mean to tell me there should be no fissure?
No glittering, compact drops of dawn?
Do you mean it is wrong, the gold-filmed skin, integument, shown ruptured?
For my part, I prefer my heart to be broken.
It is so lovely, dawn-kaleidoscopic within the crack.

When Christiaan Barnard's father proposed to his future wife, he did so under a pomegranate tree: he broke open a fruit and offered it to her, saying, "Maria, so is my heart open to you." Which brings us round to the broken heart again (see page 121). Fruit is eminently breakable and woundable, so it lends itself to all the Christian imagery of the wound that gives access to love. It has to be broken to be eaten; to make wine, to give of itself. George Herbert offered his heart to God on a plate of fruit. And fruit is eminently adaptable: Javier de la Garza's *Aparición de la Papaya* (1990) has a plump, cut-open papaya in a crown of thorns hanging in the sky above a field of cactuses, with a devoted Mexican maid gazing serenely on.

The peach was sacred to Isis, according to Plutarch, because it looked like a heart: "The peach has fruit that vies with the heart, leaves that vie with the tongue; would that these two were in harmony with all things."

THE MONKEY AND THE CROCODILE

A monkey lived very happily in a mango tree, looking out over the ocean. One day a crocodile appeared in the sea beneath him, looking for food. A mango dropped, and the crocodile swam quickly to catch it. The monkey picked another mango and calling "Hey, Crocodile!" he threw it—right to the other side so the crocodile had to splash and scurry again to catch it. How the monkey laughed! And he picked another mango, and calling again to the crocodile he threw it—right out to sea! The crocodile scurried, the monkey laughed and laughed—and dropped another mango, right beneath his feet. The crocodile scurried in, splashing and panting, ate the mango, and then looking up said: "Kind monkey, thank you for the fruit you have given me. In return, let me offer you a trip to Crocodile Island, just over the horizon, where you can meet our king as a reward for your kindness."

The monkey was intelligent but he was curious too, and he climbed upon the crocodile's back and balanced there carefully while they swam out to sea. And after a while the monkey said to himself: "Oh dear. I have been very foolish."

When the coast was far behind them and Crocodile Island was nowhere to be seen, the crocodile stopped and said: "You know, Monkey—the Crocodile King has been very sick. The only thing that can cure him is to eat a monkey's heart."

"Oh dear!" cried the monkey. He thought quickly. "If only you had told me that before I would have brought my heart with me!"

The crocodile was extremely surprised.

"Quick, my friend!" cried the monkey. "Let us return at once and get it, then we can save your king's life."

The crocodile was perturbed. How could the monkey be happy to give up his heart? And how could he have left it behind? But—if he had left it behind, then of course it could not be so important to him . . .

The crocodile turned back.

When they returned to the mango tree, the monkey leaped from the crocodile's back into the branches, crying "I'll be back in a moment." Then as soon as he was out of reach and out of earshot, he called his friends to him and said, "Go and gather up all the bad mangoes, the soft and rotten mangoes, the smelly mangoes, and when Crocodile calls for me, throw them at him as hard as you can!" So the monkeys armed themselves with mangoes, and when the crocodile called, "Monkey, my friend, where are you?" the monkey shouted, "Here I am, and here is my heart for you!" and the crocodile was pelted with the rotten fruit. And he never bothered those monkeys again.

This is from West Africa; versions of the same story are known in Indonesia, Zanzibar, Latvia, Japan and the Philippines, and in Jewish, Buddhist and Spanish-American traditions. In Japan the Queen of the Sea wants the monkey's liver; in Swahili it is a shark who wants the heart for his sultan. In one Indian version the monkey lives on the bank of the Ganges, and the crocodile wants his heart for his wife. The monkey explains that if their hearts were inside them when they jumped about in the trees they would get knocked to pieces, and directs him to a fig tree, saying, "There are our hearts." Having met Indian monkeys (a gang of them once stole my bedclothes while I was asleep on a roof) I quite believe this.

In another version the Monkey King makes friends with a porpoise because of the charming noises the porpoise makes when he eats the *udumbara* fruit that the monkey throws him. The porpoise's jealous wife falls ill and demands soup made from the lotus-like heart of the monkey. The Monkey King escapes as usual and tells the porpoise the story of the lion, the jackal and the ass: the lion is sick, and requires the heart and ears of a donkey to cure him. The jackal brings a donkey to him; but the lion is too weak to kill it and only scares it away. The jackal tricks it into coming back again, and this time the lion kills it. Tired by the effort, he goes to bathe, leaving the jackal to guard the donkey meat. The jackal eats the heart and ears; the lion, on returning, wants to know what has happened to them. Says the jackal, "The creature never possessed ears or a heart, otherwise how could he have been stupid enough to return when he had once escaped?"

HEART OF OAK

Heart of Oak is from a sea song written in 1759: "Heart of Oak are our ships, Heart of Oak are our men," and used in David Garrick's pantomime *Harlequin's Invasion*. As the timbers were the best and strongest, so were the crew. In Ghana there is a football team called Hearts of Oak of Accra. The Scots team name Heart of Midlothian is from the old Tollbooth Prison in Edinburgh, now demolished, and Sir Walter Scott's novel.

5

THE HEART AS A
MUSICAL INSTRUMENT

In the summer of 2001 the Irish band U2 was performing on a massive crimson stage, its outline picked out with white light bulbs. The shape? A heart, both filled with and surrounded by a sea of audience. Bono and the Edge stood near the tip, singing their hearts out, in a video made for the human rights organization Amnesty International: so, compassion, music, a place for people to be, a moment of expression and communication, a universal symbol—just the heart, doing its usual job.

The heart is and always has been a musical organ for the simple reason that it makes a noise: *debdeb, lubdub.* As air was supposed in ancient times to pass through the heart, of course it should be a pipe. It beats a rhythm, so it is a drum, and for less obvious reasons it is also a harp.

In the Old Testament, it sings like a pipe in mourning, and in Jeremiah: "I am pained at my very heart, my heart maketh a noise in me, I cannot hold my peace because thou hast heard, oh my soul, the sound of the trumpet, the alarm of war." St. Paul, in his epistle to the Ephesians, speaks of the melody of the heart.

One of the sweetest, saddest images in Sufi music is of the *ney,* the reed flute, representing the voice of the human heart yearning for God, from whom the heart has become separated as the reed is separated from the bed where it grew. Rumi was one of many Sufi poets who wrote about this—he brought in the wound and the flame too:

> Listen to the lament of the reed,
> to its sad tale of separation,
> Crying, "Ever since from the reedbed born
> My lament hath caused men to mourn.

Mine is the voice of sorrow in every land
The pain of loss in every man
Mine is the wound that will not heal
The mysterious pain that all men feel.
And I am a flame dancing in love's fire
That flickering light in the depths of desire
To know the pain the severance breeds
Listen to the song of the reed."[*]

How did it become a harp, with strings? The heart shape is somewhat harp-like, and inside the chambers are the filaments which the Hippocratics called "the guy-ropes and stays of the heart." Tendons or nerves were formerly supposed to brace the heart within the body, holding it in position, which was so important for emotional and moral stability. The heart was already a communicator, speaking through the vessels for ancient Egyptians; it clearly has rhythm. Before you know it, the emotional heart has heartstrings, to be plucked by sad stories and played on by sentimental music. John Ford, in *The Broken Heart,* wrote of "The silent griefs which cut the heartstrings"; a fiddler's

song of 1604 asks, "How can he play whose heartstrings broken are?" Thomas Watson saw the heart as an instrument that needed tuning, and Margaret Cavendish compared the heart to a harp. The Emblematists adopted it: Henry Hawkins's Jesus "sings in the Quire of the hart, and plays on the harp while angels sing." Three hundred years later Roberta Flack sang of a musician "strumming my fate with

Jesus playing his harp in the heart, from Hawkins's *The Devout Hart.*
© *The British Library 1578/15*

---

[*]If you want to hear this sound, get hold of a recording by Kuddsi Erguner, the Turkish *ney* player. He calls his music *zikr qualbi* (the remembrance of the heart).

his fingers, singing my life with his words": reading her book of the heart and playing on her heartstrings at the same time.

PULSES, HEARTBEAT AND MEDITATION

Mei Ching, the Chinese *Book of the Pulse* (A.D. 280), is a twelve-volume work which likens the human body to a musical instrument "of which the different pulses are the chords. The harmony or discord of the organism can be recognised by examining the pulse, which is thus fundamental for all medicine." The pulses of the wrist can be read in three places and at three depths in each place, and each of these pulses will be recorded according to strength, duration, resonance, rhythm and texture. The pulse which speaks for the heart is the *tsun,* the one closest to the hand on the left wrist. Learning the subtleties of pulse-reading is a life's work, and even then, as Confucius said, "Man will never understand his own heart, for he has only his own heart with which to understand."

The simple pulse, the beating of the drum of the heart, is the repetitive rhythm which leads and propels meditation—the voyage into the heart—in all religions: Islamic *zikr,* Buddhist chanting, yogic pranayama and mantras, Orthodox heart prayer, the counting of the beads of the rosary, the Hail Marys, the copying out of sutras by Buddhist calligraphers and, in own its way, the relaxation response of one modern religion-substitute, medicine.

One Muslim ritual is the recitation of the Qur'an; the flowing, hypnotic rhythm of the Arabic words has often been compared to the heartbeat. Grief caused by the separation from God is assuaged by remembering God: "Verily in the remembrance of Allah do hearts find rest." This remembrance is *zikr*—remembrance, the mental and verbal repetition of a verse of the Qur'an or one of the names of God. Muslims are required by the Qur'an to repeat basic truths "in their mind and heart" in daily life, and also to act on their beliefs because "God does not accept belief if it is not put into deed, and does not accept deed if it does not conform to belief." (Similarly, as Yunus Emre, the Turcoman dervish much admired by Rumi, wrote, "No man may injure a heart, then pay the price in prayer." So the heart is an organ both of consciousness and of conscience.) The *zikr* can be a purely private devotion or a public and communal spectacle, part of a religious festival. Then it is often accompanied by music and physical movement, by dancing or whirling like the Mawlawis (dervishes) or the Sufis of al-Ghouri in Cairo. The whirling imitates the move-

Turning Dervishes, by Amadeo Preziosi, Italian, 1857. © *Stapleton Collection / Bridgeman Art Library*

ment of the universe, the open right hand faces upward to God and the sky, the left faces down to the earth and mankind. The dervish's body becomes a channel through which divine grace can flow down to the world: man ascends, God descends. At the same time the movements induce a concentration, a trancelike rhythm and ultimately ecstasy, in which the dancer draws near to God. Al-Ghazzali wrote:

> The heart of man has been so constituted by the almighty that, like a flint, it contains a hidden fire which is evoked by music and harmony, and renders

261

man beside himself with ecstasy . . . the effect of music and dancing is deeper in proportion as the natures on which they act are simple and prone to emotion; they fan into a flame whatever love is already dormant in the heart, whether it be earthly and sensual or divine and spiritual. Sufis . . . by this means stir up in themselves greater love towards God, and, by means of music, often obtain spiritual visions and ecstasies, their heart becoming in this condition as clean as silver in the flame of a furnace, and attaining a degree of purity which could never be attained by any amount of mere outward austerities. The Sufi then becomes so keenly aware of his relationship to the spiritual world that he loses all consciousness of this world, and often falls down senseless.

The visions and ecstasies and falling down senseless of a twenty-first-century clubber awash on drink, drugs, sexual desire and loud music are by no means the same thing, though perhaps it is the same appetite, misdirected, which achieves them. Rumi and Hafez give descriptions of medieval drunkenness and frolics. This is by Rumi:

Last year I admired wines. This,
I'm wandering inside the red world.
Last year, I gazed at the fire.
This year I'm burnt kebab.
Thirst drove me down to the water
where I drank the moon's reflection.
Now I am a lion staring up totally
lost in love with the thing itself.
Don't ask questions about longing
Look in my face.
Soul drunk, body ruined, these two
sit helpless in a wrecked wagon.
Neither knows how to fix it.
And my heart, I'd say it was more
like a donkey stuck in a mudhole,
struggling and miring deeper.
But listen to me for one moment,
stop being sad. Hear blessings
dropping their blossoms
around you. God.

Sufis believe that all earthly love, of its nature mortal and finite, yearns to become divine love, eternal love, with God as its object—exactly the opposite of what has happened in the "civilized world" of the modern West, where rather than singing and dancing to the glory of God and in search of our higher natures, we are truly stuck on the animal level, singing and dancing to the glory of more vodka, an instant shag, and the godlike powers you feel when driving an extremely fast car (or would, if only you could get out of this tailback).

THE DRUM

Each society adapts the heart to its own instrument: across Africa it has been the drum. The influence of ancient Egypt trickled up the Nile; the Bambaras of what is now Mali recognized the organs: they put the will in the kidneys, judgment in the liver, fear in the bladder and courage in the heart. Across West Africa the Ashanti, the Ewe of Togo and the Yoruba of Nigeria held the heart in high esteem. The Ashanti Adinkra symbols, a set of traditional designs which record proverbs, include the shape and idea of the heart in several forms. Symbol 1, *Sankofa,* is the symbol of positive reversion: "Go back and take." It is interpreted as meaning go back to the past and learn there what you need for the future, a symbol of revival and new life. It is very popular among black Americans yearning for their lost heritage. Symbol 31, *Akoma,* is the heart plain and simple; the symbol means *nya akoma,* take heart: be patient and tolerant in the face of emotional stress and provocation. Symbol 2, *Nyame Dua,* is God's Tree, made up of four hearts meeting at their points to make a flower shape. It represents the stakes that support an earthenware jar full of water for purification rites. Symbol 17, *Akoma Ntoaso* (Linked Heart), signifies understanding and agreement between couples and family. How much of this familiar symbolism is due to northern influences—Christian and Muslim—and how much to its own universal truth is impossible to say.

For the Yoruba the heart is the physical counterpart of the *emi,* the soul or vital force; the blood is seen as essential in the service of the body. "A heart without blood is lifeless, blood without a heart is idle and useless . . . both are regarded as agents of the soul in the physical plan," wrote M. Akin Makinde. "The life of a man is in his bloodstream." As well as the body and the *emi* there is the *ori,* the inner head—Greece and Africa are not so far apart. The chest,

SANKOFA **AKOMA** **AKOMA NTOASO**

as in Europe, symbolizes a good and warm life filled with friends and lovers. The following is from a Yoruba Ifa divination song:

> Pakelemo, Ifa priest of chest [*aya*]
> Performed Ifa divination for chest
> When chest was weeping because he had no friends . . .
> Chest performed sacrifice,
> And chest made friends.
> Pakelemo, the good father,
> We thank you.

Most African religion, native or introduced, and much healing, sorcery, fun and celebration take place to the beat of drums. A heart and a drum clearly correlate: they beat and they are effective—alive—only when they beat.

African drumming has a strong and deep relationship with the heartbeat, which takes in identity, the emotions and communication. In West Africa drums kept soldiers in contact with each other in the jungle; they mourn at funerals and sing at weddings; they inspire entranced dancing, fulfilling a similar spiritual urge to the Sufi dervishes. In every medical tradition the pulse tells of life, death, ill health and good health. African drums play a similar role, talking to the parts of the company or the community. A talking drummer in Ghana will speak via the drum to a dancer as he dances: encouraging him, admiring him, telling him what to do and telling what he is doing. "The first word was drum's word," wrote Larry Neal in "Kuntu." Archie Shepp, the saxophonist, said that when performing, "I feel I am a drum. I try to become a drum." The drums of restless natives scared the pants off colonials as they sat on their verandas because they were the heartbeat of the people (like the tell-tale heart of Poe's story), and like the heartbeat they spoke of courage, love, fear, anger: all the intense passions. The Jamaican writer Leonard E. Barrett decided "to identify myself with my African heritage, setting loose the rhythm that I felt throbbing within me." And, of course, the great African photojournalism magazine was called *Drum*.

Zora Neale Hurston called the drum the instrument that Africans had "brought to America in their skins," humanizing it when she spoke of the "furious music of the little drum whose body was still in Africa, but whose soul sang around a fire in Alabama." Slave work songs and spirituals, sung to the rhythm of physical work, using a veil of genuine spiritual needs and desire, often in emblematic biblical words, to disguise revolutionary declarations of rights and identity, are heart songs par excellence, "breathing the prayer and complaints of souls boiling over with the bitterest anguish. Every tone was a testament against slavery, and a prayer to God for deliverance from chains," as escaped slave Frederick Douglass put it. The following are lines from spirituals:

> You got a right,
> I got a right
> We all got a right to the tree of life.

> Oh write my name
> Oh write my name
> The angels in heaven going to write my name . . .
> Write my name in the book of life
> Yes write my name in the dripping blood
> The angels in heaven going to write my name.

> Between the earth and sky
> Thought I heard my Saviour cry
> You got a home in that rock, don't you see?

Between heaven and earth, in Jesus' body, is the wound, the cleft in the rock where the dove nestled, the route to the heart and love of God, which is home. Also, like the home built upon a rock, this is a declaration of steadfastness, a determination to hold on to the ideas of freedom and justice. As James Weldon Johnson wrote, in "St. Peter Relates an Incident":

Heart of what slave poured out such melody
As "Steal away to Jesus"? On its strains
His spirit must have nightly floated free
Though still about his hands he felt his chains.

While the body is bound, the heart can fly. Singing about stealing away to Jesus and being happy in heaven in the great by and by concealed a more mortal longing to steal away from the plantation to seek freedom and justice.

When a magnificent troupe of twenty or thirty or forty African, Latin American or Japanese drummers perform, the hearts of the audience seem to beat in synchrony. Within the ensemble, and within the audience, a massive, beating communion takes place. The highest purposes and fruits of this lie in the ancestor religions that originated in Africa and traveled with slavery to Latin America and the Caribbean: Kumina and Pukumina in Jamaica, voodoo in Haiti, Shango in Trinidad, Santeria in Cuba, Candomble and Macumba in Brazil. In Kumina, for example, a person in need of knowledge would dance into a drum-accompanied trance, with the help of a medicine man, in order to be possessed and helped by ancestors. Leonard Barrett describes the drummer as "indispensable. He . . . sets the mood and controls the spirits that possess people; it is he who controls the movements of the people under possession . . . the drummers prepare the human bodies to receive the spirit." Maya Deren, chronicler of voodoo, wrote that the drum "empties the head and leaves one without a centre around which to stabilise oneself . . . the person remains defenseless, buffeted by each stroke, as the drummers set out to beat the *loa* [god, mystery, soul of the cosmos] into one's head."

Andrew Neher produced "a physiological explanation of unusual behavior in ceremonies involving drums" which can be applied to the ceremonies of African origin and also to Sufis, and thus through to the quieter rhythms of chanting and repetition in prayer and meditation. (Even in the restrained Anglican Church before the host is given out you sometimes hear the little bell— God's bicycle bell, my father called it—showing that God is arriving.) Neher listed the effects that drumming could have: visual experiences—colors, patterns and movements; kinesthetic sensations such as swaying and vertigo, spinning and jumping; general emotional disturbance, including fatigue, confusion, anger, pleasure, loss of sense of time, hallucinations and seizure. This may be true but, like Jeremy Bentham (who described the scent of new-mown

A WORD ON VOODOO

In voodoo, that potent mix of Christianity and West African religion, the heart is the symbol of Erzulie, "the divinity of the dream, the Goddess of Love, the muse of beauty"; with "exclusive title to that which distinguishes humans from all other forms: their capacity to conceive beyond reality, to desire beyond adequacy, to create beyond need." Erzulie is not the mother, the fertile earth goddess, so much as the mistress, the queen of infinite luxury. Champagne must always be ready for her, though she doesn't let anybody drink strong liquor in her presence; she likes to be fanned and to be sprinkled with water. She eats cakes and loves dancing, and she wears three wedding rings, one for each husband, who were important voodoo *loas,* or gods.

Any of her devotees might become her lover. As goddess of love, her heart is so full of love that this is not promiscuity any more than her luxury is vanity—she is just extremely generous, and she has more than enough of everything. Her wealth is the dream of the poor men who serve her.

In her book *The Voodoo Gods*, Maya Deren explains how as the goddess of the heart Erzulie is specifically not goddess of the body; she stands for how things could be, not for how they are: in this sense she is virgin, innocent, and thus can be associated with Mary. But the Mary she is associated with is the Mater Dolorosa; her heart symbol is pierced, as Mary's is, with the foreknowledge of unavoidable disappointment. Things are not as they could be, or should be, so Erzulie is overcome, and becomes Erzulie Ge-Rouge, weeping and furious; or Erzulie Maitresse, Erzulie Freda Dahomey, weeping with despair, whereupon her people bring her more gifts and luxuries and love.

A *vever*—a symbolic gate—for Erzulie.

267

> Deren describes the possession of Erzulie Freda Dahomey, in which after her weeping and railing her body falls limp and exhausted into sleep, her arms outflung like Christ on the cross: "The wound of Erzulie is perpetual: she is the dream impaled eternally upon the cosmic crossroads where the world of men and the world of divinity meet, and it is through her pierced heart that 'man ascends and god descends.'" In which she is totally Christ-like.
>
> Erzulie's *vever*—the symbolic signs drawn in ashes or flour at ceremonies to invoke the *loa*—is a heart. The *vever*, the design of which varies according to the practitioner, is the door through which the *loa* will be welcomed. By the end of the ritual it will have been sacrificed over and danced on—in effect, sacrificed itself.
>
> Her other emblem is the mirror: reflecting possibility rather than reality and echoing the biblical and Islamic image of the heart so pure it reflects God when he looks into it.

hay as "vegetable matter in state of recent degradation"), it misses the point. Most racism is ignorance shot through with envy, and white has stereotypically envied black in areas identified with the heart: sex, rhythm, "soul," dancing, music, the passion of ecstatic possession and its modern version in truly heartfelt music—from ancestor-worship under a sacred tree on the Gold Coast, to Kumina, to the church choir, to Aretha Franklin.

In Paule Marshall's novel *Praisesong for the Widow* the eponymous widow, a middle-class black American, absconds from a cruise ship in the Caribbean and undergoes a spiritual rebirth which culminates at the Big Drum fête, a ceremony directly linking the Caribbean descendants of slaves to Africa through blood, rhythm and half-memories. The note of the singing drum embodied

> feelings that were beyond words, feelings and a host of subliminal memories that over the years had proven more durable and trustworthy than the history with its trauma, and pain, out of which they had come. After centuries of forgetfulness and denial they refused to go away. The note was a lamentation that could hardly have come from the rum keg of a drum. Its source had to be the heart, the bruised still-bleeding innermost chamber of the collective heart.

YOGA

The Hindu version of God descending and man ascending centers, like the Sufi, in the physical rhythm of the heart and breath. Yoga, the physical practices which encourage the process, means union.

There are seven chakras (from the Sanskrit for "hub") in the human body. The dark-red heart chakra is the key to connection with all other energy centers and chakras within and outside ourselves. Mostly chakras exist on a subtle level: the heart is one of the few with a recognizable physical base (though it would be wrong to take the physicality too literally: this is a subtle system).

The mind may dwell in one or other of the chakras. The navel, reproductive organs and organ of evacuation are the lower ones: live there and you live in desire and greed. The three highest are the throat, the forehead and the top of the head: by the top, you have attained *samadhi* and know Brahman. The heart is the fourth, in the middle. In the words of Ramakrishna: "When the mind learns to dwell there, man experiences his first spiritual awakening. Then he has the vision of light all around. Seeing this divine light, he becomes filled with wonder and says: 'Ah, how blissful!' His mind does not then run to the lower centres."

Perfect concentration on the heart reveals the contents of the mind, but perfect concentration is not easy. One route is through yoga—itself a non-religious practice, but one closely associated with Hinduism and Buddhism. Yoga unites the soul and body in the physical postures (above all, through breathing and the control of the heartbeat); it unites the soul with its God through meditation: looking into the heart, which is looking into God. Once again, the heart is where God and man meet.

This is the prayer of the heart: "*Hrdaye cittasamvit . . . Hrdaye cittasamvit.*"* By repeating the words, you request the wisdom. As with the *Imitatio Christi* of medieval Christianity, as in sympathetic magic, what you think, you become. The heart is the home of emotions and the starting point of life: our minds enact what our hearts decide.

The great yogi Patanjali who lived sometime between 400 B.C. and A.D. 400, wrote:

---

*Hrdaye—of the heart, the seat of the emotions; *citta*—of the psyche, mind, intelligence, thought, emotion; *samvit*—complete knowledge and understanding.

> The mind becomes clear and serene when the qualities of the heart are
>   cultivated:
> Friendliness towards the joyful
> Compassion towards the suffering
> Happiness towards the pure
> Impartiality towards the impure.

A literal translation from the Sanskrit shows why interpretation is such an important part of yoga: "Friendliness, helpfulness, gladness, dispassion, welfare, illfare, right, wrong, regarding dwelling-on hence mind-calming." It helps to remember that *sutra* means "thread": the basis, the minimum, on which further considerations and interpretations can be hung, and the guiding line along which the yogi is led in his search for enlightenment. Patanjali's Sutra 36 reads: "Concentration may also be attained by fixing the mind upon the inner light, which is beyond sorrow." The Kaivalya Upanishad describes the light, which is related to the sun, and how to find it:

> The supreme heaven shines in the lotus of the heart. Those who struggle and aspire may enter there. Retire into solitude. Seat yourself on a clean spot in an erect posture, with the head and neck in a straight line. Control all sense organs. Bow down in devotion to your teacher. Then enter the lotus of the heart and meditate there on the presence of Brahman—the pure, the infinite, the blissful.

Praying to the Sacred Heart of Jesus is the Christian version. "Try to feel that the saint's heart has become your heart, within your own body," advised Swami Prabhavananda and Christopher Isherwood, introducing their edition of Patanjali's works, recalling the medieval Christian image of Christ swapping hearts with his chosen saints. They also quote an Orthodox Russian monk on the delights of repetition: "Frequent service of the lips," he said, "imperceptibly becomes a genuine appeal of the heart, sinks downwards into the inward life, becomes a delight, becomes as it were natural to the soul." As St. John Chrysostom wrote: "It is possible to pray at all times, and in all circumstances, and in every place, and easily to rise from frequent vocal prayer to prayer of the mind and from that to prayer of the heart, which opens up the kingdom of God within us." In order to do so, according to St. Theophan, we must "keep the heart from passionate movements, and the mind from passionate thoughts." As the sutra says: free of passion.

In Buddhism the Heart Sutra—the Sutra on the Heart of the Transcendent and Victorious Perfection of Wisdom—is the most famous, the shortest (only 217 Chinese characters—see page 209) and the most elusive scripture. It is a condensation and abbreviation of the Prajnaparamita—the Perfection of Wisdom, the 2,000-year-old central Buddhist texts. The sutra describes itself as "the great spell, the spell of great knowledge, the utmost spell, the unequalled spell, allayer of all suffering." The ninth-century cleric Kukai described it as "simple yet comprehensive . . . terse yet profound." As with many sutras, it takes the form of questions and answers, but it asks only one question: "How should a son of good lineage train who wishes to practice the profound perfection of wisdom?"

The answers given come in the form of, first, advice to deny all other categories of Buddhist philosophy; a statement "form is emptiness; emptiness is form"; and—"by the perfection of wisdom this spell has been delivered"—a mantra: "Gate gate paragate parasamgate bodhi svaha," which may be translated as: "Gone, gone, gone beyond, gone altogether beyond, O, what an awakening, all hail!" This is surely the mystical union with God, beyond this world, to which every religion looks, once again taking place in or through the heart. The Japanese courtier and calligrapher Konoe Iehiro is said to have written out the Heart Sutra every day. Nowadays, it is more often chanted. A rhythm of the heart. A song.

6

A WORD MORE ON
GEORGE HERBERT

Now that we have seen all the emblems of the heart, let's look again at how George Herbert used them. He almost certainly saw emblem literature—perhaps the "Concordance" made by the ladies of Little Gidding (now in the British Museum), which was a version of the Book of Revelation illustrated with engravings in the manner of the Heart Emblem series, including a font full of hearts into which Christ's blood is pouring. The collector Nicholas Ferrar had one: he said it was "a rich jewel worthy to be worn in ye heart of all Xtians," and was pleased to "see women's scizzers brought to so rare an use as to serve at Gods altar."

But Herbert is a better poet than any emblematist: his verse is not the thing of rote, a version like many that have gone before; it is where contemplation of now-familiar images takes wings. Out of the soil of an emblematic attitude to the Bible grows a fully human, individual, inspired devotion.

"Love Unknown," for example, is a litany of emblematic devices going back to ancient Egypt, overstuffed like a sofa, yet hugely touching. Herbert brings God "a dish of fruit one day,/And in the middle plac'd my heart." God calls servants to wash it in a font and wring it out; later it is purified in a cauldron and then, later, in bed:

> when I thought to sleep out all these faults
> (I sigh to speak)
> I found that some had stuff'd the bed with thoughts,
> I would say thorns.

The reason for all this is:

The Font did onely, what was old, renew:
The Caldron suppled, what was grown too hard:
The Thorns did quicken, what was grown too dull:
All did but strive to mend what you had marr'd.

There is a great sadness and compassion in him—often compassion for God, as is shown in this extract from "Sepulchre":

Sure there is room within our hearts good store;
For they can lodge transgressions by the score:
Thousands of toyes dwell there, yet out of doore
They leave Thee . . .
And as of old, the Law by heav'nly art
Was writ in stone; so thou, which also art
The letter of the word, find'st no fit heart
To hold Thee.

Where he asks for the law to be written on his heart, as is the custom, he sadly turns the request around and seems to ask for his own heart to be his grave-stone: a new version indeed of the book of the heart:

O smooth my rugged heart, and there
Engrave thy rev'rend law and fear;
Or make a new one, since the old
Is saplesse grown
And a much fitter stone
To hide my dust, than thee to hold.

Which adds up to so sincere a human sorrow that it would be a sin not to be-lieve him when, asking for a thankful heart, he requests one

Not thankfull, when it pleaseth me;
As if Thy blessings had spare days:
But such a heart, whose pulse may be
Thy praise.

One of the extras Herbert brings to the emblematic tradition is anatomy: as the reality of the physical heart was uncovered, the greatest poets incorporated the new knowledge into their imagery. And in "The Church-Porch" he invites us to

> Salute thyself: see what thy soul doth wear.
> Dare to look in thy chest; for 'tis thine own:
> And tumble up and down what thou find'st there.

This is "*nosce te ipsum*" on a spiritual plane. The poem was written in 1633, during the age of dissection and scientific advance; Vesalius's open-torsoed anatomical men had been strolling though their classical landscapes pointing out their own organs for a century; Harvey had identified the circulation of the blood. We may not be able literally to look into our own chests and tumble our own hearts, but what are poets for, after all?

THE FLYING HEART

As modern life values freedom above devotion, so the heart emblem which has survived in best shape is the winged heart. A young friend sends me a picture message from her mobile phone: a heart with wings flapping, cartoon-style. Bryan Ferry croons on the radio: "And oh my heart has wings, these foolish things, remind me of you." A patch on the back of my old biker jacket: a heart, wings wide, HARLEY-DAVIDSON USA written across the middle. "The very instant that I saw you," says Ferdinand to Miranda, "did my heart fly to your service." The heart sometimes has arms and, very occasionally, knees, but wings are standard issue. How else could it soar?

The hieroglyph for the ancient Egyptian *haty* sometimes appeared as a jar with a little wing on each side. To judge by looks alone it is definitely an ancestor of the modern winged heart. The ancient Egyptian *ib* could be lifted up—love lifted it, for example. Light-heartedness has been around for millennia.

The biblical heart was forever being lifted up unto the Lord like a sacrifice. The chalice of communion wine—heartlike—is lifted at the altar. And love does have wings—Cupid flew. How can a soul rise to heaven without wings? How could Christ "rise again" without wings? Of course the heart flies, and in doing so it takes on one of the oldest human fantasies, the very image of freedom.

For the emblematic heart, freedom from worldly desires combines with freedom from being earthbound to become freedom from death: eternal life—the gift of Jesus. A heart with wings takes comfort, rising above the sorrows of the earth.

Christopher Harvey (see page 228) accompanied his emblems with his own poetry: he professed to be a follower of George Herbert. The verses accompanying number 38 of the *Schola Cordis*, "The Flying of the Heart," make, like Herbert's "Easter Wings," the shape of wings:

> Oh that it were once winged like the Dove,
> That in a moment mounts on high,
> Then should it soon remove,
> Where it may lye
> In love,
> And loe,
> This one desire
> Me thinks hath imp'd* it so,
> That it already flies like fire,
> And ev'n my verses into wings do grow.

And a heart with wings, lifted up by love, is conveniently mobile for taking messages and getting from one lover to another. It suggests angels carrying the soul away to heaven on snowy white dove wings, as described in the spirituals, or the wings of Gabriel at the Annunciation. And it is flexible, as is shown in this poem by the Turcoman dervish Yunus Emre, who was much admired by Rumi:

> How wondrous this gift of God, this heart which time transforms,
> One moment awash with delight, the next steeped in woe,
> Suddenly struck dumb, all words shorn of meaning,

---

*"To imp" is a falconer's term, meaning to graft extra feathers on to a bird's wings to make it fly better. The dove, remember, nestled in the cleft of the rock.

Till suddenly silver-tongued, a balm for troubled souls.
One moment plying the starry heights, then plummeting, broken-
　　winged;
Now a mere droplet, now a vast ocean bursting its brink
Now in a mosque, its face pressed down in prayer,
Now in a monastery, sharing the Gospel with monks.

Above all a flying heart can get from place to place quickly, bearing messages and love. Hence the picture on the mobile phone.

7

A WORD ON FOLLY AND KITSCH
AND *O BROTHER, WHERE ART THOU?*
(OR, WHO DIED AND MADE REASON GOD?)

"It's a fool looks for logic in the chambers of the human heart," says George Clooney, playing Everett Ulysses Gill, hero of the Coen brothers' film *O Brother, Where Art Thou?*, a latter-day Mississippi Odyssey. Moments later he and his chain-gang escapee buddies are surrounded by white-robed Christians going down the river to be baptized, singing a beautiful swampy bluesy gospel song about being borne away on snow-white wings. Ulysses's companions race down to the river to be saved. Their sins washed away by immersion, they cry that neither God nor man has a thing on them now.

Sitting in the Odeon, thinking about the longevity of heart imagery: the sacrament of water that flowed from Christ's heart wound, about Osiris and the "cool water" for the washing of the heart, about the snow-white wings of the dove of the Holy Spirit, heading for the cleft in the rock that St. Gregory identified with Christ's heart wound, thinking about a friend who was behaving illogically, foolishly in a matter of love . . . It's a fool looks for logic in the chambers of the human heart. Saw the Fool's Head map lifting a lantern as Christ does in the emblems, but lifting it in the anonymous nun's heart, lifting it in different rooms of the mansion, in the storehouse, the bedchamber, the reception and the thalamus, the memory, the study, the place where the law is written in stone, the light flickering though the windows like a burglar's torch, like the qu'ranic image. Saw the Fool looking for logic, finding only his own reflection in the mirror of a clean and polished heart.

After Descartes reinvented reason in the seventeenth century and located it in the pituitary gland, the heart became for a while the enemy of reason, an identifiable anatomical object that was the emblem of all unidentifiable, antiscientific, irrational urges. But even as an atheist knows what God is, the most reasonable knew—and were perhaps scared of the fact—that the heart has it reasons that reason cannot know. The Fool looking for reason in the heart has clearly not read Pascal:

> We know truth not only through reason but also by way of the heart . . . it is on this knowledge of the heart and of instinct that reason has to rely and found all of its discourse. This impotence should only serve then to humiliate reason, which wishes to judge all, but not to combat our certainty, as if there were no other faculty than reason capable of instructing us.

There is, however, plenty of room for folly in the heart. The flexibility and gorgeousness of the image has led to an imaginative free-for-all, where the heart can mean, or be, anything at all. Images have always held a particular power for the illiterate; the illiterate have always needed luck as much as God's grace, and the heart easily became a ubiquitous good-luck emblem. Another version of the Mexican votive hearts led to the *corazón* of popular culture: lottery tickets, good-luck candles (*Amor! Felicidad! Pesetas!*), the sweet tawdries of modern kitsch.

Tricky to explain kitsch, but it must be done. Here's the theory: the Sacred Heart became kitsch in that moment when somebody looked at it *again* and recognized it was kitsch; a lapsed Catholic, perhaps, someone with a sentimental yearning, nonetheless genuine for being sentimental, and a desire to bring down the icon for which he yearns though he knows it will give him no satisfaction. For more people than would care to admit it, religious images are kitsch because it is easier to feel better about our loss of God if we can mock the items beloved of the most faithful, the most ignorant and illiterate—those who fall for the prettied-up, ridiculous images of the most precious thing in man's existence, the thing which may well not even exist: the love of God.

I have around me as I write the results of the free-for-all: a handful of multicoloured pressed-tin hearts adorned in various ways with flowers and crowns; a red Cellophane heart which, depending how it curls on my hand, will tell me—in Spanish—how much I am in love; a little pink plastic toy heart on legs inscribed with the words *cuore matto* (crazy heart), which jumps and chatters; a good-luck candle covered in hearts and dollar signs (*salud, amor y dinero*—health, love and money); a red fake-fur heart which trembles when you pull a string; a heart-shaped purse covered in scarlet glass beads; an amber heart from Poland; a gold crowned heart for hanging on a Christmas tree; a clear Perspex key-ring heart with a red plastic rose set in it; an eighteen-inch cardboard heart entirely swathed in sequins, glitter, tinsel, a plastic gilt Madonna, tiny pictures of saints, red Christmas-tree balls and an array of motto-cum-prayers; postage stamps (a lacy American one with roses—55 cents—and a chic French one designed by Yves Saint Laurent); a long clear tube full of gel with floating sequins—hearts, musical notes, gold discs and a tiny model of Elvis Presley (there's also a minute pink Cadillac, but it's very hard to spot); an exquisite votive silver-filigree flaming heart I got in Rome when I was eight; a string of crimson heart-shaped fairy lights; an eighteen-inch plaster Jesus opening his yellow robe to display his flaming scar-let heart; a shiny red wooden heart on a string; a large green glass heart and four tiny Venetian glass hearts, in shimmering pink and sea green; a Rwandan pin-up of Jesus with pink and white rays (for blood and water) emanating from his bosom, labeled *Yezu ndakwizera* (Jesus I have confidence in you); a gold wooden heart with a star emerging from the top; a folded and pleated pa-per garland of hearts from China; a wooden Indian printing block in the form of a heart with wings and a crown; a heart-shaped hot-water bottle; a red, heart-shaped washing-up sponge; a gel-filled heart that you boil in a saucepan and use as a hand warmer; a picture of a Ghanaian fabric celebrating the postal service, based on a pattern of interconnected hearts; a heart-shaped bulldog clip on a prong; a hollow rubber anatomically correct heart-shaped squirty bath toy; and an anatomical model of a heart, which you can open up—oh no, that's not kitsch. Or is it? Hearts litter every stage of the long path from the sublime to the ridiculous. (And I swear I have resisted *plenty* of other potential purchases during my time writing this book. Plenty.)

Dr. Boyadjian's collection in Brussels runs the length of that long path, but where my trash is mostly trash, his is historical and religious: he has church ornaments, lanterns and oil lamps in red glass, heart-shaped with radi-ant mother-of-pearl and semi-precious stones, the imprint of

Heart-shaped stamps, © *La Poste/Yves Saint Laurent*

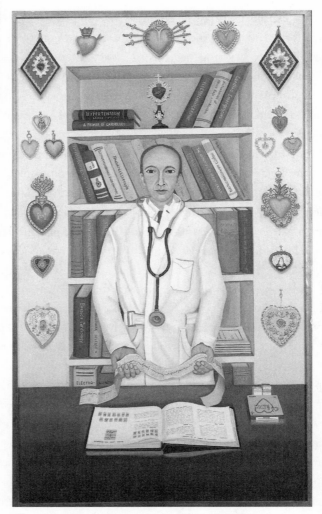

The Heart Specialist and His Hearts, by Micheline
Boyadjian, 1971: note the books on hypertension and
intravascular catheterization and the votive, flaming,
pierced, inhabited, floral hearts on the walls.
© *Musées Royaux d'Art et d'Histoire, Bruxelles*

drops of blood etched on the glass. He has holy water stoups made of porcelain: in one you dip your fingers in the wound for water to cross yourself with.
He has Austrian heart-shaped lamps with wings: the flames emerging from
the top are real; the heart holds the oil. He has a nineteenth-century board
game called Spiritual Recreation, a kind of Snakes and Ladders with hearts on

every square, and improving verses. (Snakes and Ladders is biblical: it refers to the Serpent of Eden and Jacob's Ladder.) He has framed German marriage mementos of cream satin and wax flowers; sailor's pin cushions; lockets and Valentines; boxes and jewels; a massive Austrian fireplace bearing the five wounds . . . The doctor started to collect in the fifties, and his collection is not kitsch because he didn't see it as kitsch. Now, rather sadly, it would be impossible to put all this together without kitschness being an issue.

In a church in Santa Fiora in Tuscany, as in so many Italian churches, stands the same mass-produced Jesus in his yellow robe that I have at home, his heart visible outside it, radiant with gold paint and palpitatingly red. Nearby, a blue and white ceramic "Last Supper" by della Robbia adorns a pulpit. At the center of the long table is Jesus; next to him, and resting against his chest, is St. John. He is listening with his never-sleeping eye of the heart, though looking at it you wouldn't know. Here, side by side, can be seen the most obvious and vulgar manifestation of the Christian heart and one of the sweetest and most discreet.

THE
LOVER'S HEART

1

THE HEART OF HUMAN LOVE

The heart, as we have seen, is full of love. So what is love? As Harley-Davidson riders say, if you don't understand, I can't explain. Rumi put it slightly better: "The intellect becomes like a donkey mired in mud in its efforts to explain love. It is love which explains love . . . The evidence of the sun is the sun. If you require proof, turn your face away from it." As St. Augustine heard: "I am what I am."

But here goes anyway:

Love is artificially divided into two. I described the physical heart earlier as Siamese twins; so, according to Western culture, is the emotional heart. One side is filled with Eros: a love that is romantic, sexual, selfish, passionate, mad, magical, irresistible, physical, pagan, pre-Christian, enchanting, repressed and often, when forbidden, ultimately egocentric. On the other is Agape, also known as Caritas: a love that is Christian, gentle, unselfish, forbearing, ultimately theocentric. Of course, these two have many further subdivisions, and other cultures have other approaches. But once again the heart is both.

The problem with this is that since God was so widely abolished in the West, half the heart is yearning. For many of us one of the traditional love objects is gone. We are a halfhearted generation.

The heart sexualizes spirituality, and it spiritualizes sex. The Christian heart shows the Eros in the Agape, as does the mystical Sufi heart. At the same time the heart represents the Agape within the Eros: the profession of fidelity, the declaration of loyalty underpinning passion—"true love," if you like. You don't send a Valentine to a one-night stand, no matter how orgasmic it was. The heart, sexual though it can be, is not a symbol of sex.

This poem from the sixteenth century, by Barnabe Barnes, is a nice example of sexualized Christian imagery, an erotic Holy Communion in which the lover wishes that he could be

> that sweet wine, which downe her throate doth trickle,
> to kisse her lippes, and lye next at her hart,
> runne through her vaynes, and passe by pleasure's part . . .

Spiritual love is not a substitute for human love, and vice versa. They are extensions of each other. The difference is that Cupid was an arrogant, tricking little brat who rode on dolphins, burned nymphs with his torch, fired his arrows into goodness knows whose heart without a moment's consideration, put on his dad's armor and reveled in his power over the living, the dead and even the gods. Cupid is the son of war. It's his job to cause chaos in the hearts of men—as Ovid makes clear:

> . . . the God undid his quiver and pulled out
> an arrow with my name on it.
> "Poet," he said, flexing the bow against his knee,
> "I'll give you something to sing about—take that!"
> Alas his arrows never miss. My blood's on fire.
> Love has moved in as master of my heart.

Researchers in Pisa have just recently decided that romantic palpitations—the fluttery heart of love—is chemically akin to obsessive-compulsive disorder: both are caused by low serotonin levels.

Christ's job, on the other hand, was to make peace in the heart. But the overlap is unavoidable: *Emblemata amatoria*—Emblems of Love—showed a remarkably close family resemblance between the rose-plucking, heart-shooting Cupid (god of love) and the divine Cupid or Christ child (God of Love). Henry Hawkins is less incorporative: he beseeches the angels "to drive away Cupid, that infamous princock boy, that lewd stripling, to knap his arrows asunder and to burn his quiver that he may never more come neere my hart, or offer any violence to it." But Cupid, like Christ, is used to being insulted—by Ovid, for one:

> O Cupid, you who can never be reviled as much as the situation warrants,
> O boy, loitering in my heart, why do you harm me,

A nineteenth-century English valentine showing the heart as a castle, pierced with arrows. © *The Art Archive / Private Collection*

> A soldier who has never deserted your standard, and why am I wounded in
>   my own camp?
> Why does your torch burn and your shaft pierce your own friends?

Here we have a clear if negative precursor of the heart as a house and of Christ with his flames and wounds. Later in the same poem Ovid repents his rudeness and invites Cupid and his beautiful mother to come and rule his breast. Does it sound familiar?

With this classical and Christian background it seems absurd to ask why the heart is the emblem of romantic love, at least in the West, but since I've asked, and because the heart is the emblem of human love not only in the West, the answer is:

1. Because the human heart does seem to skip a beat, or lurch, when the newly noticed love object appears: it might feel like an arrow to the heart, it is actually the effects of chemicals.
2. Because the human heart does seem to fill and glow when the familiar love object is near: this is the endorphins.

3. Because the human heart does ache when emotional pain afflicts its owner.

4. Because the human heart speeds up like anything during sex and orgasm. Someone—Woody Allen?—said that the brain is the great neglected erogenous zone, and so it is, but only the heart joins in so wildly with the actual sex—the palpitating, contracting, squeezing and pumping of fluids. The heart, the penis and the clitoris are the only organs to fill up with blood in the course of their duties.

5. Because for the past two millennia Western civilization has been predicated on a love-based religion which in many ways has used the heart as the source and object of that love.

6. And because, in an arguably less loving incarnation, followers of that religion felt the need to force it on everyone they came across as they attempted to colonize the world—and often succeeded.

7. Because for a while now Western cultures have worshipped, alongside Mammon, a notion of romantic, sexual love, and as the heart is in place as the emblem of love in the previous religion (Christianity), so it slips easily into this further territory. Though religious faith seems to decline, in many ways it simply moves around: how else did all those ancient religions end up as aspects of Christianity and Islam? Why do so many religions share so much—the significance of the heart being only one example?

8. Because everybody knows it is. The connection between the heart and love is as near to inherent, or instinctive, as an idea can be.

Some say that love was invented in Aquitaine in the eleventh century. According to C. S. Lewis, "Compared with this revolution the Renaissance is a mere ripple on the surface of literature." But in that case, what was Cupid up to all that time? What was it that Isis felt for Osiris, or Paris for Helen? What were Sappho and Catullus writing about? How could Aphrodite exist? What were Rama and Sita doing? Why did Ishtar follow Tammuz, and Orpheus Eurydice? What was going on when Ovid described "love and hate, here in my heart, at tug of war"? And why, in a story recorded in tenth-century Kashmir, does Vararuchi tell how his heart was cleft by the stroke of love's arrow when he first saw Upakosa?

Lucretius described the process of sexual love in some detail in *De Rerum Natura,* translated by Dryden in the seventeenth century: how the appearance of the woman (or boy—heterosexuality was a late invention too) shoots fiery darts into the man, injecting his heart with desire, transfixing it and filling it with the need to "inject the sprightly seed" into the body which has provoked this desire.

> Such is the nature of that pleasing smart
> Whose burning drops distill upon the heart
> The fever of the soul shot from the fair
> And the cold ague of succeeding care . . .
> When hands in hands they lock, and thighs in thighs they entwine
> Just in the raging foam of full desire,
> When both press on, both murmur, both expire,
> They gripe, they squeeze, their humid tongues they dart,
> As each would force their way to t'other's heart.

So erotic love goes from the heart, and to the heart. The "cold ague" of anxiety and fear and postcoital distress comes later.

In classical times love was a tragicomedy that you fervently hoped would not befall anyone in your family, a chaotic fall from grace, nothing but trouble. Mercutio took this view when he said:

> Alas poor Romeo, he is already dead!
> Stabbed with a white wench's black eye; shot through
> the ear with a love-song; the very pin of his
> heart cleft with the blind bow-boy's butt-shaft . . .

The "pin" of the heart is interesting: in fairy tales an enchanted creature with a pin in its head can be liberated when the pin is removed (this happened in "The Pomegranate Raja"—see page 253); the pin could be seen as an axle, the pin of a hinge, that which holds everything together. In the beautiful old ballad "Waly, Waly," the lover declares:

> But had I wist, before I kist,
> That love had been sae ill to win,
> I had lock'd my heart in a case of gold
> And pinn'd it with a silver pin.

The pin of the heart would be like the backbone of a book, holding the two sides together. And angels dance on the heads of pins . . . In all, it is something altogether too graceful and balanced to withstand the vulgar attack of a blind bow-boy's butt-shaft.

THE WIZARD OF OZ

The fate of the three companions in the children's book *The Wizard of Oz* exemplifies how traditional heart qualities have changed neighborhood. The Wicked Witch of the West, remember, destroyed the Tin Man's human body bit by bit until he was all made of tin replacements, had no heart and therefore could not love the Munchkin Maiden whose domestic services the witch was reluctant to give up. He desperately wanted a heart: to love and be loved, to unite with his fellows (and the Munchkin Maiden) and to feel that he belonged. He stood rusted up for a year, and during that time, "I had time to think that the greatest loss I had known was the loss of my heart. While I was in love I was the happiest man on earth; but no one can love who has not a heart." The Scarecrow wanted a brain: he wanted intelligence, certainty, a raison d'être. "I shall ask for brains," he said, "because a fool would not know what to do with a heart if he had one." The Lion wanted courage, confidence, identity—the strength to be himself. "As long as I know myself to be a coward I shall be unhappy," he says; "perhaps if I had no heart I should not be a coward," adding cowardice to the list of qualities that live in the heart and demonstrating once again how the heart contains its own opposite.

All the things that the companions seek—including Dorothy's wish to go back to Kansas, home being where the heart is—are traditional heart qualities. But *The Wizard of Oz* being a twentieth-century tale, the heart is now for romantic love only: the Tin Man needs it not so he can unite with God, but so he can marry his Munchkin Maiden. Intelligence, courage, faith and individuality now live elsewhere. Thus is the human soul divided.

But, in the end, the story suggests your heart's desire is in your own backyard. When the Scarecrow, the Lion and the Tin Man, with his little silk and sawdust heart and the tin patch where the Wizard put it into his chest, believe that they have what they wanted, they have it.

In medieval times the idea of Christ as a man, and Mary as his mother, and women as love objects (and thus even more valuable marriage commodities) all developed at about the same time. Love now took on a respectability; it became admirable, and ultimately overriding. Courtly love moved in with religious union, occupying the same little house in the human body, and adopted some of the seriousness of its housemate. The heart had a new job. Whether it was a promotion or a move sideways is a matter of opinion.

Sometime after Shakespeare, intelligence and understanding moved out of the heart and took up residence in the brain. Then God died (though, as ever, he is showing signs of coming back to life). Now only romantic love and the reasons that reason cannot know are still living in the Western heart, knocking about rather in its many chambers.

The traditional uses of the romantic heart continue: Irish Claddagh rings are in the form of a heart held at each side by a hand. If you wear it with the heart pointing in (up your arm) it says you're taken; the heart pointing out says you're available. It used to be thought that rings were worn on the third finger because it had a special connection with the heart. Clearly this is an old belief, and old too is the belief that it is nonsense: Sir Thomas Browne, M.D., gave four pages to refuting it in his *Vulgar Errors* of 1646. Wearing your heart on your sleeve harks back to medieval tournaments, where a knight would wear a lady's "favor"—usually a ribbon or handkerchief—pinned to his sleeve as a mark of his devotion to her. Nineteenth-century Norman hearts were a piece of jewelry in the shape of a heart broken in two. A woman would be given one half on marriage, the other when she had her first child (recalling Alice Thomas Ellis's observation that the perfect couple is not a man and a woman, but a woman and a child). Modern versions exist as pendants: two friends each wear round their neck a jagged half gold heart with half the legend BEST FRIENDS engraved on it. With printing, capitalism and adjustments in the nature of God (no more embroidery by female acolytes required), there are ever more sleeves on which hearts can be worn.

As we have seen, the romantic heart is universally used and understood in design and advertising, in games, greetings cards, bumper stickers . . . It frequently descends into kitsch (consider French artists Pierre et Gilles, tattooing, Jean Paul Gaultier, Spanish bingo cards [see Appendix II] and has been the mainstay of sentimentality for years (the Valentine industry, "Love Is . . ." cartoons, "I ♥ _____," and—on another level—Raymond Peynet's *Amants* and their delicious visual heart-puns). The love heart is a natural in animated cartoons: when Tex Avery's big bad wolf visits a nightclub and falls in love with a singer his heart does the most glorious gymnastics which funnily enough echo the descriptions of various kinds of heart pain listed in Victorian homeopathy

LOVE HEARTS

The heart of the Love Heart, the candy-colored outline encircling a fat heart bearing a message within it, has become a common motif in its own right. It's on book covers (the proof copy of my first novel, *Baby Love*, used it); it's in advertisements, on T-shirts, in clubs, on music packaging. Harrods recently ran an advertisement showing an array of Love Hearts, each with the name of a desirable designer written on it: John Galliano, Gucci. It follows on from the "I ♥ such-and-such" of the late twentieth-century bumper sticker, but is much richer, and furthermore cool (perhaps because a pastel-colored thing you pop in your mouth speaks to and of drug culture as well).

They are sweet—suggesting moral goodness and kindness—lovable and adorable like Christ's heart or a benevolent lover's. They have writing on them—recalling God's law written in the heart and the heart as a book. They declare romantic love and everyday desire. They are a method of communication: "let me tell you what's in my heart"; "open your heart to me." They are the place where lower urges (I want a sweetie) meet higher ones (I want love). They are hearts that people give to each other. And let's not forget Willie Nelson and his beautiful song "Valentine": "If anyone could, you could have a candy heart, you're the sweetest of all sweethearts." They come in fruit flavors. They don't sing, but even so the Love Heart heart is the twentieth-century version of the 5,000-year-old icon. Once again, almost everything is taken in, soaked up, held and symbolized by the heart.

And then eaten.

books: "Swings to and fro as on a string, yoyos, feels clutched as if by an iron hand."

A WORD ON VALENTINES

St. Valentine had nothing to with the heart. He was a Roman priest who was beaten and beheaded in the third century, and he is the patron of lovers merely because of a coincidence of timing. His feast day coincided with the

Roman festival of Lupercalia, during which young girls' names were written down and put in a box to be ceremonially drawn by young men during a month-long series of feasts in honor of Pan—god of chaos and wine—and Juno—goddess of marriage. The combination was a potent one. The early Fathers tried to put an end to such pagan fun; as usual, rather than ending, the habits and frolics merely adjusted a little and took on a Christian front, including the Christian symbol of love—the speared heart—which so neatly fit with the classical symbol of love—Cupid with his careless arrows.

"Valentine's Day is now almost everywhere a much degenerated festival," wrote Dr. Chambers, in his excellent Book of Days (*A Miscellany of Popular Antiquities*, 1869), "the only observance of any note consisting merely of the sending of jocular letters to parties whom one wishes to *quiz*, and this confined very much to the humbler classes." He goes on to sniff at the vast number of ridiculous caricatures and burlesque verses, the altars of Hymen, fluttering cupids and "hearts transfixed with his darts" that "maid servants and young fellows interchange . . . no doubt conceiving that the joke is amazingly good." Misson, in the early eighteenth century, recorded a more complex observance: young men and women would write their names on pieces of pa-

A "*poilu*"—a French soldier in the First World War—sends good luck to his girl: a ladybird for prosperity, a horseshoe for fidelity, a white rat for mad love and a louse for happiness, all radiating from a pierced heart. © *Wellcome Library, London*

293

CHARLES LAMB

Charles Lamb, in his essay on Valentine's Day, had this to say:

> In these little visual interpretations no emblem is so common as the heart—that little three-cornered exponent of all our hopes and fears —the bestruck and bleeding heart; it is twisted and tortured into more allegories and affectations than an opera hat. What authority we have in history or mythology for placing the headquarters and metropolis of god Cupid in this anatomical seat rather than in any other is not very clear; but we have got it, and it will serve as well as any other. Else we might easily imagine, upon some other system which might have prevailed for anything which our pathology knows to the contrary, a lover addressing his mistress, in perfect simplicity of feeling,—"Madam, my liver and fortune are entirely at your disposal"; or putting a delicate question, "Amanda, have you a midriff to bestow?" But custom has settled these things and awarded the seat of sentiment to the aforesaid triangle, while its less fortunate neighbors wait at animal and anatomical distance.

per which were then drawn by lots, whereupon both the person who drew your name and the person whose name you drew became your Valentine. "Fortune having thus divided the company into so many couples, the Valentines give balls and treats to their mistresses, wear their billets several days upon their bosoms or sleeves, and this little sport often ends in love." Samuel Pepys was dressing on Valentine's Day 1667 when "came up to my wife's bedside little Will Mercer to be her valentine, and brought her name written upon blue paper in gold letters, done by himself, very pretty, and we were both well pleased with it. But I am also this year my wife's valentine, and it will cost me £5." Later, "I find that Mrs. Pierce's little girl is my valentine, she having drawn me, which I was not sorry for, it easing me of something more that I must have given to others." Either way, Pepys had gotten off cheaply: of Miss Stuart, who became Duchess of Richmond, he wrote: "The duke of York, being once her valentine, did give her a jewel of about £800; and my lord Mandeville, her valentine this year, a ring of about £300."

The first person you saw on Valentine's Day would be your husband; if you pinned bay leaves to your pillow that night and dreamed of him you would marry him . . . The idea was that February 14 was the day the birds choose their mates, and so should we, according to this verse by John Donne:

From "An Epithalamium" on the Lady Elizabeth and Count Palatine being married on St. Valentine's Day:

Haile Bishop Valentine, whose day this is,
All the Aire is thy Diocis,
And all the chirping Choristers
And other birds are thy Parishioners
Thou marryest every yeare
The Lyrique Larke, and the grave whispering Dove,
The Sparrow that neglects his life for love . . .

2

LOVE NEEDS AN OBJECT

Love needs an object, anything will do
When I was a child I loved a pumping engine,
Thought it every bit as beautiful as you.

W. H. AUDEN

Love needs an object, and it may be God, and it may be the boy next door. The inheritor of the poetic tradition of romance and religion, the bastard offspring of St. Augustine, Hafiz, Herbert and Donne, is funnily enough country and western music, with its taste for imagery, form, moral narratives and elegant conceits. When you hear Connie Francis sing that her heart has a mind of its own, or how she's breaking in a brand-new broken heart; or Kitty Lester commending the strength of feeling in "Love Letters Straight from the Heart"; or Randy Travis declaring that it's written in stone how he feels for you; or that great song "My Tears Have Washed 'I Love You' from the Blackboard of My Heart," the ghosts of ancient imagery are up there on the hardwood floor two-stepping with the best of them. And when Hank Williams sings that "Your Cheating Heart" will tell on you, it could be a soundtrack for the ancient Egyptian psychostasia.

In another Hank Williams song, "Cold Cold Heart," the woman can't forgive a former lover who done her wrong, and therefore can't open up to poor Hank, who wants to melt her cold cold heart. John Hiatt continues the image in a different setting in "Icy Blue Heart," which Emmy Lou Harris sings in icy blue tones, about a man wondering whether it would be worth melting what's been frozen for years into a river of tears. (Matthew Arnold used a similar image, saying of Wordsworth: "He spoke, and loosed our heart in tears." Frozen tears, incidentally, are an image used by the Ndembu people of Zambia; one of the wooden figures, known as Pieces of Perception, used by diviners. But I digress.) He's felt the chill, he says, that can follow the first kiss when there's not enough heat in the fire burning there. Either of these songs could be illustrated by Amor with his little bellows; by Iesule and his fluttering flames of love, trying desperately to warm up the isolated sufferer. But then in "Heart on Fire" we hear the other side of the story: Gram Parsons and Emmy Lou mourn and object to the heart being aflame with love, and want the lover to let this cold heart be: this takes us straight back to the reluctant heart of the *Schola Cordis,* which won't admit Christ, with his uncomfortably bright lantern and his irritating flames. And they have a point: Jim Morrison and a thousand other pants-on-fire singing seducers hark on the warmth and the passion (the rhymes in English help: burn, yearn; fire, higher; flame, shame), forgetting that human love is not like religious fervor. The Burning Bush burns without destroying, but in carnal love,

> When your heart's on fire,
> You must realize,
> Smoke gets in your eyes ...

Later on in that song of 1932—the first worldwide number-one hit for a black band (the Platters)—love flies away and the flame dies. Smoke in your eyes is a multilayered image: it brings tears to your eyes, makes you cry, it hurts, it stops you from seeing clearly and it's a form of self-deception, stopping you from seeing what's going on. Remember the smoke rising from Hafiz's winding sheet ...

The temperature of the heart, perhaps because it correlates so nicely with sexual temperature, almost swamps the imagery of modern love songs. But the others are still there, lurking quietly. Blondie's "Heart of Glass" goes back to John Donne and the biblical and Sufi image of the heart as a mirror. Here, the perfect heart of glass in which God saw his own reflection transmutes into a cold, hard, fragile and dangerous thing, where reflection is rejection, not recognition. In "Heart Like a Wheel" Kate and Anna McGarrigle describe a classic heart pilgrimage: the heart's like a wheel because if you bend it, you can't mend it—remember the heart on the anvil; then it's all at sea, it's in a sinking ship on an ocean. Hafiz's heart was a wheel too:

> My heart wheeled round in circles
> Like a compass twirled in the fingers

Till it fell down giddy and lay still
The minstrel sang such a ghazal
Of the sorrows of love
That blood oozed down on the eyelashes
Of every learned scholar in the world.

When Tammy Wynette sang,

Don't open the doors to heaven, if I can't come in,
Don't touch me, if you don't love me, sweetheart,

she was singing a worldly love song, but one replete with biblical imagery: of the heart wound which is the gate of heaven; of the connection between touching and wounding through the Latin *stringere* (to press, to pinch); of the ancient link through touch, to wound, to connection, to love, to ecstasy, to salvation.

It's not only country: the very phrase "rock 'n' roll" originated in black churches—the swaying of the spirit, the heart being moved. Bruce Springsteen's "Hungry Heart" could hold one of those sacramental picnics illustrated by the Painting Nun; it could be plowed and sown as it was in the Heart Emblem series, and sprout good wheat to feed itself. It's in no danger of being the smug, fat heart of the Old Testament. "Take these chains from my heart and set me free," sing karaoke aficionados up and down the land, almost certainly not considering Donne's "Take mee to you, imprison mee, for I/Except you'enthrall mee, never shall be free" (another version is Kris Kristofferson's "Freedom's just another word for nothing left to lose," from "Me and Bobby McGee"), or Shakespeare's "Prison my heart in thy steel bosom's ward," or the emblematic heart freed from the love of worldly things by the love of God, his hand coming down from a cloud and cutting the chains that bound the heart to a treasure chest or an orb. Who of the many who sang "Drown in My Own Tears" knew of Sir Cueur, knocked into the Stream of Tears by the knight Soucy (see page 304)?

In "Getting Mighty Crowded," a tragically neglected soul classic with a straightforward heart-as-a-house motif, Betty Everett sings of packing up her memories, turning in her keys and moving on out of his heart. She's going to "leave the neighborhood" and "find another heart where [she] can live all by [herself]." Clearly she would never have made a nun.

Christ holding up a glass heart full of animals and healing a sick woman with the fluid from his heart wound: the biblical references include Matthew 12, in which Christ heals the sick on the Sabbath, and Hebrews 4, which says: "the word of God is a discerner of the thoughts and intents of the heart. Neither is there any creature that is not manifest in his sight, but all things are naked and opened unto the eyes of him with whom we have to do." The glass heart is transparent, and the "creatures" are the nasty qualities we met before in *The Heart of Man* on page 208.

© *Wellcome Library, London*

RED AND BLUE

Blue, like the Blues, represents melancholy and pain; blue is cold, which is sad and lonely; blue is bruised and battered; blue is also without oxygen, like a blue baby or a dying person's lips. The blood coming back to the heart for oxygen is blue; filled up again with what it needs it is red. If oxygen = love = *pneuma*/vital spirits, then red is full and rich and equipped and united and loving, and blue is poor, deprived, loveless, alienated from humanity. Pursuing this idea, the left heart is the red, oxygenated side (red is also the color of port, as in port and starboard); the right heart, where the tired, needy, deoxygenated blood comes in, is the blue side. Red and blue, left and right. There may be a Labor Party political broadcast lurking in there somewhere, but I don't think I will pursue it.

Janis Joplin is a willing Aztec when she wails, "Take it, take another little piece of my heart now, baby"—human sacrifice by installments. When Mick Jagger shouts, "Can You Hear Me Knocking?" who recalls the lover asking to be let into the heart in the Song of Solomon? The Yardbirds had their "Heart Full of Soul," a lyric any twelfth-century mystic would go along with. Annie Lennox mused about an angel playing with her heart, echoing Herbert's encouragement to "tumble up and down" what we find in our chests. The ancient Egyptians told us why it was bad to leave your heart anywhere—a couple of thousand years later Tony Bennett sang of how he left his in San Francisco, and now an airline uses a picture of a lonely little heart with a lost property label on it to advertise flights there. (San Francisco is named after the first saint to have Christ's heart-wound reproduced on his body, in a country where the first appearance of whose name on a map was on a heart-shaped map. And Christ did leave his heart in various saints.) And who did write the Book of Love?

While on the subject of the ridiculous: "Boom boody-boom boody-boom boody-boom (Goodness Gracious Me)," in which Peter Sellers does his silly Indian doctor impression, Sophia Loren palpitates breathily—the title is her description of what her heart is up to—and the goings-on between her cleavage and his stethoscope remind us why René Hyacinthe Laennec invented it in the first place.

The "St. Louis Blues" tells of a mean man who's "got a heart like a rock cast into the sea," which picks up two emblematic roles of the heart: as the rock for writing on (what is strong and firm for the law is hard and mean to a lover, and also very heavy) and being thrown into the sea during its trials (cut off and lost to love, until Jesus rescues it).

But ninety percent of modern heart imagery is about love, and the broken heart—the heart ruined by love—is paramount: "What Becomes of the Broken-hearted?" "Only Love Can Break Your Heart," "Heartbreak Hotel," "Unbreak My Heart" . . . This broken heart is where Christ the true lover makes his entrance, but over the years Jesus has lost most of his sex appeal and many people have lost him; instead you have Tammy Wynette singing, "I'm a Christian, Lord, but I'm a woman too"; and Christian rock is not just a contradiction in terms, it's also a bad joke. In rock 'n' roll only Bob Dylan, bigger than both, and Nick Cave, darker than the devil, have done anything to suggest that the devil hasn't had all the best tunes since 1950.

Blues and soul music have always been about God. Soul's own John Donne/St. Francis figure (live a wild life, then turn to God) is Al Green (see page 137): "Take me to the River, drop me in the water, washing me down," he sings; or, "It's you that I want but it's Him that I need." Like Donne, Green became a preacher, and the powerful double direction of his love only strengthened his art too. The Bee Gees wrote "How Can You Mend a Broken Heart?" but sung by Al Green it becomes a plainsong for posterity.

Some messages hardly change. Bob Marley probably would have known that his lyrics to "One Love," the bit about one heart and everyone getting together and being all right, echo Jeremiah: "And I will give them one heart, and one way, that they may fear me for ever, for the good of them, and of their children after them." And how about these two: Hafiz's "He cannot perish whose heart holds the life love breathes" and Gloria Gaynor's "As long as I know how to love I know I'm still alive"?

I won't give you a list of every love song with the image of a heart in it. Just remember, next time you hear one, the journey the heart has taken. And here, for the quintessential rock 'n' roll attitude to the heart, are the sleeve notes from Steve Earle's 1997 album *El Corazon*:

The Greeks were right! It's the heart that matters. Don't try to tell me it's all in my head, 'cause thinking too much only gives me a headache (a minor annoyance) and I know where I hurt when promises are broken and dreams die and the lump in your throat when your firstborn starts walking or talking back, that's your heart, fool, ten sizes too big, bangin' away at your chest, hollerin' "Let me out of this box and I'll really fuck you up!" And sometimes you do and sometimes you don't and sometimes your little bitty ass mind'll fool you again and tell you "I'm running this motherfucker" but just let the beast out of the box and hide and watch how fast ol' bad ass brother brain'll cut and run. But heart is dumb animal, muscle and blood, a pit bull on a mission and he's hangin' in like Gunga Din, good to the last drop of blood.

Or, as the Jesuit M. C. d'Arcy wrote: "Thought is always a post-mortem, and it misses the immediacy of individual experience . . . if this frustration be apparent even in the mind's masculine activity, much more is it so in the desire of the heart."

La Rochefoucauld was even more succinct: "The mind is always the heart's dupe."

RENÉ D'ANJOU'S SMITTEN HEART

René, duc d'Anjou, King of Naples and Sicily (though mostly only in name), produced a sweet early love story: *Le Livre du Cueur d'Amours Espris* (The Book of the Heart Smitten with Love). It is a perfect example of the God/romance crossover, about winning union not with God but with a woman—though her name is Sweet Grace. Though Sir Cueur does go to Mass frequently, these are not the *Pilgrim's Progress* adventures that Daniel Cramer's heart was having 150 years later. It is a story of human love: sad, beautiful and terminally allegorical.

René was born in 1409; he married his cousin Isabel of Lorraine when he was ten. While imprisoned by Philip of Burgundy at Dijon he began to paint, possibly with the encouragement of Jan van Eyck, who was in Philip's service at the time. Isabel protected his interests; he was released, and after ruling for four years he had to return to France. He married again after Isabel's death and wrote and painted—including his own tomb ornament, a painting of himself half skeleton, with his crown falling off.

Hope Rescues Sir Cueur from the River of Tears, by René d'Anjou (from a facsimile edition of *Le Livre du Cueur d'Amours Espris*). © *Private Collection/ Bridgeman Art Library*

Le Livre du Cueur d'Amours Espris is the story of a dream: one night, as René sleeps, Amor (Love) appears to him, takes his heart from his breast and hands it over to Desire.

The heart is Sir Cueur, a knight in armor, his helmet adorned by his heart, with golden wings and wreathed in pansies (*amoureuses pensées*—loving thoughts). Desire is his pageboy, dressed in white with red and gold flames lapping at his tunic skirts. His horse, *Franc Vouloir,* wears cloths embroidered with gold and scarlet winged hearts. Together they must rescue the Lady Sweet

Grace (*Dame Doulce Mercy*) from *Ruffus, Honte* and *Crainte*—Denial, Shame and Fear—the enemies of Love, who are keeping her in the *Manoir de Rebellion*. Their adventures are many, as they meet *Jalousie*, a nasty dwarf in lion skins who directs them into the *Forêt de Longue Attente* (the Forest of the Long Wait) rather than the *Château de Bon Repos* (the Castle of Good Rest), and get into trouble with the *Fontaine de la Fortune*—bad fortune, as it turns out. Desire goes to sleep during these travails. But they are continually helped and encouraged by the *Dame Espérance*—Lady Hope—so though Sir Cueur is knocked into the Stream of Tears by the knight *Soucy* (Worry) and gets sidetracked by Wrath (who fights him) and Sorrow (who tricks him into falling into a pit because he took pity on her), he is rescued by Pleasure and Pastime, Honor, Valor and Renown, and manages to bypass the *Plaine de Pensée Ennuyeuse* (the Plain of Tiresome Brooding). Eventually our heroes reach the *Hôpital d'Amours* (the Hospital of Love) run by *Pitié* (Compassion), who shows them round and introduces them to the residents: Paris, Theseus, Heracles, Tristan, Lancelot, Caesar, Charles VII of France and one René d'Anjou. In the graveyard behind rest Ovid, Petrarch and Boccaccio (all of whom knew something of the symbolic power of the heart), to name but a few. Thence they go on to rescue *Doulce Mercy*. Having conquered Shame and Fear, and assisted by Desire, Modest Plea and Compassion, Sir Cueur is able to kiss her: but alas they are waylaid and he loses her forever to Denial. Desire is killed, Compassion takes charge and Sir Cueur is taken back to the *Hôpital d'Amours* and checked in.

René, meanwhile, wakes up and calls his valet, desperate to check that his heart is still in the right place. Much of the story is illustrated by the most exquisite illuminations you could care to see, which are probably by René himself. It's worth comparing them with Walter Crane's illustrations for *Cinderella*, and with Tenniel's White Rabbit in *Alice in Wonderland*—and, of course, the Jack of Hearts.

René, by the way, was the owner of a relic purporting to be the very vessel which held the water that Christ turned to wine at the wedding in Cana, a heart-alike if ever there was one. He bought it in Marseilles for 200 gold crowns. He died in 1480 and directed in his will that his heart should be buried in the Chapel of St. Bernardine at Angers, with the same masses, processions and lights as would attend the burial of his body.

3

THE HEART EATEN FOR LOVE

Now here is something rather strange, which I had never come across—perhaps unsurprisingly. Here is the little-known school of funny, romantic, touching and peculiar stories about love and cannibalism.

THE LAY D'IGNAURÉ (EARLY THIRTEENTH CENTURY)

A Breton knight, Ignauré, *fleur de la noblesse, dont le coeur est galant,* the gallant-hearted flower of the nobility, was in love with twelve (married) ladies of the Château de Riol. For a year he kept them all happy. One day the ladies decided to play a confession game, with one of them playing the part of the father confessor. It became clear that they all had this same secret lover. They ambushed him, revenge in their hearts and knives in their hands. The priest-playing lady challenged him: *"A vous j'avais donné mon coeur!"* "Madame," he replied, *"je suis votre ami, votre vassal et votre chevalier, et d'un coeur entier, sincère et parfait!"* and so on to each of them in turn: *"Et vous et toutes les autres, sans restriction, je les aime; toutes sans aucun doute, ainsi que pour leur plaisir et leur jouissance!"* I love you all, he said, without restriction, without any doubt, for your pleasure and joy, you and all the others. As they came to kill him he said that if he were fully armed on the field of Aquilea he would come here and put himself at their mercy; he didn't deserve such an honor, he said, to die at such fair hands—he would become a martyr, and be placed with the saints. Whereupon they all began to weep, and as they loved him, they required him only to choose between them. He chose the one who played the father confessor—though, he said, he was very sorry to give up the others. But then . . .

"Mice who have only one hole do not have a long life!" Paying all his attention to the one lady, he was found by her husband *"en galante posture"* with his *amie* and imprisoned. This lady told the others that they should all mourn, as they had all had pleasure with him. The wives, then, all swore to fast: "These ignoble debauchees have all sworn not to eat until the moment when it will be known whether he will die or live," said one of the husbands. "In four days, we will take from him precisely this fifth member that gave each of them so much pleasure. We will make a meal out of it for them, we will add to it his heart. We'll fill twelve plates, and we will get them to eat it, for we cannot better avenge ourselves!" The meal was delicious. But the women didn't notice because their hearts were *rassasie*, wondering what the news would be. After the feast, when the priest-player inquired after Ignauré, her husband said: "Madame, you have eaten the object of your great desire, which gave you so much pleasure you wanted nothing else—*vous avez mangé l'objet de votre grand désir, qui vous plaisait tant, car vous ne souhaitiez rien d'autre* . . . have you had enough, the twelve of you?"

The women who loved Ignauré were distraught. Everyone wept to hear them. They "swore an oath that they would never eat again, unless they were given such a precious dish." And they starved themselves to death.

LE ROMAN DU CHÂTELAIN DE COUÇI ET DE LA DAME DE FAYEL (LATE THIRTEENTH CENTURY)

The Châtelain de Couçi went off on a crusade, and his mistress, la Dame de Fayel, cut off her hair, bound it with gold and gave it to him as a sign of her love, saying that with her hair went her heart: "If without killing myself I could tear it out, I would give it to you!' Alas, the châtelain was wounded in battle by an arrow; sick, he instructed his servant Gobert to take out his heart as soon as he was dead and to embalm it with spices. The servant, with a sad heart, agreed. A letter was to go with the heart: as he had been a faithful lover and chevalier, and as she had given him her noble brilliant hair and her heart, which was "*li fins grains sans paille, gemme, zaphirs, rose nouvielle*" (wheat without chaff, a precious stone, sapphires, a new rose) and which he guarded, he now sent her his heart, because "*c'est vos, s'est drois que vous l'ailes!*" (it is yours, it is right that you have it).

Carrying the heart with her hair and the letter in a little silver box, Gobert did as he promised, but he was intercepted by the Seigneur de Fayel, madame's husband, who bullied the servant into giving up the box and the story. The seigneur had the heart prepared; the dame ate it and found it so delicious she asked, "Does it cost so much, is that why we don't have this dish more often?" He tells her that she has eaten the heart of him whom she loved the best, the Châtelain de Couçi:

> Dame, ne soiies en esfroi,
> Je vous affi en boinne foi
> que vous en ce mes mengastes
> le coer celui que meius amastes:
> C'est dou Castellain de Couchi
> dont on vous siervi ore chi.

The lady was *boulversé*, her heart was *boulversé*—filled with "*grief doel amer.*" His proof that he was truly hers proved a dolorous gift. After this "*gentil viande*," she never ate any other food. She died of her misery.

At this her husband's heart was *boulversé* in turn; he buried her with great honor, but her family accused him of killing her, and he agreed to leave the country, as the chevalier had in the first place. He was never happy again and died soon afterward.

An English version of this tale was published in Belfast in 1875 under the title *The Knight's Heart*: the author (calling himself QED) sent a copy to Gladstone. It has all the qualities of the worst Victorian poetry, including length: there are eight pages of the lady's grief—though Gladstone might have liked that. A historical Sire de Coucy, Enguerrand, the last scion, was taken by the Turks near Nicopolis and died in captivity in 1397. His heart was sent home to be buried at the Church of the Célestins at Villeneuve, near Soissons, which he had founded.

IN EACH of these stories the husbands attempt with this one terrible act to humiliate their wife's lover by dishonoring his mortal remains; to regain control of their wife's body, which has been (or wanted to be) unfaithful, by directing for themselves the entry of the lover's body—well, body part—into their wife's orifice; to punish and degrade both wife and lover; to observe the physical union of wife and lover; and to celebrate their rival's death. But it is all wrong and perverse, and it backfires utterly. Nobody can control the heart of another. All these wives reject their husband and choose to join the lover in death. The husbands, both those who murder the lover and those who take advantage of his death, lose their wife, their love: the husbands' own act unites the wives with their lovers. The wives, however, have in a way only consumed what is already theirs—particularly the Dame de Fayel. Her beloved could not have been more literal in the gift of his heart. "It is right that you have it"— and have it she did.

Bata drank his refreshed heart in a bowl of clear water: for him this presaged a rebirth and an opportunity for him to take vengeance. In reality, vengeance ends in death, not in rebirth. For these wives, once they had eaten the forbidden fruit, as for Adam and Eve there was no turning back. By eating their lover's heart they are more bound to him than they were to their husband by the sacrament of matrimony. They had no choice.

There is also a Christian parallel—perhaps even parody—in the *Lay d'Ignauré*, both with Christ's life and with the lives of nuns. A group—a community even—of twelve women (as in twelve disciples) living and bound together by love for one man (who is killed violently for love; whose flesh—the particular parts representing love and manhood—they consume at the Last Supper they ever eat; and in whose love for all of them they believe profoundly) cut themselves off from husbands and marriage.

THERE ARE many versions of these tales. The Fourth Day of Boccaccio's *Decameron*, written in the fourteenth century, is the day of stories of those whose loves had unhappy endings. One is the story of Tancred, the Prince of Salerno, who was altogether too attached to his daughter Ghismonda, among whose many qualities is listed "rather more intelligence than a woman needs": the heart-eating is played out between the father's jealousy and the daughter's determination. Another is that of Guiglielmo Guardastagno and Guiglielmo Rossiglione (Guillaume de Guardestaing and Guillaume de Roussillon), astonishingly similar to the provençal troubadour biography of Guillaume de Cabestanh, from Roussillon, who fell in love with Seremonda, the wife of his friend Raimon, the Seigneur de Château Roussillon. Raimon killed Guillaume, then *"trais li lo cor del cors . . . et fez lo cor raustir, e far pebrada e fez lo dar a manjar a la molher"*—took out the heart of hearts . . . had it roasted, made with pepper, and had it given to the woman to eat. And she said,

"Seigneur, you have given me such a good meal that I shall never eat another," and threw herself off the balcony. According to a longer (and probably later) version, the news reached King Alphonse of Aragon, who confiscated Raimon's lands and castles and put him in prison, and had the lovers buried by the door of the church of St. Jean in Perpignan, and required all *chevaliers* and *dames* of Roussillon to remember the anniversary of their death. Stendhal translated one version of the story in his *De l'Amour* (Chapter LII). The difference is, Guillaume de Cabestanh existed; he was a twelfth-century troubadour, a love poet who dedicated two of his verses to his friend Raimon. He is listed among those who fought at the Battle of Las Navas de Tolosa in 1212, and records suggest his wife married again, so perhaps she didn't jump out the window. When and why the story of the *coeur mangé* attached itself to him we do not know, but some of his poetry remains: his beloved, he wrote, was "*Blanc e lis plus qu'us altamist*" (whiter and smoother than an amethyst), and when his heart opened up his love expanded without and within, he was full of and surrounded by love, more than hyssop is with flowers—"*claus et cins d'amor plus que de flors ysops.*"

True or fictional, the story is older still, and international: a version called *Guirun* was cited in 1150; there is the history of Linauré (is this the same name as Ignauré?), another provençal troubadour, from about 1190; there are German, Swedish and Spanish versions; and the Punjabi story of *Rasalu*. Jean-Pierre Camus, Bishop of Belley and friend of Francis de Sales, published in 1630 a book of cautionary moralizing tales called *Les Spectacles d'Horreur où se descouvrent plusieurs tragiques effets de notre siècle* (Visions of horror, which reveal many tragic aspects of our century). Spectacle number 3 is a complete horror called *Le Coeur Mangé*. Scholars have gone round in circles trying to work out which story is rooted in which: in my favorite interpretation Rasalu arrived from India in the south of France and the name became Roussillon, attaching itself to Guillaume de Cabestanh, who came from near Roussillon, and hence on to Boccaccio and Camus. But who knows?

In all these stories, the husbands do not recognize that by burying the lover's remains inside their wife they are uniting the two more than ever, and making a tomb out of their wives' own bodies. It is a consummation of a kind, and also recalls the Christian tales of lady saints who take Christ's heart into their bodies. Shakespeare's Sonnet XXXI is also interesting in this respect: the love object's

bosom is endearèd with all hearts . . .
Thou art the grave where buried love doth live,
Hung with the trophies of my lovers gone,
Who all their parts of me to thee did give . . .

He clearly means that what he loved in them he sees now in her, but it's a risky strategy to call your beloved a tomb of ex-girlfriends. George Sand, on breaking up with her lover Jules Sandeau, declared: "My heart is a cemetery." Someone told him about this years later: "a necropolis," he suggested.

The next appearance of the *coeur mangé*—or *cuore mangiato,* as we are in Italy—is Dante's extraordinary response to the occasion when Beatrice first said hello to him, in his *Vita Nuova.* So miraculous was the greeting that, overcome with bliss, he rushed home and fell into a deep sleep, wherein appeared this vision:

> I seemed to see a cloud the colour of fire and, in that cloud, a lordly man, frightening to behold, yet he seemed also to be wonderously filled with joy. He spoke and said many things, of which I understood only a few; one was "*Ego dominus tuus.*" I seemed to see in his arms a sleeping figure, naked but lightly wrapped in crimson cloth, looking intently at this figure. I recognised the lady of the greeting, the lady who earlier in the day had deigned to greet me. In one hand he seemed to be holding something which was all in flames, and it seemed to me that he said these words: "*Vide cor tuum.*" And after some time had passed, he seemed to awaken the one who slept, and he forced her cunningly to eat of that burning object in his hand; she ate of it timidly. A short time after this, his happiness gave way to bitterest weeping, and weeping he folded her arms around this lady. And together they seemed to ascend towards the heavens.

What was all that about? Dante wondered too, and wrote a sonnet putting the question, which he offered to the community of poets, seeking their "elucidation in reply": "suddenly Love appeared before me," he wrote, ". . . joyous, love seemed to me, holding my heart within his hand, and in his arms he had my lady, loosely wrapped in folds, asleep. He woke her then, and gently fed to her the burning heart; she ate it, terrified. And then I saw them disappear in tears."

He received many answers. One man wrote, "I think you beheld all worth," and became Dante's first friend. "*Dominus tuus,*" in a cloud, with a heart, might be God, but Dante wrote that though nobody worked it out, now "it is very clear even to the least sophisticated." The lord is Love, demonstrating Dante's poetic vocation. The poet's heart is his words, his connection with other people, his poetry, his self, offered up for humanity to share and consume. And Beatrice, nervously at first, consumes his offering, inspiring Dante to set off on the long poetic quest described in *The Divine Comedy.*

Why then does Love, the poetic vocation, retire in tears with the lady? I don't know.

4

SOME HEART METAPHORS,
SOME LONG-LASTING IMAGES,
SOME LOVE SONGS

I'll leave you with the words of poets, because poetry, more than history, anatomy, religion or analysis, is the language of the heart. See how universal it is, in time and place. See how much we all share.

> Thief of my heart, it's only fair
> You should give me yours, or cherish mine for ever.
> OVID, *AMORES*, C. 20 B.C.

> My true love has my heart, and I have his,
> By just exchange, one to the other given.
> I hold his dear, and mine he cannot miss:
> There never was a better bargain driven.
> My true love hath my heart, and I have his.
> His heart in me, keeps me and him in one,
> My heart in him, his thoughts and senses guides:
> He loves my heart, for once it was his own,
> I cherish his, because it in me bides.
> His heart his wound receivèd from my sight:
> My heart was wounded with his wounded heart,
> For as from me, on him his hurt did light,
> So still methought in me his hurt did smart:
> Both equal hurt, in this change sought our bliss:
> My true love hath my heart and I have his.
> SIR PHILIP SIDNEY, 1581

Alas, madam, for stealing of a kiss
Have I so much your mind there offended?
Have I then done so grievously amiss
That by no means it may be amended?

Then revenge you, and the next way is this:
Another kiss shall have my life ended,
For to my mouth the first my heart did suck;
The next shall clean out of my breast it pluck.

SIR THOMAS WYATT, C. 1530

The Message
Send home my long strayd eyes to mee,
Which (Oh) too long have dwelt on thee;
Yet since there they have learn'd such ill
Such forc'd fashions,
And false passions,
That they be
Made by thee
Fit for no good sight, keep them still.

Send home my harmlesse heart againe,
Wich no unworthy thought could staine;
But if it be taught by thine
To make jestings
Of protestings,
And crosse both
Word and oath,
Keepe it, for then 'tis none of mine.

Yet send me back my heart and eyes,
That I may know, and see thy lyes,
And may laugh and joy, when thou
Art in anguish
And dost languish
For some one
That will none,

Or prove as false as thou art now.
JOHN DONNE, 1611

Your cheating heart will make you weep
You'll cry and cry and try to sleep
But sleep won't come the whole night through
Your cheating heart will tell on you.
FROM "YOUR CHEATING HEART" BY HANK WILLIAMS, 1953

Thou canst not every day give me thy heart,
If thou canst give it, then thou never gavest it:
Loves riddles are, that though thy heart depart,
It stayes at home, and thou with losing savest it:
But wee will have a way more liberall,
Than changing hearts, to joyne them, so wee shall
Be one, and one anothers All.
FROM "LOVERS INFINITENESSE" BY JOHN DONNE, 1611

Two souls with but a single thought,
Two hearts that beat as one.
FROM *INGOMAR THE BARBARIAN* BY MARIA LOVELL (D. 1877)

Maid of Athens, ere we part,
Give, oh give me back my heart!
Or, since that has left my breast,
Keep it now, and take the rest ...
FROM "MAID OF ATHENS" BY BYRON, 1810

Now you've got the best of me
Come on and take the rest of me,
Oh baby, oh baby ...
FROM "THE REAL THING," 1976

... my heart through which her heart has passed
Or will pass whether she likes it or not
Still vouches from far away in impossible hours
For the echo that exists only in grottos

On rainbow evenings
But I swear the nights, the nights are too much . . .
ANDRÉ BRETON, 1926

Hearts are not had as a gift but hearts are earned . . .
FROM "A PRAYER FOR MY DAUGHTER" BY W. B. YEATS, 1919

I lost my heart, dear,
Yes I must have lost my heart there—
Near your small hut beside the well . . .
Why else does my heart sink and swell
When you scoop water from the well?
TEE AH POON

Go, let the fatted calf be killed;
My Prodigal's come home at last;
With noble resolutions filled,
And filled with sorrow for the past.
No more will burn with love or wine:
But quite has left his women and his swine.

Welcome, ah welcome my poor Heart;
Welcome; I little thought, I'll swear,
('Tis now so long since we did part)
Ever again to see thee here:
Dear Wanderer, since from me you fled,
How often have I heard that thou wert dead! . . .
FROM "THE WELCOME" BY ABRAHAM COWLEY, 1647

When I was one-and-twenty
I heard a wise man say,
"Give crowns and pounds and guineas
But not your heart away;
Give pearls away and rubies
But keep your fancy free."
But I was one-and-twenty,
No use to talk to me.

When I was one-and-twenty
I heard him say again,
"The heart out of the bosom
Was never given in vain;
'Tis paid with sighs a plenty
And sold for endless rue."
And I am two-and-twenty,
And oh, 'tis true, 'tis true.

FROM *A SHROPSHIRE LAD* BY A. E. HOUSMAN, 1896

Give all to love;
Obey thy heart . . .

FROM "GIVE ALL TO LOVE" BY R. W. EMERSON (D. 1882)

Holy Sonnet XIV
Batter my heart, three-person'd God; for, you
As yet but knocke, breathe, shine, and seeke to mend;
That I may rise, and stand, o'erthrow mee, and bend
Your force, to breake, blowe, burn and make me new.
I, like an usurpt towne, to'another due,
Labour to'admit you, but Oh, to no end,
Reason your viceroy in mee, mee should defend,
But is captiv'd and proves weake or untrue.
Yet dearely "I love you," and would be lov'd faine,
But am betroth'd unto your enemie:
Divorce mee, untie, or breake that knot againe,
Take mee to you, imprison mee, for I
Except you'enthrall mee, never shall be free,
Nor ever chast, except you ravish mee.

JOHN DONNE, 1617

"Plants and trees are not of one fragrance
Flowers and leaves are of different colours."
I sent these words to my former lover
To let him know my heart remembers him.

HSIAO-YEN (FIFTH CENTURY)

About to go on a long campaign
My lover sent me twin inscribed brocades.
Toward the time of departure
He also left me his loving you pillow.
His inscription I always press to my heart
His pillow makes me dream we sleep together.
On, on, each day further on,
The more I feel my pining keen.

PAO LING-HUI (FIFTH CENTURY)

The heart at forty has its own ways of laying the mind to waste
Which all our fund of experience cannot alter . . .

The time to love
is when the heart says so
Who cares
If it is muddy August
Or tepid April?
Love is a country with its own climate.

TAUFIQ RAFAT (D. 1998)

The Gateway
Now the heart sings with all its thousand voices
To hear this city of cells, my body, sing.
The tree through the stiff clay at long last forces
Its thin strong roots and taps the secret spring.

And the sweet waters without intermission
Climb to the tips of its green tenement;
The breasts have borne the grace of their possession,
The lips have felt the pressure of content.

Here I come home: in this expected country
They know my name and speak it with delight.
I am the dream and you my gates of entry,
The means by which I waken into light.

A. D. HOPE (D. 2000)

True hearts have ears and eyes, no tongues to speak;
They hear and see, and sigh, and then they break.
FROM "A SILENT LOVE" BY SIR EDWARD DYER (D. 1607)

My tired heart eternal silence keeps.
I know not who has slipped into my heart;
Though I am silent, someone in me weeps.
HAFIZ

SHAKESPEARE

Shakespeare was the perfect observer of the crossover and combined role of the heart; of human love, physical reality and morality in one place. Here is one small example. Juliet, learning that Romeo had killed her cousin Tybalt, cried out: "O serpent heart, hid with a flow'ring face!"

The honest and beautiful exterior—a flow'ring face, suggesting fruitfulness, innocence, paradise—hides the wickedness within. Betrayal of a friend is a terrible offense because love and honor both live in the heart. The serpent ousted by Christ when he "fixes" the heart is here destroying human love. Yet here the serpent actually *is* the heart: so the love is in the serpent. This *might* not be phallic, but it reminds me of Blake's sick rose (the flow'ring face) and the invisible worm. The serpent under the flow'ring face recalls the snake of Eden in the Tree of Knowledge. Juliet has just acquired knowledge which ends her joyous state of innocent love for Romeo. Through his sin, his betrayal of her, she falls. It is the antithesis of Christ's redemption: it is sex, loss of virginity (deflowr'ing), death . . .

And then she says: "God pardon him! I do, with all my heart; And yet no man, like he, doth grieve my heart."

And then we're into the territory of the wounded heart and what the nightingale owes the rose in exchange for the opportunity to suffer.

Sonnet XLVI
Mine eye and heart are at a mortal war,
How to divide the conquest of thy sight;
Mine eye my heart the picture's sight would bar,

My heart mine eye the freedom of that right.
My heart doth plead that thou in him dost lie—
A closet never pierced with crystal eyes;
But the defendant doth that plea deny,
And says in him thy fair appearance lies.
To 'cide this title is impannellèd
A quest of thoughts, all tenants to the heart;
And by their verdict is determinèd
The clear eye's moiety, and the dear heart's part:
As thus—mine eye's due is thy outward part,
And my heart's right thy inward love of heart.

Sonnet XLVII
Betwixt mine eye and heart a league is took,
And each doth good turns now unto the other.
When that mine eye is famished for a look,
Or heart in love with sighs himself doth smother,
With my love's picture then my eye doth feast,
And to the painted banquet bids my heart;
Another time mine eye is my heart's guest,
And in his thoughts of love doth share a part.
So either by thy picture or my love,
Thyself away art present still with me;
For thou no farther than my thoughts canst move,
And I am still with them, and they with thee;
Or, if they sleep, thy picture in my sight
Awakes my heart to heart's and eye's delight.

Sonnet CXXXIII
Beshrew that heart that makes my heart to groan
For that deep wound it gives my friend and me!
Is't not enough to torture me alone,
But slave to slavery my sweet'st friend must be?
Me from myself thy cruel eye hath taken,
And my next self thou harder hast engrossed.
Of him, myself, and thee, I am forsaken—
A torment thrice threefold thus to be crossed.

Prison my heart in thy steel bosom's ward,
But then my friend's heart let my poor heart bail;
Whoe'er keeps me, let my heart be his guard,
Thou canst not then use rigor in my jail.
And yet thou wilt, for I, being pent in thee
Perforce am thine, and all that is in me.

Sonnet CXLI
In faith I do not love thee with mine eyes,
For they in thee a thousand errors note;
But 'tis my heart that loves what they despise,
Who in despite of view is pleased to dote.
Nor are mine ears with thy tongue's tune delighted;
Nor tender feeling to base touches prone,
Nor taste, nor smell, desire to be invited
To any sensual feast with thee alone.
But my five wits, nor my five senses can
Dissuade one foolish heart from serving thee,
Who leaves unswayed the likeness of a man,
Thy proud heart's slave and vassal wretch to be.
Only my plague thus far I count my gain,
That she that makes me sin, awards me pain.

Totem
To ward it off (whatever it was) or to attract it
You painted little hearts on everything.
You had no other logo.
This was your sacred object.
Sometimes you painted around it the wreath
Of an eight-year-old's flowers, green leaves, yellow petals.
Sometimes, off to the side, an eight-year-old's bluebird.
But mostly hearts. Or one red simple heart.
The frame of the big mirror you painted black—
Then, on the black, hearts.
And on your old black Singer sewing-machine—
Hearts.
The crimson on the black, like little lamps.

And on the cradle I made for a doll you painted,
Hearts.
And on the threshold, over which your son entered,
A heart—
Crimson on the black, like a blood-splash.
This heart was your talisman, your magic.
As Christians have their cross you had your heart.
Constantine had his cross—you, your heart.
Your genie. Your Guardian Angel. Your Demon Slave.
But when you crept for safety
Into the bosom of your Guardian Angel
It was your Demon Slave. Like a possessive
Fish-mother, too eager to protect you.
She devoured you.
Now all that people find
Is your heart-coloured book—the empty mask
Of your Genie.
The mask
Of one that opening arms as if to enfold you
Devoured you.
The little hearts you painted on everything
Remained, like the track of your panic.
The splashes of a wound.
The spoor
Of the one that caught and devoured you.

TED HUGHES, 1998

MARY QUEEN OF SCOTS

Mary Queen of Scots wrote this to her husband the Earl of Bothwell, when he
unexpectedly failed to appear one evening in 1567:

Mon coeur, mon sang, mon ame et mon souci,
Las, vous m'avez promis qu'aurions ce plaisir
De deviser avec vous à loisir
Toute la nuit où je languis içi
Ayant le coeur d'extrème peur transi
Pour voir absent le but de mon désir . . .

My heart, my blood, my soul and my care,
Alas, you promised me we would have the pleasure
Of playing with you, at leisure
All the night that I languish here,
Heart transfixed with extreme fear
To see absent the thing of my desire.

Later, imprisoned, she wrote:

Un coeur, que l'outrage martyre
Par un mépris ou d'un refus,
A le pouvoir de faire dire:
Je ne suis plus ce que je fus.

A heart, that outrage martyrs
By a treachery or by a refusal,
Has the power to say:
I am not any more that which I was.

And later, from her last sonnet, "Ode to Francis II":

Que suis-je hélas? Et de quoi sert ma vie?
Je ne suis fors qu'un corps privé de coeur,
Une ombre vaine, un objet de malheur,
Qui n'a plus rien que de mourir en vie . . .

So what am I? To what purpose my life?
I am but a body deprived of a heart
A vain shadow, an object of unhappiness,
Who has no more than to die in life . . .

And if you ask how I regret that parting:
It is like the flowers falling at spring's end
Confused, whirled in a tangle.
What is the use of talking, and there is no end of talking,
There is no end of things in the heart.
FROM "EXILE'S LETTER" BY RIHAKU (EIGHTH CENTURY)

The Heart of Man

There is the other universe, of the heart of man
That we know nothing of, that we dare not explore
A strange grey distance separates
Our pale mind still from the pulsing continent
Of the heart of man
Fore-runners have barely landed on the shore
And no man knows, no woman knows
The mystery of the interior
When darker still than Congo or Amazon
Flow the heart's rivers of fullness, desire and distress.

D. H. LAWRENCE

RELIQUARY

We've seen how the symbolic heart gets around. So too does the physical. Hearts do not always rest in the grave where they would be expected to.

Evisceration of corpses seems to have started in the later Stone Age; it was central to ancient Egyptian ritual. The Romans preferred cremation, and early Christians buried the body whole. They did, however, build churches over the tombs of saints. The Emperor Constantine, dying in 337, was accorded the great honor of being buried in the vestibule of his Church of the Apostles in Constantinople, and gradually after that rich, important or very religious people wanted to be buried inside churches, particularly the beautiful new churches which were built after the safe passage of the first millennium. A sweet-smelling corpse—the odor of sanctity—was a sign of sainthood, but mostly bodies did smell: hence the "stinking rich." To preserve the atmosphere of the churches it proved necessary to remove the viscera. At the same time, why should they—the heart in particular, still necessary for the resurrection of the body—be honored less than the rest of the body? From this grew the practice of separate heart burial.

The guts needed to be buried quickest; a body could sometimes be embalmed and sent elsewhere; but the heart, symbol of the person in all the ways we have seen, could be pickled, sent, given, kept, eaten, or worn round the neck—almost like an amulet.

One of the first hearts to be so honored seems to have been that of Robert d'Arbrissel at Anjou in 1117. He founded both a monastery for men—Fontevrault, where many royal hearts ended up—and a *madeleine* for penitent women, at Orsan. Both institutions wanted his remains: his body was buried at the former and his heart, in a silver heart-shaped case, at the latter. This allowed him to show his loyalty to different places, to receive prayers from several congregations and to provide relics (preferably miraculous) for a number of places. In 1490 the people of Toledo kept the heart of a murdered boy as a charm against the Inquisition; the soldiers of St. Louis wanted to keep his heart in their camp to bring blessings and protection for them. Sometimes monasteries would agree to swaps, or remains could be bought and sold. Hearts often brought with them a dowry for the upkeep of their monuments, which might attract pilgrims—and business.

During the crusades European soldiers who died in the Holy Land generally had to be buried there. (Up until the nineteenth century plague laws usually regulated the repatriation of bodies.) Their hearts, however, if the dead were rich enough and someone cared enough, could be dried or pickled for ease of transport. William Mandeville, Earl of Essex, who died in 1198, asked on his deathbed for his corpse to be sent home from Gisors to Walden in Essex: told that it could not be done, he replied: "If you cannot, it is because you have no mind to effect what I, a dying man, desire; then take my heart and carry it thither." And so it duly went, with half his fortune. Small effigies of knights found in European churches mark the tombs of returned hearts whose bodies were lost.

Heart-shaped grave markings, however, do not necessarily denote that only the heart is buried there. In the Languedoc, in southwestern France, black iron crosses from the 1930s carry white enamel hearts inscribed with the details of the deceased, recalling all the imagery of the written-on heart, and in the United States hearts have ornamented grave markings since the eighteenth century. Biblical texts relating to the heart, and sentimental verses based on them, are even more common than the shape itself: "They are not dead who live on in our hearts"; or "God took him from our home but not from our hearts."

Other devouts preferred to die at home and have their hearts sent to the Holy Land: the great enemies Edward I and Robert the Bruce both expressed this desire, though neither achieved it.

Hearts were sometimes marked with brasses: that of Anne Muston, who died in 1496, bore the legend: "Here lieth the bowels of Dame Anne." Many of these tombs were very elaborate: urns on top of pyramids or columns were not unknown, and boxes were made of dull lead or gleaming gold, or ivory, crystal, terra-cotta or wood. An urn on a marble obelisk in St. Nicholas's Chapel at Westminster Abbey contained the heart of Anna Sophia Harlay, who died aged twelve months in 1605. Sometimes an effigy of the deceased would hold the heart in its hands, either on the breast or up in offering, perhaps implying Lamentations: "Let us lift up our heart with our hands unto God in the heavens." The heart of Elizabeth I's lady-in-waiting Blanche Parry is at Bacton church in Herefordshire: her effigy appears to be offering the heart in a case to a statue of Elizabeth. Funerals, too, could be showy: at the funeral of the Bishop of Winchester's heart in 1555, the church was draped in black, and there was a sermon, dirges and bell-ringing. After his murder the heart of Henry IV of France, accompanied by monks in black velvet, four Jesuits and 400 cavaliers, was paraded through the streets in a silver-gilt case. The heart of a duke of Brittany, who died as a baby in 1705, was carried in a coach on the knees of the Great Almoner of France, accompanied by sixty *mousquetaires* in black and sixty in gray, fifty gendarmes and fifty light horse, twenty-four pages on horseback, footmen, flaming torches, notables and the Duke of Bourbon.

Apocryphal stories tell of nineteenth-century rakes, the Hellfire club, drinking-toasts-to-their-mistresses-from-a-human-skull type, who took their ancestors' hearts from crypts and chapels and ate them, but I have not found any reliable accounts. J. E. Jackson in his guide to Farleigh Castle wrote:

> About 1650 there were in this vault [of the chapel] some glazed earthenware jars covered with white leather, one of which, being broken by accident, discovered a heart preserved in liquor. There was also till 1822 (when upon an attempt being made to steal the lead coffins it was carried away) a cylindrical urn of lead holding the like contents.

The vault was closed to visitors in the mid-nineteenth century after "some experimentalists" poked a stick into one of the lead coffins in order to "taste the embalming liquor."

In 1299 Pope Boniface VIII forbade the dismembering of the dead: he described it as cruel, profane, abominable in the sight of God, impious to the deceased and barbarous, and threatened excommunication to those who practiced it. Pope Benedict XI modified this for the sake of cases where it was difficult to get the body to the burial ground (King Philip le Bel, to be precise). Pope John XXII kept up the ban, and made large sums from granting one-time licenses to break it, including one to the Bishop of Moray for separating Robert the Bruce's heart and sending it against the Saracens, and two for Queen Isabella. There was a strong business aspect: monasteries would fight over the remains of the rich. The nuns at Val de Grâce had a monopoly on the hearts of the French royal princes and princesses from their foundation up until the Revolution, and again almost immediately after the hearts were "cleared out" in 1793. Edward I delivered his wife's heart to the Church of the Dominicans and his mother's to the Gray Friars on the same day. The friars, wrote Rishanger, the St. Albans chronicler, of this occasion, "are wont to claim something for themselves of the mighty dead, like dogs who wait greedily to receive each his own particular morsel of the carcase." About 150 hearts belonging to members of the Austrian royal family are at the Church of the Capuchins in Vienna.

According to Ambrose Paré, principal surgeon to the kings of France in the sixteenth century, the heart was at that time usually kept aside for embalmment and disposal "as the kinsfolk think fit." This was only the case for the (not-so-stinking any more) rich: even in 1281 it cost £6 5/4d to embalm Cicely Talmadge of Suffolk, and for Henry VI, in 1471, it was £15 3/6d halfpenny. The surgeon who embalmed the heart of the Marquis of Montrose (see below), hanged at Edinburgh in 1650, received £25, to include the cost of the spices. The height of the popularity of separate heart burial was during the seventeenth century, and the hub of it was France: no doubt the growing popularity of the cult of the Sacred Heart of Jesus contributed, though anybody who died abroad was likely to want to send their heart home. Catholics—despite all the reluctance of the popes through the ages—were more inclined than Protestants. And curiously enough the viscera of some twenty popes who died between 1590 and 1830 are buried in urns in the crypt of Sts. Anastasio and Vincenza in Rome.

But fashions change: by the nineteenth century even queens (Caroline, who died in 1821, and Adelaide, in 1849) expressed a wish to be buried without what one marchioness called "ripping, imbalming or spicery."

Many museums and collections include human hearts; only since the Alder Hey scandal has it come to light that they are not all ancient and forgotten. In Bristol and Liverpool in the late 1990s, immense pain and outrage was caused when it emerged that the hearts of hundreds of children who had died in hospital had been kept, without parents' knowledge or permission, "for research," and then not even used. The scandal spread, and one father camped outside the hospital in Liverpool for eight days in protest, surrounded by flowers and photographs, ten years after his daughter died. As one mother said: "If they had asked . . . we would have said no because we believe that the heart is the soul of the person." The strength of the reaction shows that the ritual of a proper burial is still important to us. In the past murderers and traitors were denied burial, or drawn and quartered, as a part of the punishment: they were deemed unsuitable material for resurrection. It was on their bodies that surgeons trained.

A FEW FAMOUS HEARTS

The Lion Heart of Richard was buried at Rouen Cathedral, at his instruction, "*en remembrance d'amour*"—because of the town's loyalty and cordiality to him. Its original silver casket was sold to raise money to ransom St. Louis and the heart was lost, but in 1838 it was recovered, inside a statue: the silver box which contained it was in a lead box inscribed "*Hic Jacet Cor Ricardi Regis Anglorum.*" It was examined and, according to Mr. Albert Way, it seemed to be "reduced to the semblance of a dried reddish leaf." Alternatively, it is under the altar at All Hallows, Barking, where a lamp was still burning for it in the 1920s. His body was buried under his father's feet at Fontevrault.

HIS BROTHER, King John, died of pique and peaches: he lost all his treasure in a Lincolnshire bog while trying to secret it away, threw a fever, "imprudently" ate peaches and died. His heart was buried at the Cistercian Abbey of Crokesden, Staffs, to whom he also bequeathed land worth £10 a year.

SWEETHEART ABBEY—Dulce Cor—near Dumfries was founded around 1269 by Devorguilla, wife of John Baliol, as a resting place for her husband's heart. A ballad records the embalming of his heart:

> Or he was laid in sepulture
> She gart opyne his body tyte
> And gart take his heart out quite.

She kept the heart in an ivory box enameled with silver, which she liked to have on the table when she ate. When she was buried it was placed in her own coffin next to her heart.

HENRY D'ALMAYNE was murdered at San Lorenzo in Viterbo in 1271 by the sons of the Earl of Leicester. His heart was sent in a golden vase to Westminster Abbey and set in a gilt statue on the tomb of Edward the Confessor. The legend read, "I bequeath to my father my heart pierced with the dagger." (His father Richard, brother to Henry III, then died of grief, and his heart was buried in Oxford under a pyramid.) According to another version, the cup was set in a pillar on the old London Bridge. Dante referred to the heart "on the banks of the Thames" in the *Inferno*. No one knows where it is now.

ELEANOR OF CASTILE, the original Infanta of Castile whose name developed into the Elephant and Castle, married Prince Edward and went with him on his crusade in 1270, where she famously either did or didn't suck poison from his wound and save his life. Her body was buried at Lincoln and her heart at the Church of the Dominicans in London, a place brimful of royal hearts, and destroyed during the Dissolution. Master Adam, the queen's goldsmith, made a gold angel to hold her heart; like so many "heart cases," it fell victim to politics and iconoclasm.

KING EDWARD I of England, Hammer of the Scots, wanted his boiled-down bones to be carried into battle against Scotland by his army and his heart taken to the Holy Land by 140 knights and their retinue. He appointed £2,000 in silver for the costs, and "eternal damnation on any who should expend the money on any other purpose." His son ignored this and buried him in Westminster Abbey.

ROBERT THE BRUCE, his great enemy, also wanted his heart taken to Jerusalem. The heart headed south with Sir James Douglas, in a silver—or gold—box which he wore round his neck. The legend goes that Douglas got caught up in a battle between the King of Castile and the Saracen King of Granada, during which, surrounded by the enemy and seeing that all was lost, he took his precious necklace and threw it in front of him, crying, "Onward as thou wert wont, I will follow or die!" He died. The heart was found beneath his corpse and taken up by Sir Simon Locard of Lee (or Sir Alan Cathcart, or Sir William Keith), and carried back to Melrose Abbey in Scotland where, after being the subject of much dispute, it was finally reburied in a new box in June 1998. Locard changed his name (to Lockheart) after the incident, and included a heart in a fetterlock and the motto *Corda serrata pando* in his coat of arms. The Douglas arms include a crowned human heart, and the family owns a sword, dated 1329, emblazoned with two hands holding a heart.

Mrs. Hemans wrote about Bruce's heart:

Heart! That didst press forward still,
Where the trumpet's note rang shrill,
Where the knightly swords were crossing,
And the plumes like sea foam tossing;
Leader of the charging spear,
Fiery heart!—and liest thou here?
May this narrow spot inurn
Aught that so could beat and burn?

THE HEART of King Edward II, murdered in 1327 with a red-hot poker (for his homosexuality with Piers Gaveston), may have ended up in a silver vase under the breast of his queen, Isabella, in an alabaster tomb at the Church of the Gray Friars at Newgate in London. Her lover, Roger Mortimer, was buried there too. Nothing remains. Marlowe's Edward II says: "My heart is an anvil unto sorrow."

THE HEART of St. Teresa is at the convent of Avila in Spain, in a heart-shaped rock-crystal urn, set with precious stones. Dr. Boyadjian saw the heart and reported:

The eye of the cardiologist, looking closely at this heart which has been preserved in alcohol since 1582, was overwhelmingly surprised to notice a split, a tear in the myocardium of the left ventricle, and after four centuries pronounced this audacious diagnosis: Teresa of Avila could perhaps have died from a coronary thrombosis with rupture of the heart: the arrow which pierced her heart during her illness was probably the manifestation of an attack of angina.

CATHERINE OF ARAGON is said to have died of cancer of the heart: the candlemaker who cered and wrapped her in lead said that all her body was sound except the heart, which was black and hideous.

HENRY VIII's body is at Windsor; his heart at Whitehall. The heart of his elder brother Arthur was buried in the beautiful pink church of St. Laurence in Ludlow in 1502. Arthur, aged fifteen, had honeymooned at the castle there with Catherine of Aragon; the following year he "departed out of this transitory and uncertain life," according to a sign seen "over y seats of ye north side of the High Chancel" in Ludlow in 1684, but washed over in 1748 and forgotten. Stukeley, in 1723, was told that "they took up his heart not long since in a leaden box"; Emily Sophia Hartshorne, an enthusiastic if not always accurate Victorian cordophile, reported in 1861 that the heart had been taken up "some years ago," and that the sexton "embezzled" the silver case and lost his job as a result. When I visited Ludlow in 2000 the rector's wife told me a similar story of a nineteenth-century workman rebuilding the floor, who found the heart in its pretty silver box and pawned it in the town. The rector had to go and redeem it. The stories go round and round.

THE HEART of Elizabeth I ("I know I have the body of a weak and feeble woman, but I have the heart and stomach of a king, and a king of England, too") is in an urn near that of her sister Mary, which was put in a velvet box bound with silver. A record survives of the expenses: "for half a yard of velvet, black, for covering a box for the queen's heart; of the queen's store, one quarter of sarsenet, red, for to wrap the queen's heart in. John Grene, for a box, and covering the same, 3s 4d. Mary Wilkinson, four yards of passamayne lace to garnish the same. Canopy of blue velvet. Hatchments and mantellets. The coat and banner of arms." The diary of Dr. William Taswell, rector of Newington, records the tale of a naughty schoolboy from Westminster who in 1670, when the vault was opened for the funeral of the Duke of Albemarle, found the urns. "I dipped my hand into each, and took out of each a kind of glutinous red substance somewhat resembling mortar. Mary's urn contained less moisture."

MARY STUART, Queen of Scots, is buried nearby. In 1562 she told Lord Cecil: "I have a ring with a diamond fashioned like a heart; I know nothing that can resemble my goodwill unto my sister [Elizabeth, technically her cousin] better than that." She wrote her cousin a poem to accompany the gift, in which the diamond speaks of wanting to "unite their hearts as one," "for I'd have two great jewels in one setting bound." She had wanted her heart to be buried with the body of her childhood sweetheart and first husband, Francis II, at Saint-Denis. His heart, meanwhile, was enshrined at the Church of the Célestins in Paris, near that of his father Henry II. Mary's request was denied, and her heart buried at Fotheringay, where she was executed. Her body was buried in Peterborough before her funeral because she was decomposing in a manner likely to cause an explosion. (Elizabeth's body did this too. So did Oliver Cromwell's—three years later it was dug up and hung at Tyburn.) Her son moved her to Westminster, near the cousin who executed her.

EDWARD, Lord Bruce of Kinloss, was a childhood friend and soon-to-be brother-in-law of one Sir Edward Sackvile who, in drink and having squabbled with a Scotsman, declared against "beggarly Scotsmen" in general. Bruce hoped he did not include all Scotsmen in this; Sackvile said he made no exception for a Scotsman who sits in his friend's house and talks of him puritanically behind his back. From this insult in the end resulted a duel, at Bergen. Lord Bruce saw in his mirror that morning a death's head, and indeed it

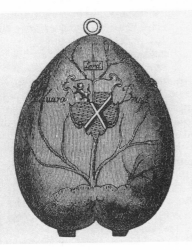

Edward Bruce's silver heart-case, found at Culross Abbey. © *The British Library 9010.h.9*

was he who died. He was buried at Bergen (with a death's head in a mirror on his monument) but his heart, so his family believed, was sent to the abbey church of Culross in Perthshire. In 1806 it was decided to look for his heart, and two feet below the floor were discovered two large flat stones, curiously bound together with iron. The searchers separated them, and found a cavity between them in which was a silver heart-shaped case, engraved with Bruce's name and arms (upside down, from a modern point of view, resting on its curves rather than its point, and with a stylized cardiac artery growing up it like a tree. Inside was an embalmed heart, in its liquid.

IN A PASSAGEWAY under the quadrangle of Somerset House in the Strand, built into the wall, is an old gravestone: *"Cis Gisent les entrailles de feu hault et puissant seigneur messiere Jacques d'Angennes..."* Not so *haut* or *puissant* now. He was the Marquess de Poigny, French Ambassador to England from 1634.

WHEN SIR EVERARD DIGBY was executed the hangman, as was the custom in the case of traitors, took out his heart while he was still living and held it up to the crowd, crying, "Here is the heart of a traitor!" Sir Everard, it is said, replied: "Thou liest!"

JAMES GRAHAM, Marquess of Montrose, Viceroy of Scotland for Charles I, was sentenced to hang and be beheaded, and then his limbs hung again, in different towns. At his first hanging a copy of a book he had published of his heroic actions was tied round his neck: he thanked them, saying he was prouder of wearing that than of wearing the Garter. His heart (the Heart of Montrose) was kept for many years in a box made from the blade of his sword.

SIR NICHOLAS CRISP, an abominably wealthy slave trader and royalist, who built the slave fort of Coromantin on the coast of Ghana and financed Charles I (to the tune of £100,000 a time) when Parliament wouldn't, had his heart placed in a monument to the king's memory which he had erected in the church he built at Hammersmith. Every year on the anniversary of its entombment it was given a glass of wine to refresh it. The drink (for which he provided in his will) was served for 150 years, after which the heart was deemed to be decayed, and encased in lead.

CHARLES II's heart was left behind by mistake when his body was taken to Westminster before burial; it had to be carried down by water the next night. It was given to the Dean and placed in Henry VII's chapel, enclosed in silver and wrapped in purple velvet (this was the style for royal hearts for the next hundred years: they would be placed either in the coffin or on it or at its feet).

WILLIAM KING was principal of St. Mary Hall, Oxford (now part of Oriel), in the eighteenth century, and his heart was in a silver urn in the chapel there. Apparently it could be heard beating, late at night.

IN 1760 HOGARTH engraved a heart on the gravestone of his bullfinch, in Chiswick.

PAUL WHITEHEAD (d. 1774) was a poet and a crony of the notorious Sir Francis Dashwood of Medmenham Abbey, to whom he left his heart in his will. It was wrapped in lead, put in a marble urn and enshrined in the mausoleum at West Wycombe with great festivities, including grenadiers, French horns, bassoons, choristers, fifers, muffled drums and the Dead March. Six soldiers carried the urn on a black crepe-draped bier; bells tolled, twenty more soldiers marched by with their firelocks reversed. Large guns were discharged, volleys were fired every three and a half minutes, and the marching went on for two hours. (It was the habit of "the Monks of Medmenham" to mock the rites of the Catholic church.) Whitehead's inscription read

Unhallowed hands, this urn forebear,
No gems, nor orient spoil
Lie here concealed; but what's more rare,
A heart that knew no guile.

Whitehead's heart used to be taken out and shown to visitors; but it disappeared in 1829, believed stolen.

THE BODY of Voltaire was stolen from the Pantheon in Paris in 1814; his heart was returned in 1864.

GEORGE BUBB DODINGTON, who paid for the Medmenham mausoleum, put his wife's heart in an urn on top of a great pillar in his garden at Hammersmith.

THE HEART of the French boy-king Louis XVII was saved and pickled in alcohol by the royalist doctor who carried out the postmortem on the boy, who died of tuberculosis in prison in 1798, after his parents Louis XVI and Marie-Antoinette were guillotined. The corpse was thrown into a common grave. The heart was stolen by a medical student, declared a fake by the French Bourbon family, adopted by the Spanish Bourbons and transferred to the Royal Crypt at Saint-Denis in 1975, where it is held in a crystal reliquary engraved with the sun, stars and the monogram LXVII. It looks like a piece of dark stone. In 2000 it underwent DNA testing, which showed that it had the same genetic material as locks of Marie-Antoinette's hair, thus quashing the hopes of at least a hundred claimants to the Bourbon inheritance.

WHEN NAPOLEON died on St. Helena in 1821, no one knew what to do with his heart (he had wanted it sent to Maria Louisa at Parma; his gentlemen wanted to keep it for themselves), so it was put in a silver vase, with spirits to preserve it, while awaiting instructions. Thereafter its history is unclear. It may have been buried with him in Paris in 1861; it may have been eaten by Dean Buckland of Westminster Abbey, whose legendary intention it was to eat everything that could conceivably be called edible.

AFTER THE POET SHELLEY drowned off Viareggio in 1822, his body and those of his companions were not washed up for ten days. Shelley was burned on the beach by Edward Trelawny, with Lord Byron and Leigh Hunt. The wine, oil and salt poured on the body "made the flames glisten and quiver," wrote Trelawny.

> The heat from the sun and fire was so intense that the atmosphere was tremulous and wavy. The corpse fell open and the heart lay bare . . . Byron could not face this scene; he withdrew to the beach and swam off . . . what surprised us all was that the heart remained entire. In snatching this relic from the fiery furnace my hand was severely burnt; and had anyone seen me do the act I should have been put into quarantine.

It was, wrote Hunt, "alike beautiful and distressing." Shelley's ashes were buried in Rome; his heart was given first to Hunt and then, after some dispute, to his widow, Mary. She kept it in her desk, wrapped in a copy of his poem "Adonais," which includes these lines:

> From the contagion of the world's slow stain
> He is secure, and now can never mourn
> A heart grown cold, a head grown gray in vain.

Lord Chancellor Bacon, in his *History of Life and Death,* observed: "I have seen the heart of one that was bowelled, as suffering for high treason, that being cast into the fire leaped at the first at least a foot and a half in height, and after, by degrees, lower and lower, for the space, I remember, of seven or eight minutes." Leonardo da Vinci wrote: "The heart is of such density that fire can hardly damage it. This is seen in the case of men who have been burnt, in whom after their bones are in ashes the heart is still internally bloody." He believed that nature made it so to resist the enormous heat that the heart itself generates when transforming arterial blood. It is said that the hearts of Joan of Arc, Savonarola, Zwingli and Cranmer all refused to burn.

DAVID LIVINGSTONE's heart underwent a curious reversal of the crusader tradition. When he died, at Chitambo between Lake Tanganyika and Lake Nyasa in East Africa, his heart was taken out by his loyal servants and buried in a tin box under a mpundu tree (*parinari curatellifola*). His name was carved on the tree:

"Livingstone, May 4 1873." His servants—almost eighty of them—dried his empty body in the sun, mummified him, wrapped him in calico, bark, sailcloth and tar, disguised him as ordinary trade goods and transported his body 1,500 miles cross country, under the Union Jack and the flag of the Sultan of Zanzibar, led by a drummer. This was at considerable risk to their health and safety, as nobody liked a corpse passing through their territory. On one occasion their secret cargo was found out, and they had to pretend to bury him. At Bagamoyo, which means "Lay down the burden of your heart," they handed him over to Catholic missionaries, who sent him to Britain by ship. He was buried in Westminster Abbey in April 1874, nearly a year after his death. In 1899 the mpundu tree was dying; Robert Codrington cut away the inscription, and it is now displayed at the Royal Geographical Society.

THOMAS HARDY died of a heart attack. He wanted to be buried at Stinsford in Dorset, where four relatives lay, including his first wife, Emma.

> Tired, tired am I
> Of this earthly air
> And my wraith asks: why
> Since these calm lie
> Are not five out there?

he wrote, putting it somewhat more prosaically in his will. However, he was deemed too grand a national asset to rot away in Dorset, and it was decided that his heart should remain with Emma and that his cremated body should be buried next to Dickens in Poets' Corner at Westminster Abbey. A surgeon came to remove the heart; it was wrapped in a small towel and placed in a biscuit tin, then in a proper casket. The heart and the body were buried at the same time. Pallbearers for the heartless corpse included the prime minister, the leader of the opposition, Sir James Barrie, John Galsworthy, Rudyard Kipling, George Bernard Shaw, Sir Edmund Gosse and A. E. Housman. In London it rained; in Dorset the sun shone. (According to the librarian at Westminster Abbey, there is a legend that the cat got the heart off the kitchen table while the surgeon was drinking a stiff medicinal gin after the removal.)

HERE IS the dedicatory verse from Emily Sophia Hartshorne's charming work, "Enshrined Hearts of Warriors and Illustrious People" (1861):

To my Mother
From long forgotten stories of old days
Was won this chronicle of human tears
Withered, not perished, Hearts are here enshrined
Surviving all the change and chance of years,
And (from the past) to living hearts appealing
By kindred love, and holy human feeling.

AFTERWORD

This harmonious creation of muscles born in dialogue, this unity of continual disunity, this little theatre of life where every contraction led to its opposite—constant as the tides, inevitable as the seasons, enduring forever ...

CHRISTIAAN BARNARD

When I started this book I did not expect it to have a point. Serendipitously, I have found that it has.

The heart is the place of union, and it is in two parts, so it is uniting constantly with itself too. It is the very image of love and friendliness, and it is double. It is body and soul, it is God and man, Aristotle and Descartes, ancient and modern, sacred and profane, physical and emotional, hard and soft, male and female, recipient and creative, suction and expulsion, sex and purity, conjoined twins, red and blue, left and right, hot and cold, flesh and blood. Even its sound is double—*lubdub*. It cleaves to itself—cleave being one of few words which mean their own exact opposite: to cling together and to cut asunder.* It cleaves like the Platonic divided soul searching for its other half; like Eve cleft out of the flesh of Adam's breast; like the ever-healing, never-healing wound, the cleft in the rock; like man and woman, self and other, the internal seed of the opposite. It represents both our artificial divides and our longing for unity, which between them, I suspect, make up the human condition.

At its longest, this book ran to 180,000 words. I would happily have written to twelve volumes, which could lurk on the shelves in the British Library for the

---

*Others are *secrete*: to hide away, and to ooze; *sanction*: to permit and to deny; and *bound*: to be tied, and to leap. All can be applied to the heart.

next 400 years, waiting for people like me (or you?) to come across it and delightedly brush off the cobwebs. But we wanted to give you a book you could hold in your hands, so some of the stories and aspects of the heart have escaped for now, sacrificed so that this heart can fly . . .

I have so loved writing this book. I feel now as if I am at the end of a long love affair, and I don't want to let it go. It has filled my heart with joy over and over. The number of times I've laughed out loud in the library—is it vain to say so? I don't think so. Let me quote John God:

> Though rude be my stile, and knowledge be scant,
> Yet of the matter there nothing doth want.

And whoever speaks against this book, may Thoth challenge him to single combat, as they used to say in Thebes.

APPENDIX I

COEUR DE PORC À L'ORANGE
(from a recipe of Jane Grigson's)

One heart per person is ample—and four would do for five people.

4 pigs' hearts
½ lb. chopped onions
a rasher or two of bacon, coarsely chopped
2–3 oz. butter and oil
1 heaped tbsp. flour
¾–1 pint stock
6 oz. glass red or white wine
1 clove garlic, chopped
salt and pepper
marmalade (the bitter, chunky kind)
juice and peel of 1 orange
orange liqueur
chopped parsley for garnish

Cut the surplus fat off the hearts, brown them with the chopped onion and
bacon in a large heavy frying pan, in the butter and oil. Remove the meat and
onions to a heatproof casserole dish, stir enough flour into the pan juices to
make a roux, and add stock and wine enough to make a sauce. Add garlic, salt
and pepper to taste, and a tablespoon or two of marmalade.

Pour this into the casserole and simmer gently over low heat until the hearts are done—about 1½ hours. Remove the hearts, slice them thinly and arrange in a shallow ovenproof dish. Skim fat off the sauce, and taste. If the sauce is a bit tasteless, boil it down hard until it improves, flavoring it finally with orange juice, orange peel and liqueur. Barely cover the hearts with this sauce, putting the rest into a sauceboat to pass separately.

Warm through in the oven, and sprinkle with chopped parsley. Serve with boiled potatoes and an orange and tomato salad.

A Spanish bingo card, 1980s.

APPENDIX II

HOW TO WIN THE LOTTERY

According to the Italian tradition of Smorfia, the "Cabbala of the Lotto," any dreamed-of object signifies a particular number, which you should use on your lottery ticket. Here are the numbers of the heart:

Heart: 71

Dolorous heart: 3 or 32

Sick heart: 20 or 26

Painted heart: 66

Passionate heart: 5 or 41

Bleeding heart: 5 or 18

Wounded heart: 54 or 84

Flaming heart: 10 or 35

Animal heart: 28 or 43

Silver heart: 11 or 12

Golden heart: 16 or 64

Heart in love: 11 or 77

Human heart: 70 or 75

Heart of wax: 7

Heart of wood: 26

Cow's heart: 48

Hard heart: 20

Ungrateful heart: 71

Votive heart: 45

The Heart, from *Traite de Médecine* by Aldebrande de Florence, 1356. © *Biblioteca del Palacio de Ajuda, Lisbon / Bridgeman Art Library*

SELECTED BIBLIOGRAPHY

A full bibliography for this book would be nearly as long as the book itself. Even so, it is with reluctance that I give you only this limited list, as my debts to all those I have read are immense. The following books come absolutely recommended:

On the history of anatomical knowledge of the heart, R. K. French's *The History of the Heart*.

The heart in books, as opposed to the heart as a book, is another book: to be precise, it is *The Language of the Heart* by R. A. Erickson.

Encyclopaedia of Medicine by Roy Porter.

On the heart as a book, *The Book of the Heart* by Eric Jager.

On *nonenarbeiten, Nuns as Artists: The Visual Culture of a Medieval Convent* by Jeffrey F. Hamburger.

For a full and fascinating firsthand account of watching a heart transplant, "Transplanting a Heart" by Sherwin B. Nuland, in the *New Yorker*, February 19, 1990, reproduced in his book *How We Live*.

On firsthand experience of a heart transplant, Claire Sylvia's autobiographical work *A Change of Heart*.

On the meanings of the heart in ancient Egypt, *Le Coeur dans les Textes Egyptiennes* by Alexander Piankoff.

On Aztec ritual, *The Florentine Codex* (vol. II) by Fray Bernardino de Sahagún.

On sacrifice, *Human Sacrifice* by Nigel Davies.

On eating the heart, *A Perverse History of the Human Heart* by Milad Doueihi.

On Erzulie, *The Voodoo Gods* (formerly *Divine Horsemen*) by Maya Deren.

On the Book of the Dead, *The Hieroglyphic Vocabulary of the Theban Recension of the Book of the Dead* by E. Wallis Budge.

Witchcraft, Magic and Alchemy by Grillot de Givry.

The Rosicrucian Emblems of Daniel Cramer edited by Fiona Tait and Adam McClean.

The Devout Hart by Henry Hawkins.

Le Roman du Châtelain de Couçi et la Dame de Fayel, edited by Jakemes Makes (Société des Anciens Textes Français).

Le Lay d'Ignauré in *Le Coeur Mangé: recits érotiques et courtois, xiii et xiii siècles* edited and translated by Danielle Regnier-Bohler.

In Search of Hafiz edited by A. J. Alston (Shanti Sadan).

De Motu Cordis by William Harvey.

One Life by Christiaan Barnard (this is one of the most extraordinary books I've ever read).

The Heart's Code by Paul Pearsall.

The Essential Rumi translated by Coleman Barks.

Ocean of Story by Nicholas Penzer.

CREDITS

$\mathbf{T}$he author and publisher would like to express their thanks to the following for permission to quote copyright material:

Marian Reiner and the author for "Sometimes," from *I Feel the Same Way* by Lilian Moore © 1967, 1995 Lilian Moore. Coleman Barks for translations of Rumi, © Coleman Barks. The University of Arkansas Press for lines from "Corrinna in Vendome" by Pierre Ronsard, translated by Robert Mezey © 2000. Pollinger Limited and the estate of Frieda Lawrence Ravagli for "The Heart of Man" and lines from "Pomegranate" by D.H. Lawrence. Viking Penguin, a division of Penguin Putnam, Inc. for lines from "One Perfect Rose" by Dorothy Parker © 1926 renewed 1954 by Dorothy Parker, from *The Portable Dorothy Parker* by Dorothy Parker, edited by Brendan Gill. Used by permission. Penguin Putnam, Inc. for lines from "St. Peter Relates an Incident" by James Weldon Johnson. *The Guardian* and Colin Blackstock for "Woman Frozen in Lake" © *The Guardian*. Farrar, Strauss and Giroux, LLC for excerpts from "Red" and "Totem" from *Birthday Letters* by Ted Hughes © 1998 by Ted Hughes. Random House for lines from "Heavy Date" by W.H. Auden. Thunder's Mouth for lines by Larry Neal. The estate of Christiaan Barnard for extracts from *One Life*. Westview Press for lines from "Scarlet Memorial" by Zheng Yi. Little, Brown & Co. Inc. for material from *A Change of Heart* by Claire Sylvia © 1997 Claire Sylvia and William Novak. Steve Earle and Warner Brothers Records, Inc. for lines from Steve Earle's liner notes from *El Corazon*.

Lafleur Music Ltd and Boosey & Hawkes Music Publishers, Ltd. for lines from "These Foolish Things Remind Me of You" by Jack Strachey and Eric Maschwitz © 1936 Lafleur Music Ltd. Gibb Bros. Music/BMG Music Publishing International, Ltd. for "How Can You Mend a Broken Heart," words and music by Barry Gibb/Robin Gibb © Gibb Bros. Music/BMG Music Publishing International, Ltd. (All rights reserved. Used by permission.) MPL Communications Inc./Peermusic (UK) Ltd. for "Heartbeat" by Montgomery & Petty. (Used by permission.) Handy Brothers Music, Inc. for "St. Louis Blues" by William Handy. International Music Publications Ltd. for "Sam Stone," words and music by John

INDEX